Mark Twain in the Margins

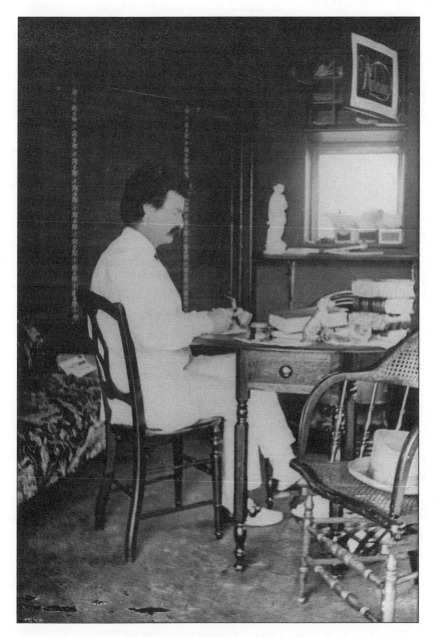

Frontispiece: A young Mark Twain writing in the study at Quarry Farm, c. 1874. Note the books on the writing table. Courtesy Mark Twain Archives, Elmira College.

Mark Twain in the Margins

The Quarry Farm Marginalia and
A Connecticut Yankee in King Arthur's Court

Joe B. Fulton

THE UNIVERSITY OF ALABAMA PRESS

Tuscaloosa and London

Portions of chapter five have appeared previously in *American Literary Realism* and are
reprinted here by permission.

Typeface: ACaslon

∞

The paper on which this book is printed meets the minimum requirements of
American National Standard for Information Science–Permanence of Paper for
Printed Library Materials, ANSI Z39.48–1984.

Library of Congress Cataloging-in-Publication Data

Fulton, Joe B., 1962–
  Mark Twain in the margins : the Quarry Farm marginalia and A
Connecticut Yankee in King Arthur's court / Joe B. Fulton.
      p. cm. — (Studies in American literary realism and naturalism)
  Includes bibliographical references and index.
    ISBN 0–8173–1033–9 (alk. paper)
    1. Twain, Mark, 1835–1910. Connecticut Yankee in King Arthur's
court—Criticism, Textual. 2. Twain, Mark, 1835–1910—Books and
reading. 3. Twain, Mark, 1835–1910—Technique. 4. Realism in
literature. 5. Fiction—Technique. I. Title. II. Series.
    PS1308 .F85 2000
    813'.4—dc21
                99-050647

British Library Cataloguing-in-Publication Data available

For Blaine and Phyllis Fulton
and for Hallie, Rory, and Felicity

In humanis itaque artibus universis
non convenientibus causis nunquam utique proveniret effectus.
          —Galen, *On Antecedent Causes*

Contents

Illustrations

Acknowledgments

For a genetic analysis like this one, it is particularly appropriate to employ as an epigraph the cautionary statement of Galen. For we in fact cannot trace *all* of the influences that cause any worthwhile endeavor, let alone the composition of Twain's "wonder book," *A Connecticut Yankee in King Arthur's Court*. Nor can I personally track the legion of those who have influenced this study; I will have to be content with identifying some of the main sources of assistance.

Many scholars have generously shared their time and expertise. Howard Baetzhold read an early draft and provided encouragement and helpful criticism. I would also like to thank Twain scholars Hamlin Hill and Dennis Berthold for their encouragement in the earliest stages of my composing of this book. Alan Gribben of Auburn University provided both encouragement in my study of the marginalia and the inspiring example of his own meticulous scholarship. I also thank Leland S. Person of the University of Alabama for his continued supportive presence; Person's example of thoughtful, thorough scholarship has been the compass guiding my own scholarly endeavors.

The crew at Elmira College deserve special recognition, for this study could not have been written without their assistance. Gretchen Sharlow, director of the Center for Mark Twain Studies at Quarry Farm, is the foremost expert on the Langdon/Crane/Clemens connection in Elmira and graciously arranged my two research visits to the farm. Mark Woodhouse, whose wry sense of humor rivals that of his namesake, directs the Mark Twain Archives and arranged for the photographs appearing in this volume. Mark spent many hours on the phone with me, verifying my transcriptions of passages in Lecky, Macaulay, and Carlyle. We did not begin speaking in archaic English, as Twain and Cable did, but we considered it. I would also like to thank Jervis Langdon Jr. and his family, whose generosity has done so much for our understanding of Mark Twain.

My friends and colleagues at Dalton State College have likewise been supportive. The administration of the college provided travel funding for my trips to Elmira and also generously provided two student research assistants, Will Burke and Katherine Clinton. I need to thank my students, too, whose enthusiasm for Mark Twain approaches my own; my students should thank Mrs. Dorothy Ittner of John A. Logan College, for she taught me that teaching begins one student at a time. Divisional secretaries Dudd Dempsey and Cheryl Guider helped with so many details on so many occasions I could not possibly enumerate them. Head librarian Harriet Mayo has been exceedingly accommodating about ordering books for my research. Serials librarian Judith Weber and interlibrary loan librarian Barbara Durham have facilitated the completion of this work with their good humor and technical expertise. My colleague Dr. Robert Weathersby has encouraged my work at every stage with his interest and friendship.

I also want to thank the good people at The University of Alabama Press, whose efforts have made this book possible. Director Nicole Mitchell and Editor in Chief Curtis L. Clark were supportive from my initial contact and throughout the process. Mindy Wilson, assistant acquisitions editor, helped with a variety of technical details in the preparation of the manuscript. Dr. Gary F. Scharnhorst, editor of the Studies in American Literary Realism and Naturalism series, offered both encouragement and advice in the preparation of this study. Finally, Joe Abbott, copy editor for this book, taught me a good deal about the editing of manuscripts. *Mark Twain in the Margins* is better for his efforts.

The members of my family have influenced this work in countless ways. My brothers and sisters are among my most ardent supporters. My parents, Blaine and Phyllis Fulton, have been wonderfully supportive and encouraging with this project and with the more momentous project of raising a family. The wife of my youth, Hallie, has become the wife of my middle age and remains my most faithful friend. Rory and Felicity, our "Tom" and "Becky," are my greatest teachers and remind me about eternal values. Rory also taught me an important lesson about realism.

Showing me one of his drawings, he said, "It's a talking tree." I responded by saying, "Hello, talking tree. I'm pleased to meet you!" My son looked at me as if I were the dunce of the class: "Papa, it's only a *picture* of a talking tree." Perhaps that will be the subject of my next book.

Dalton State College
Dalton, Georgia
July 4, 1999

Method of Transcription

The marginalia discussed in this study are part of a wealth of material discovered at Twain's summer home in Elmira, New York. The marginalia, collectively referred to as the Quarry Farm marginalia, unsettle the usual view of Twain as a writer whose sources were primarily personal and experiential. Twain's comments written in the margins of books that contributed to his own work surprise, even stun, long-time readers of his prose.

In addition to the comments he wrote in the margins, Twain impressed marginal lines and underlining in many sections of the histories he studied. In many instances it is possible to demonstrate that passages he marked contributed in significant ways to the manuscript. Twain scored many full pages of Lecky's discussion of infant damnation in *History of the Rise and Influence of the Spirit of Rationalism,* for example. While transcribing the infant damnation passages, I began to wonder if the painstaking donkeywork of the transcription was worthwhile; then I found the several references to infant damnation in the portion of the *Connecticut Yankee* manuscript Twain had written that same summer. Twain had not marked the passages in desultory fashion but so he could return to them as he wrote his book; by using the appendixes in the back of this book, students and scholars can follow Twain's lead and return to these scholia as they compose their own studies of this great American writer.

This study, then, is both an analysis of the marginalia and a resource for those interested in further study. Accordingly, in the appendixes I indicate each mark in the books by the usual page.lines method. For example, "23.1–12, 14–18" indicates that on page twenty-three, marginal lines span lines one through twelve and fourteen through eighteen. I then provide the text, or a description of it, corresponding to the marks. I also indicate any underlining within the quoted passage and include volume, chapter, and chapter titles, if any. This information is referred to throughout the study. Scholars can either use the appendixes for their reference, or they may obtain the same editions Twain read and employ the appendixes located in the back of the volume to locate the full text corresponding to Twain's markings.

Abbreviations

I
Following the "Compass of Fact"

Rethinking Mark Twain's Composing Process

> I have begun a book, whose scene is laid far back in the twilight
> of tradition: I have saturated myself with the atmosphere of the
> day & the subject, & got myself into the swing of the work.
> —Mark Twain to Charles Webster, February 13, 1886
> (*MTN&J* 3:177)

In the *Poetics* Aristotle asserts that the historian "describes the thing that
has been" and the poet the "thing that might be" (637). Samuel Lang-
horne Clemens, Mark Twain, did both. Time and again Twain claimed
he wrote only about things as they had been, and he liked to portray
himself as both a historian and a rough, unlettered writer who wrote
from experience—as, in some sense, the historian of his own life and
time. In fact, recent discoveries of books bearing his marginalia demonstrate that Twain combined the vocation of the historian with the vocation of the poet under the rubric of aesthetic realism. Albert B. Paine was
at his most perceptive when he wrote that Twain composed "fictional
history" (1269). Twain's fictional history encompasses the polarities of
Aristotle's definition, and this study will maintain that Twain was both
that experiential writer he claimed to be *and* the careful craftsman his
manuscript and marginalia prove him to be.

Moreover, I will maintain that Twain's aesthetic was one of literary
realism. As concerned as Twain was about grounding his writing in actual events, his ultimate purpose was to convey a sense of plausibility, a
sense that even if the events he related did not actually happen, they
might have. The present study is particularly called for because of recent

misrepresentations of Twain's aesthetic. Scholars have adopted uncritically Twain's claim that he was a "jack-leg" novelist and have concluded that he had no theoretical interests worthy of analysis. Michael Davitt Bell's *The Problem of American Realism* is only the most direct of such salvoes and poses a problem for any scholar discussing Twain's realism. Twain fails to reach the Howellsian standard, Bell maintains, and "it simply will not do to imagine that Twain's scattered critical writings reveal a realist in principle" (45).

Certainly, we should not expect from Mark Twain—of all writers—any theoretical writing approaching the depth, breadth, and dryness of William Dean Howells or Henry James, the two preeminent American theorists of realism. Nevertheless, Bell's assertion smacks of nearly intentional disregard for Twain's lengthy record of aesthetic commentary. In addition to Twain's letters, books, and autobiographical writings, a small, representative sampling of his stories and essays treating aesthetics ought to be required reading for any scholar of American realism: "Journalism in Tennessee" (1869), "The Story of the Good Little Boy Who Did Not Prosper" (1870), "A Couple of Sad Experiences" (1870), "Post-Mortem Poetry" (1870), "Report to the Buffalo Female Academy" (1870), "How I Edited an Agricultural Paper" (1870), "A Memory" (1870), "A General Reply" (1870), "License of the Press" (1873), "About Magnanimous-Incident Literature" (1878), "Reply to a Boston Girl" (1880), "Concerning the American Language" (1882), "General Grant's Grammar" (1887), "Reply to the Editor of 'The Art of Authorship'" (1890), "What Paul Bourget Thinks of Us" (1895), "Fenimore Cooper's Literary Offenses" (1895), "Fenimore Cooper's Further Literary Offenses" (1895), "How to Tell a Story" (1895), and "William Dean Howells" (1906), to name just a few. One ought to at least glance at such primary sources as Jim McWilliams's *Mark Twain in the* St. Louis Post-Dispatch, *1874–1891*. Similarly, in his compilation of Twain's interviews, Louis J. Budd lists fully 278 items, reprinting some of the most significant. Many of them are "manifestos in miniature" of Twain's aesthetic. True it is that Twain's aesthetic pronouncements are scattered widely—very widely. How, then, can one justify not reading them?

That Twain had any serious conception or theoretical understanding of his writing is derided by other scholars than Bell. Implicitly, many critics share Bell's assumption that there is one true American realism and that Howells is its prophet. Thus, the definition of realism routinely applied to Twain really belongs to Howells and no one else. Too many scholars look to Twain's writing not for Twain's thinking about realism or aesthetics but for Howells's prescriptive definition. David Shi thus labels Twain "a truant member" of the realist school (107). Similarly, Sarah Daugherty asserts that Howells "could hardly have seen himself and Clemens as members of the same literary school" (19). Bell, of course, excludes Twain entirely for failing to reach the Howellsian standard of moralism.

Subjecting Twain's fiction to Howellsian realism is an obviously flawed approach, particularly given some of the criticisms made over the years regarding Howells's thinking. Luc Herman's assessment in *Concepts of Realism* is exemplary: "The manifesto betrays all the contradictions that lie at the heart of Howells's practice during the period under consideration. His program of realism itself is flawed because of its ideological limitations" (34). In 1898 Henry James reviewed Howells's *The Story of a Play* and criticized the "suffusion of that 'romantic' to which the author's theory of the novel offers so little hospitality" ("Dialect" 256–57). Call it irony, but James weighed Howells on the scale of Howellsian realism and found him wanting, just as Twain has been found wanting by those selfsame weights and measures.

Margaret Anne Doody neatly identifies one source of this difficulty. As she points out, realism "is a development emanating *from* the Novel itself. 'Prescriptive Realism' extrapolated certain elements of the Novel, reinterpreted them and treated them as rules or invariable conditions" (478). Thus was a "school" of realism born out of a movement. One of the ironies is that most practitioners of realism eschewed both moralizing over ethics and theorizing about aesthetics. As Harold Kolb so aptly puts it, "The philosophy of American realism, to borrow Carlyle's term, is 'descendental,' or, more accurately, nontranscendental" (38). Lilian Furst notes that, with the exception of Henry James and Edmond Duranty, "the realists did not present a systematic theory in the shape of manifestos or treatises" (*Realism* 27). One might cavil and add Howells to the list, as well as the Japanese realist Tsubouchi Shoyo, whose theoretical work *Essence of the Novel* (1885) inaugurated Japanese realism the same year that *Adventures of Huckleberry Finn* (1885) appeared in the United States. But Furst's point holds: generally, the realists were by nature and outlook uninterested in theory, abstractions, and rules. As Warner Berthoff maintains in *The Ferment of Realism*, the realist novel has "a certain built-in indifference to ought and must" (6). Twain's bias against pure theory, far from banishing him from the realist "school," actually makes him a charter member.

If some critics can be faulted for not taking Mark Twain's humor seriously, their approach represents a larger movement to ignore the claims made by any realist. *The Realistic Imagination* finds George Levine concerned "not with a definition of 'realism,' but with a study of its elusiveness" (7). Dieter Meindl, too, states that "Today, definitions of realism address themselves to the question of, rather than the objects of, representation" (103). J. P. Stern is only slightly more stentorian when he labels realism "philosophically incurious and epistemologically naive" (54). Recalling Bell's argument, Christopher Prendergast—in his study of Balzac, Stendhal, Nerval, and Flaubert—states that "Mimesis is back on the agenda as a *problem*" (213). "The corpse," he observes mordantly, "keeps springing back to life" (213).

Dare I say it? The reports of realism's death are exaggerated. Despite the carping and criticism, there are compelling reasons to take the claims of the realists seriously, and this is particularly true of Twain. The present study is crucial for two reasons. Primarily, I will examine seriously and rigorously Twain's claims about his writing, scrutinizing these claims in light of the *Connecticut Yankee* manuscript and the marginalia discovered at Quarry Farm. This is an enterprise similar in scope and method to Victor Doyno's *Writing Huck Finn*, which offers us, as he puts it so well, "the rare opportunity to look over the author's shoulder while he creates" (xi–xii). I also hope this study will reinvigorate a discussion about realism generally. Critical debate on "the question of realism" has grown too ironic, too knowing, and too dismissive. This attitude has become so pervasive that few critics even grapple significantly with the aesthetic or theoretical works by the realist authors they treat; critics have their own theories to test, so why bother with those of the writer? Realism is an important subject, and it is essential that critics at the very least examine thoroughly what kind of realism the writers *thought* they were writing and *claimed* to be writing. I hope to make Twain a case study in this regard.

A CONNECTICUT YANKEE IN KING ARTHUR'S COURT AND TWAIN'S COMPOSING METHODS

In a story that has achieved the status of folklore, Mark Twain attributed the origin of *A Connecticut Yankee in King Arthur's Court* (1889) to a sudden rainstorm that forced him to seek shelter in a Rochester, New York, bookshop. Twain and George Washington Cable were then appearing on the lecture circuit, billing themselves as the "Twins of Genius." After completing *Connecticut Yankee*, Twain recalled that rainy day in November 1884 when "Cable got a *Morte d'Arthur* & gave it me to read." So smitten was Twain by the language that the two men took to conversing in archaic English, hailing one another as "Sir Mark" and "Sir George." Years later, at a memorial service for his friend, Cable elaborated on this crucial moment in the genesis of the book:

> Presently I went over to him and said I had not found anything that I thought would interest him, and asked him if he had found anything. He said no, he had not; but there was a book he did not remember any previous acquaintance with. He asked me what that book was.
>
> "Why," I said, "that is Sir Thomas Malory's *Morte d'Arthur*." And he said: "Shall we take it?" I said: "Yes; and you will never lay it down until you have read it from cover to cover." It was easy to make the prophecy, and, of course, it was fulfilled. He had read it in a day or two, when I saw come upon his cheekbones those vivid pink spots which every one who knew him intimately and closely knew meant that his mind was working with all its energies. I said to myself: "Ah, I think Sir Thomas Malory's *Morte d'Arthur* is going to bear fruit in the brain of Mark Twain."[1]

If one considers Malory's book the "tree," *Connecticut Yankee* is strange fruit, indeed. In his important article on the recovery of Twain's copy of *Morte d'Arthur*, Taylor Roberts contends that Malory's book "provided the chief inspiration for Mark Twain to write *A Connecticut Yankee in King Arthur's Court*" (166). The operational word is *inspiration*, for Malory's work certainly inspired Twain, but the picturesque tale of *Connecticut Yankee*'s origin obscures other, more vital sources of the book's power. Despite the presence in *Connecticut Yankee* of "authentic" language and even whole pages of narrative lifted directly from *Morte d'Arthur*, other sources predominate, and they are primarily not original sources. They are, as James Williams notes, works of "modern historians" (102).[2] In the main these sources treat the seventeenth, eighteenth, and nineteenth centuries, a far cry from the sixth-century Camelot of Malory's work.

The sources of *Connecticut Yankee* have, in fact, never been identified fully. In *Mark Twain's Library: A Reconstruction* critic Alan Gribben laments that those seeking information on Twain's reading during the composition of *A Connecticut Yankee in King Arthur's Court* "will be dismayed at the relative scarcity of facts" (1:xxxiv). Howard Baetzhold, too, in his standard reference, *Mark Twain and John Bull,* identifies a wide range of probable sources but admits that, "How much of his own borrowing was 'unconscious' and how much deliberate, no one can tell for certain" (xiii). Other than Twain's borrowings from *Morte d'Arthur,* the list of confirmed sources of incidents in the novel is short, and marginalia known to be penned between the novel's commencement in December 1885 and its completion in May 1889 have been thought equally rare.

The seeming absence of scholia has exacerbated a misunderstanding for which Twain himself is in large measure responsible. A number of critics have discussed Twain's conscious creation of an "unread" persona, but the myth has been a long time dying. Many years ago Minnie Brashear established that Twain's debt to reading was greater than he acknowledged publicly: "As a young journeyman, he sought out books to supplement his impressions, and as an experienced writer Mark Twain was accustomed to draw from his reading to fill out his own narratives" (223). Baetzhold's *Mark Twain and John Bull* likewise clarifies the importance of Twain's reading and has been a standard work since its publication in 1970. Sherwood Cummings, too, has been an important voice among those who make it their work to uncover the breadth and depth of Mark Twain's reading. Over the years a significant minority of critics has rejected the received notion that Mark Twain's reading was either nonexistent or "crankily limited to a few favorite subjects," as Cummings characterizes the thesis of those who promote Twain's "jackleg" identity (43). Chief among the scholars who have examined Twain's reading is Alan Gribben, who has engaged in a crusade to dispel the myths, vigorously assailing the identification of Twain as an unread writer. Although some critics and biographers—notably A. B. Paine—are partly to blame, Gribben credits Twain's "repeated professions of ignorance" as "the ultimate source of the widely accepted representation of him as an unread man."[3] Gribben hypothesizes that perhaps Twain "doubted that his readers would identify with a well-read author" and so manipulated his public image to appeal to the widest possible audience (*Library* 1:xxv). After his death, Twain's image was manipulated for him by larger institutional forces as well. Nancy Glazener observes that Twain and James "were maintained as canonical only insofar as they could be distanced from the literary establishment of the *Atlantic* group: Twain, as I have hinted above, because of his association with western humor, an extraliterary tradition, and James because of his expatriation" (251). Seemingly, only by being classed as "extraliterary" could Twain be a part of our national literature. Just as some individuals have tried to remove Twain's books from libraries, there has been a pronounced critical tendency to remove Twain the writer from the library, disassociating him from all aesthetic connections whatsoever.

Despite herculean efforts by a few critics over the last six decades, scholars—against mounting evidence to the contrary—have consistently adopted, adapted, and promoted Twain's portrayal of himself as an unread, untutored, writer who wrote off the cuff and solely from experience. Robert Wiggins, in *Mark Twain: Jackleg Novelist*, begins reasonably, asserting that "I do not take Twain's term *jackleg* as necessarily one of disparagement. It does serve to suggest that he was an improvisor" (viii). Ultimately, however, Wiggins says of *Connecticut Yankee* that "knowledge of history is not the limit of Twain's ignorance," and he "could not have been entirely aware of the implications of the story he constructed" (79). Guy Cardwell, too, has argued in *The Man Who Was Mark Twain* that although Twain was "widely read in a variety of fields . . . the profundity of his reading in any field remains debatable" (44). Although acknowledging the "corrections," Cardwell, in his chapter "An Adam from the Western Garden," reenvisions Twain as the "principal hero of the myth of the West" (45). Similarly, Richard Lowry begins his study *Mark Twain and Modern Authorship* by repeating that "personal experience" was the "raw material" for Twain's books and that this is "obvious to even his most casual reader" (3). Lowry builds his argument by accepting Twain's disingenuous claim that he knew little or nothing about books. Some critics have gone to greater lengths, portraying Twain as a kind of bumbling, fumbling fool who was fortunate enough to set words on paper, let alone understand them. Richard Bridgman bases *Traveling in Mark Twain* on the unlikely idea that Twain remained alienated from conscious understanding of events in his narratives: "Those hazy moments in his travels came when Mark Twain encountered or thought of something that was sufficiently compelling for him to want to record it; yet when he translated it onto the page, it remained problematic, for his conscious mind had not yet mastered it" (4).

Given Twain's extensive use of outside sources, and the records he kept in his writing journals, one has to question the attribution of an unconscious, psychological method of composition when the conscious forces are so readily apparent. Forrest Robinson, however, similarly analyzes Twain's travel narratives, citing them as evidence of the writer's "entanglement in the fabricated web of reality" ("Innocent" 29). Robinson's Twain is a confused Twain caught in a word web of his own spinning and having no "conscious rhetorical strategy" (28); his narratives are "striking confirmation of Mark Twain's notorious blindness to the deeper drift of his writing" (43). In his article "An 'Unconscious and Profitable Cerebration': Mark Twain and Literary Intentionality," Robinson goes to even greater lengths to preserve his critical agenda of exploring Twain's unconscious motivations. Alternately magisterial and insulting in his intemperate attack on Henry Wonham's *Mark Twain and the Tall Tale*, Robinson claims, "There is little suggestion that he [Twain] regarded himself as a highly self-conscious writer and much to indicate that he took just the opposite view" (368). Robinson bases his argument in large part on such writings as "Reply to the Editor of 'The Art of Authorship,'" in which Twain focuses on the unconscious aspects of composition, ending with the claim that "doubtless I have methods, but they begot themselves, in which case I am only their proprietor, not their father" (946). Robinson misses the obvious irony of Twain's *conscious* misrepresentation of his composing process; moreover, the discussion of how he assembles "brick by brick" the "style" of his works is suggestive of the individual facts he required to ground his fiction (945). Those "bricks" are the facts or even events from history. This all proceeds, Twain argues, "as his reading goes on," and one senses some truth lurking behind Twain's tall tale (946).

Although Robinson labels Wonham's arguments "essentially groundless" and "indefensible," it is in fact Robinson who accepts without question Twain's misrepresentations of his composing process. Wonham describes the tall tale as "a speech act that exploits the complacency of listeners who invest too much confidence in the teller's apparent compliance with the 'cooperative principle'" (23). Robinson, one might say, is the greenhorn taken in by that old yarn spinner, Twain. Indeed, Robinson makes only the barest pretense of examining Twain's lengthy list of aesthetic commentary and makes no effort to examine such criticism in light of the writer's application of his ideas. To do so would undermine his contention that Twain was an unconscious and experiential writer. In particular, Robinson, like many other critics, has adopted Twain's claims about his art without examining them in connection with *the only empirical evidence available to scholars: Twain's marginalia, manuscripts, and finished works.*

Even those who take a generally positive view of Twain's methods of composing do so in a strikingly backhanded way. Very recently Barbara Ladd reinterpreted the term *jackleg,* calling it Twain's "attempt to legitimate the jack-leg and his product" (126). Ladd seems to say Twain is a jackleg *and* that is how he wished to be perceived. Brook Thomas, too, suggests the positive aspects of the term by stating that "in a culture of professionalism, in which racism persists," the term *jackleg* disassociated Twain from the larger society and "may not be completely pejorative" (230). Even Shelley Fisher Fishkin takes at face value Twain's claim that he merely transcribed vernacular voices in such works as "A True Story," "Sociable Jimmy," and, most notably, *Adventures of Huckleberry Finn:* "What enabled Twain to transform the voice of a black child into the voice of a white one so effortlessly, confidently, and, possibly, unconsciously?" (*Black* 28). That, however, is "the ruse of realism," as Robert Holub offers in his discussion of German prose realism: readers only "think that they are viewing an unmediated social reality" (35). Critics, apparently, are not immune. New Historicists like Fishkin, Robinson, Thomas, and others are especially prone to identifying largely unconscious sources for Twain's works; Twain breathed in, as it were, a zeitgeist that reveals itself passively in his work.[4]

But what of Twain's closest friend and most perceptive critic, William Dean Howells? Howells said of Twain,

> Of all the literary men I have known he was the most unliterary in his make and manner. I do not know whether he had any acquaintance with Latin, but I believe not the least; German he knew pretty well, and Italian enough late in life to have fun with it; but he used English in all its alien derivations as if it were native to his own air, as if it had come up out of American, out of Missourian ground. His style was what we know, for good and for bad, but his manner, if I may difference the two, was as entirely his own as if no one had ever written before. ("MMT" 266)

Taken in by Twain's projection of himself as an "unliterary man," Howells makes several related claims about Twain's "manner" of writing, which we might understand as his composing process. Most significantly, he argues that Twain wrote "as if no one had ever written before" (266). That is, Howells identifies Twain as a "natural" or "experiential" writer whose way of writing owes nothing to other writers. Likewise, Twain's substance, according to Howells, is not constructed out of materials lent from other writers but crops up "out of Missourian ground," from the natal material of experience itself. Twain would surely have approved heartily of this analysis, for he insisted that his inspiration came from real life, from "out of Missourian ground," as it were; consequently, one would not necessarily suspect many literary sources for incidents in his books. A few years after the publication of *Connecticut Yankee* Twain wrote a letter outlining his qualifications as a writer. He discussed "personal experience" as crucial in "the building of novels" and asserted that "I surely have the equipment, a wide culture, and all of it real, none of it artificial, for I don't know anything about books."[5]

Twain's attitude is particularly significant when one considers that it bears on how he wrote his books or, more to the point, how he would have others believe he wrote them. In a letter to an aspiring writer Twain offered the sensible-sounding advice, "Whatever you have *lived,* you can write . . . but what you have not lived you cannot write, you can only pretend to write it—you will merely issue a plausible-looking bill which will be pronounced spurious at the first counter" (*LLMT* 228).

How, one wonders, did Twain "live in" and acquire intimate familiarity with the age depicted in *The Prince and the Pauper* (1881)? The action of the book occurs during the time of Henry VIII, a period alien to the Missourian ground of Twain's youth. Quite simply, Twain did it by engaging in historical research: "I was reading ancient English books with the purpose of saturating myself with archaic English to a degree which would enable me to do plausible imitations of it in a fairly easy and unlabored way" (*Autobiography of Mark Twain* 268). In consulting such books as *The English Rogue,* Twain, as Leon T. Dickinson observes, "was interested not only in making it authentic, but in making it appear authentic" (105). Even books like *The Innocents Abroad* (1869), *Roughing It* (1872), *A Tramp Abroad* (1880), *Life on the Mississippi* (1883), and *Following the Equator* (1897), which seem to emerge from Twain's own experience, were written with the aid of books about travel and history.[6] Before his return to the Mississippi during the composition of *Life on the Mississippi,* Twain wrote James Osgood, his publisher, to "set a cheap expert to work to collect local histories of Mississippi towns and a lot of other books relating to the river for me" (*MTLP* 158). This hardly sounds like the unconscious Twain described by Bridgman and Robinson. Victor Doyno comments wryly that *Adventures of Huckleberry Finn* is still thought by many to be "somehow non-literary," even though "the words '*book*' or '*books*' occur forty-nine times" (199). Michael Kiskis discusses "the need for external aids" as central to Twain's "career as a writer" (35), noting that Twain even relied on a variety of sources when writing his own autobiography! The handful of perceptive scholars who have rolled this Sisyphus rock up the Mark Twain mountain have had it rolled back down on them and occasionally thrown at them by pervasive individual and institutional efforts to marginalize the conscious aesthetics of Twain; the meiotic view of Twain as a slipshod experiential writer needs to be qualified with a view of Twain as a researcher and conscious craftsman.

Connecticut Yankee is even more pronounced in its dependence on other texts. Clark Griffith calls it "the most bookish of all Mark Twain's books; in ways that have never been sufficiently recognized, it is a book about waking up inside a book" (85). While writing his bookish book, Twain made notes in his journal for a proposed article in the *Princeton Review* about his composing process:

> If you attempt to (build) create & build a wholly imaginary incident, adventure or situation, you will go astray, & the artificiality of the thing will be detectable. But if you found on a *fact* in your personal experience, it is an acorn, a root, & every created adornment that grows up out of it & spreads its foliage & blossoms to the sun will seem realities, not inventions. You will not be likely to go astray; your compass of fact is there to keep you on the right course. Mention instances where you think the author was imagining. Others where he built upon a solid & actually *lived* basis of fact. (*MTN&J* 3:343)

Easily dismissed as one of those "scattered texts," this excerpt is crucial to our understanding of Twain's theory and practice of the writer's craft. Twain's argument here has a long pedigree, going back at least as far as Aristotle, who cautioned writers to see "everything with the vividness of an eye-witness" (*Poetics* 646). And yet, on the surface at least, there ripples a troubling discord, for Twain wrote this passage in early November 1887.[7] During the summer of that year, he was engaged in research for *Connecticut Yankee*. His reading included Thomas Babington Macaulay's

The History of England from the Accession of James II, which he read and annotated extensively for the purpose of "building" his novel, *Connecticut Yankee.* Twain studied Macaulay's *History,* leaving behind as evidence of his research annotations, scorings, and underlinings in four of the five volumes. Macaulay's methods of writing influenced *Connecticut Yankee* stylistically, and a number of the passages Twain marked cropped up as incidents in the manuscript. Twain's assertions in the draft for the *Princeton Review* are strange indeed when one considers that he was, even as he wrote the draft, engaged in composing a book founded on sources outside his own experience. A year after the publication of *Connecticut Yankee,* Twain claimed in "The Art of Authorship," facetiously and to further an "unread" public persona, "I am not sure that I have methods of composition" (945). Within a few years, Twain would call himself a "jackleg" novelist, again differentiating his creative process from that of more refined authors. That mocking sobriquet, which he must have hoped on some level people would reject, has stuck with him. Everyone, it seems, was convinced. After his death, even his daughter Clara maintained, "He had no determined method of writing" (*MFMT* 79). Twain's public pronouncements about his composing process seem so at odds with his actual practice that one might forgive those who have disregarded his vast record of aesthetic commentary; it might be better to neglect his comments entirely than to accept them out of context and at face value.

And yet there is perhaps some solution to the seeming incongruity of Mark Twain's theorizing in the *Princeton Review* draft and his actual practice. In the draft he first discusses his composing process in organic terms, calling a fact from experience "an acorn, a root" and asserting that "every created adornment that grows up out of it & spreads its foliage & blossoms to the sun will seem realities" (*MTN&J* 3:343). Here one thinks of Whitman (heresy when discussing realism) or of the English romantic poet Keats, who said that poetry should grow "as naturally as the Leaves to a tree."[8] Twain imagines that experience plants each fact as a seed, a seed that grows naturally—as Howells might say—"out of Missourian ground." Extending the metaphor, books are the "fruit" of an author's life. At the same time, Twain seems concerned by the author's control over the material. Writers will not, he says, "go astray" if they construct their narratives on the facts of personal experience. By referring to the "compass of fact," Twain seems to suggest that his central concern is staying "on the right course." The source of the fact seems a secondary concern next to the fact itself. In his analysis of *Life on the Mississippi* Earl Briden notes the "skeptical countervoice that quietly questions the status of his 'facts'" (231). That questioning results, I believe, from the immense weight Twain placed on those facts, particularly in books founded on otherwise subjective impressions. Jason Horn analyzes Twain's use of research in the planning of his writing, calling it a "shuffling of fact and fiction" (73). Horn's discussion of Twain's interest in the pragmatism of William James and his philosophy of "fact" and "truth" is particularly fascinating (95). Horn's argument that for James a fact begins as simply true and then generates multiple interpretations parallels in some ways my assertion that for Twain the individual fact acts as a guide, substituting in important ways for "actually lived" experience on which he often based his work. One is reminded of the important analysis Michael Kiskis has made of Twain's autobiography and of the writer's reliance on "external aids" (35). This "need to identify, include, and expand on external sources and influences" (35) that Kiskis observes is, I believe, central to Twain's aesthetic, "The Compass of Fact." As Paine observed, whether talking of *Roughing It* or autobiography, Twain wrote "fictional history, with fact as a starting point" (1269). In any event Twain identifies the fact as the point d'appui of his artistry. Twain's compass of fact served the writer as an aesthetic needle, directing him into believable realms. As he said in his draft for the *Princeton Review,* he wanted his writings to "seem realities" (*MTN&J* 3:343).

Perhaps this comment helps explain the persistent conundrum of Twain's realism. It is true that Twain's works are not exclusively realistic and that his writing contains elements of romance. Richard Chase says of Twain's writings on aesthetics that he pleads "not for realism as such but for realism as the only way of effectively assimilating the miraculous" (148). Twain's synthesis, one might say, of the romantic and the realistic is one element of his aesthetic, but Chase's observation barely plows the surface of the Missourian ground. Twain blends the techniques of romance and realism within his fiction, linking a romantic concept of inspiration with a very realistic concept of how fiction should be made. The resemblance to Keats in the draft for the *Princeton Review* should surprise us very little, for behind the romantic trope of organic growth lies the litmus test of the archrealist Howells, who asked in April 1887: "Is it true?—true to the motives, the impulses, the principles that shape the life of actual men and women?" Developing his idea, Howells contends that "we know of no true picture of life—that is, of human nature—which is not also a masterpiece of literature."[9] Howells, then, argues that realism deals not just with the exterior elements of society but also with truths of human character. Twain uncovers these truths of human character by studying the history of humankind; after all, what is history if not the "story" of human nature?

Twain's devotion to "local particularism" and the "objective representation of contemporary social reality" reveals itself most obviously in his historical research. The contemporary nature of *Connecticut Yankee* will be qualified later, but the dogged pursuit of that reality is essentially the same for Twain as for any other realist. Twain combines the science of history with the art of fiction. As Katharine Kearns observes, the "realist's imperative to present what actually happens—ordinarily, every day, humanly—is very close to the historian's mandate to present what actually happened" (51). Hayden White, in his book *Metahistory,* dismisses the notion that "the historian 'finds' his stories, whereas the fiction writer 'invents' his." For White this "conception of the historian's task . . . obscures the extent to which 'invention' also plays a part in the historian's operations" (6–7). Twain's use of history is likewise misunderstood, although it inverts White's paradigm: in many cases Twain does not just "invent" his stories from experience but "finds" them in history. Twain wrote Mary Mason Fairbanks in 1868 that "the end & aim of my ambition is to be authentic" (*MTL* 2:189). That desire for authenticity led Twain to study all elements of humanity, particularly its history. At many points in his career Twain thought of himself as a historian in much the same way that Balzac, Eliot, and James conceived of themselves as historians. Horst Kruse, for example, details the extraordinary lengths Twain went to while writing *Life on the Mississippi* in order to produce a "standard work" and establish himself as the "authoritative historian" of the river (6).[10] Thus, Twain really did write fictional history, as Paine had observed.

Twain's compass of fact, his historical research, can be understood partly as an attempt to create what James called "the illusion of life" ("Art of Fiction" 173) and, hence, a believable book. At the same time, Twain speaks of the compass of fact in much the same way that other realists speak of "truth"; the compass is both a means and an end. Verisimilitude becomes in this way something of an article of faith for the realists. They believed they could create plausible stories through realistic practices and that those practices, including a quasi-scientific approach to their subjects, would enable them to uncover truths about human existence. For this reason George Lukács's opinion that the "essence of true realism" is the "writer's thirst for truth, his fanatic striving for reality," although vague—as such definitions must be—is still the most satisfying description of realism anyone has offered (*Studies* 11). Twain's "fanatic striving" for any given project involved reading books on the subject, studying the language spoken by certain individuals, and occasionally even traveling to study the life firsthand. For *Connecticut Yankee* Twain studied a variety of historical sources for both language and incidents, for he wanted to comprehend, as he wrote in 1886 to Mary Mason Fairbanks, "the *life* of that day . . . to picture it; to try to get into it; to see how it feels & seems" (*MTMF* 258).[11] That same year he wrote his publisher, Charles Webster, that he had "saturated" himself with "the atmosphere of the day & the subject" (*MTN&J* 3:177). Twain's effusive comments find him following the compass of fact in part so he could write a believable book but also because he believed that by doing so he could seize on truths of what Balzac called *La Comedie Humaine*.

For Twain, then, the compass of fact meant much more than relying on childhood memories. His conception of realism differs significantly in this regard from Henry James's assertion that a writer "can write solely of what his fleshly eyes have seen" (*LHJ* 1:30). For his travel books *The Innocents Abroad*, *Roughing It*, *Life on the Mississippi*, *A Tramp Abroad*, and *Following the Equator*, Twain consciously set out to acquire the experience that he could transmute into art, but even then the compass of fact meant consulting books on travel and history. Nancy Cook observes that "Mark Twain represents the author as *maker* of books, one who performs a number of tasks throughout the publication process" (151). The comment is apropos, for it suggests the way Mark Twain proceeded with the compass of fact while writing, making, and building his works. For *The Prince and the Pauper* the compass of fact meant research into the day and time and compiling lists of authentic language culled from books so that the end result would be "authentic." Similarly, Twain wrote to Henry Rogers about *Personal Recollections of Joan of Arc* (1896) in terms that recall the concept of the compass of fact: "the first two-thirds of the book were easy; for I only needed to keep my historical road straight" (*MTHHR* 125). And for *Connecticut Yankee* Twain consulted books as he sought the elusive compass of fact that would make even the story of a Yankee traveling back in time to Arthurian England credible, authentic, and perhaps even profound. In each of these books Twain combines the "science" of history with the art of fiction.

QUARRY FARM

Set on a hill overlooking the Chemung River valley and the city of Elmira, Quarry Farm was the residence of Livy's adopted sister, Susan Crane.[12] For some twenty summers the Clemens family made Quarry Farm its retreat, vacationing there from June to September. The wheel tracks of the long, circular drive, although now overgrown with grass, are still visible, and one fancies a carriage may arrive from Hartford at any moment. Twain describes a typical day at Quarry Farm in a letter dated July 10, 1887, to Mrs. Orion Clemens:

> This is a superb Sunday for weather—very cloudy, and the thermometer as low as 65. The city in the valley is purple with shade, as seen from up here at the study. The Cranes are reading and loafing in the canvas-curtained summer-house 50 yards away on a higher (the highest) point; the cats are loafing over at "Ellerslie" which is the children's estate and dwelling house in their own private grounds (by deed from Susie Crane) a hundred yards away from the study, amongst the clover and young oaks and willows. Livy is down at the house, but I shall go now and bring her up to the Cranes to help us occupy the lounges and hammocks—whence a great panorama of distant hill and valley and city is seeable. The children have gone on a lark through the neighboring hills and woods. It is a perfect day indeed. (*MTLAP* 2:488–89)

Twain wrote this letter from Quarry Farm, where he spent every summer from 1885–1889, the period during which all but a few chapters of *Connecticut Yankee* were written. One might miss the significance of this letter and dismiss it as merely a well-written description of a pleasant day— until one compares its tone to some of those Mark Twain sent from Hartford. The letters from Hartford differ greatly from those written at Quarry Farm. In one letter dated November 16, 1886, to "Mother" Fairbanks, for example, Twain spoke of plans for *Connecticut Yankee:* "I expect to write three chapters a year for thirty years; then the book will be done. I am writing it for posterity only; my posterity: my great grandchildren.

It is to be my holiday amusement for six days every summer the rest of my life" (*MTMF* 257–58). Although he perhaps jokes about his lack of progress, Twain clearly recognizes that he can get no work done in Hartford and that the only work he anticipates accomplishing will be at Quarry Farm. Similarly, he wrote Mrs. Fairbanks from Hartford a year later, in November 1887: "I go from the station, Monday 12:30, to my office, East 14th street, & from there to Chickering Hall at 2 or 2.15 (according as office business crowds me or doesn't); & from Chickering to the station at 4, to catch the 4.30 train home, to meet a business engagement here next morning. (This kind of rush is why parties write no books.)" (*MTMF* 262).

The following October, after a very productive summer at Quarry Farm, Twain wrote from Hartford to Susan Crane's husband, Theodore, complaining of the "noise of the children and an army of carpenters" that interrupted his work on *Connecticut Yankee* (*MTLAP* 2:500). Twain made the now notorious statement, "I want to finish the day the machine finishes, and a week ago the closest calculations for that indicated Oct. 22—but experience teaches me that their calculations will miss fire, as usual" (*MTLAP* 2:500). The "machine" was the Paige typesetter, into which Twain sank much of his time, energy, and fortune. James Cox labels Twain's process of composition at this moment "a dumbly driven effort going on almost outside himself" and asseverates that "the novel had come to be identified with the machine" (209). But Cox's criticism goes on almost outside of Twain and his situation. Twain's letter voices the frustration of an author who lacks the aesthetic space in which to write. The real focus of the letter is the noise in Hartford and the complaint that the surroundings are not conducive to creative work. Twain was, after all, writing to Theodore Crane, his host and companion at Quarry Farm.

Even Kenneth Andrews, who discredits those who argue for the blunting effect of life in Hartford's Nook Farm milieu, observes that the years of *Connecticut Yankee*'s composition constitute "the longest period between 1867 and 1910 in which Mark published no books" and that this was due to his view of himself as a "captain of industry" (185). That identity existed primarily in Hartford and rarely intruded on life in Elmira. Laura Skandera-Trombley's *Mark Twain in the Company of Women* provides a well-reasoned alternative to the theses of Van Wyck Brooks and Bernard DeVoto, but if she has revealed the positive role of the women in Twain's life as "co-constructors of his text," she has also illumined the importance of the Quarry Farm milieu (20). As she notes, "Clemens wrote his novels under carefully controlled conditions. He required two outwardly paradoxical elements: quiet isolation for concentration, and the comforting, boisterous presence of his family. He had both elements at Quarry Farm" (24). Quarry Farm offered Twain the quiet he required but also such family events as the "cat procession," the outdoor game "English Kings" he himself devised and played with his children, and the nightly reading of the day's work to those gathered on the front porch. The farm offered both the octagonal study for Twain and "Ellerslie" for his children, the playhouse they named after a castle in Jane Porter's *Scottish Chiefs*.[13]

However much Twain may have publicly misrepresented his reading habits and methods of composition, that is, *how* he wrote his books, he accurately portrayed *where* he wrote them: "'About four months in the year,' said he, 'is the time when I expect to do my work, during the summer vacation, when I am off on the farm at Elmira.' 'Yes,' he continued, when I expressed surprise, 'I can write better in hot weather. And, besides, I must be free from all other interests and occupations.'"[14] Twain made these statements in an 1885 interview, during the earliest stages of the composition of *Connecticut Yankee*. The very next summer, in an interview at Quarry Farm, he went even further: "The three summer months which I spend here are usually my working months. I am free here and can work uninterruptedly, but in Hartford I don't try to do any literary work. Yes . . . this may be called the home of *Huckleberry Finn* and other books of mine, for they were written here."[15]

As Skandera-Trombley aptly puts it, Quarry Farm was a "locus of creativity" for Twain (37), and Twain clearly recognized this. Quarry Farm, in fact, played a more significant role in Twain's writing than has generally been acknowledged. Although the Paige typesetter is alternately credited or faulted for many elements of *Connecticut Yankee*, most of the novel was written at Quarry Farm, away from the cares of the city, the claims of business, and the promises of inventors. Twain called the farm "Rest-&-Be-Thankful" and even proclaimed it "divine" in a letter to his Hartford pastor, Joe Twichell, when inviting him to visit "and take a foretaste of heaven" (*MTLAP* 1:166). Walter Blair connects the pastoral descriptions of nature in *Tom Sawyer* (1876) and *Adventures of Huckleberry Finn*—usually attributed solely to the writer's childhood—to

Twain's adult experience: "the boy voices attitudes like those of his creator on escaping from Hartford to the solitude of Quarry Farm" (101).
Indeed, the view of the Chemung River from the study and the front
porch of the farmhouse almost certainly stimulated Twain's memories of
the Mississippi. In short, Elmira served as no secondary, no lesser Hartford and offered an entirely different environment where much could be
attempted, much done; although Twain called both home, Quarry Farm
and Nook Farm share little more than the word *farm* in their appella-
tions.

The Cranes, then, provided Mark Twain with a creative retreat that
witnessed the writing of large portions of his most important works:
*Roughing It, The Adventures of Tom Sawyer, Life on the Mississippi, Adven-
tures of Huckleberry Finn,* and *A Connecticut Yankee in King Arthur's Court,*
among others. Throughout the summers, Twain climbed the slate steps
still visible behind the house to reach the octagonal study especially built
for him by his hostess. This study, somewhat inaccurately described in
1885 by Charles Clark of the *Critic* as "modelled exactly on the plan of a
Mississippi steamboat's pilot house" (77), symbolically conjoins the two
most significant strains of Twain's composing process: experience and
research. In a letter to Dr. John Brown of Edinburgh, who had treated
Livy in Scotland in 1873, Twain describes the summer days when he
would "spread the study door wide open, anchoring my papers down
with brickbats and write in the midst of the hurricanes."[16] Among these
papers and brickbats were books belonging to the Cranes, which Twain
often toted to the study and wrote in as he composed his novels. According to Clara Clemens, "Aunt Sue" called Quarry Farm "'Do as you
Please Hall,' for she wished everyone to feel complete liberty to act and
think as he would" (*MFMT* 59). Twain apparently took this invitation at
face value and did as he pleased, for he exercised "complete liberty" when
writing in books belonging to Susan and her husband Theodore.

A few of the borrowed volumes left with Mark Twain, never to return.
Scholars have long been aware, for example, that the heavily annotated
copy of Lecky's *History of European Morals* recently sold by the Mark
Twain Research Foundation in Perry, Missouri, originally belonged to
Theodore Crane.[17] But many more volumes endured at Quarry Farm,
occupying undisturbed their spaces in the Cranes's library for more than
a century. Quarry Farm remained in the Langdon family until 1982,
when Jervis Langdon Jr. donated the property to form the Elmira Col-

lege Center for Mark Twain Studies. The library, which includes books that Twain read and annotated, was made available to scholars and provides materials for a reinterpretation of Mark Twain's composing process, and of *Connecticut Yankee* in particular.

MARK IN THE MARGINS

Although Quarry Farm provided a retreat from a hectic life in Hartford dominated by business meetings and visitors, in a very real sense Twain was never alone even in the solitude of his octagonal study. Wherever he turned he was surrounded by the books he had removed from the Cranes's library and was confronted by the strong opinions and personalities of the men who had written them: Lecky, Macaulay, and Carlyle.

With each volume he read Twain engaged not with dry historical fact but with the stories of real men and women experiencing the rush of history. With notable exceptions critics from Howells to the present have minimized the importance of Twain's historical research. Howells observed that Twain "read, or read *at,* English history a great deal" and goes on to speak of the "game of English kings (like the game of Authors) for children" that the author invented ("MMT" 306). Even more patronizing is Guy Cardwell's summary of Twain's reading: "Scanning the accounts of his reading or possible reading, one is struck by how few marginalia there are, by how little interest these scholia possess, and by how high a proportion of the books he knew were rubbishy and deservedly ephemeral" (44–45).

With the discovery of the new marginalia at Quarry Farm, a "new," revised Mark Twain is slowly emerging from the margins as critics become more aware of the depth and breadth of his reading. The author's debt to the historians he studied during the composition of *Connecticut Yankee* is immense. As Twain advanced beyond his sources through the grand alchemy of the artist, the compass of fact kept him on his course as he composed the novel. *Connecticut Yankee* exists, as E. M. Forster said of novels generally, "bounded by two chains of mountains . . . the opposing ranges of Poetry and of History" (18). This study includes appendixes that list and describe each mark left in the books Twain borrowed from the Cranes's library during the composition of *Connecticut Yankee:* William Edward Hartpole Lecky's *History of the Rise and Influence of the Spirit of Rationalism* and his *A History of England in the Eighteenth Cen-*

tury, Thomas Babington Macaulay's *The History of England from the Accession of James II,* and Thomas Carlyle's *The French Revolution.* Twain's reading of these books, and his annotations in them, can be dated with relative precision, spanning each summer of the book's composition save 1886, when Twain decided, as he told an interviewer, to "loaf all summer."[18] It will become readily apparent that the marginalia should hold great interest for scholars and in fact will force a reinterpretation of *Connecticut Yankee*'s composition and ultimate import.

Twain's deep, self-conscious interaction with his historical sources, and the record of this in his scholia, must call into question several assumptions made of his book. Readers have been troubled, for example, by the incongruity of Twain's "reading *at* history" and the many anachronisms of *Connecticut Yankee.* Twain, of course, recognized this, and in a draft preface wrote an unusual qualification: "The strange laws which one encounters here and there in this book, are not known to have existed in King Arthur's time, of course, but it is fair to presume that they did then exist, since they still existed in Christian lands in far later times—times customarily called, with unconscious sarcasm, 'civilized and enlightened.'"[19]

Twain's approach leads Harold Aspiz to call the novel "a gay abjuration of historicity" ("Lecky's" 17), and in a sense this is so.[20] Twain certainly does abjure the strict chronological approach of what happened and when, but I hope to show that he does this precisely to create a place that encompasses all of history. One ought, perhaps, to note that Twain's assumption that the laws did exist in King Arthur's time *because* they existed at a later time seems a pointed jab at the idea of meliorism; he anticipated the jibes of critics by pointing out that if things improved because of the influence of Christianity, these oppressive laws *must* have existed in prior ages, for they most certainly *did* exist in the later "civilized and enlightened" world he satirized. It is partly true, as Barbara Foley contends, that *Connecticut Yankee* "evade[s] a direct confrontation with the historicity of the present and the recent past" (166); indeed, the confrontation is much larger. In Auerbach's terms the novel achieves "omnitemporalness" without sacrificing "everyday life" (161). In "The *Bildungsroman* and Its Significance in the History of Realism," Mikhail Bakhtin offers the term *synchronism* to denote "the coexistence of times at one point in space" (41). That point in space is Camelot, and Twain strived to create a synchronic world to convey a sense of human time. Twain was less concerned with history than with historicity, "how it feels & seems" to be within history (*MTMF* 258).

Critical debate over *Connecticut Yankee* centers on the question of whether Twain meant to satirize the Arthurian age, nineteenth-century Britain, nineteenth-century America, or some combination. In his seminal study, "The Meaning of *A Connecticut Yankee*," Everett Carter divides critics into "hard" and "soft," depending on their interpretation of Twain's intent. But the novel itself, because it melts history into one pot, generally confutes any such attempts to read the book as a criticism of any given historical era, although such reading is often done. In *Mark Twain's Ethical Realism: The Aesthetics of Race, Class, and Gender,* I interpreted the novel as a debate between sixth-century England and nineteenth-century America and argued that Twain's concern is the insufficiency of any moment in time. My study of Twain's marginalia has convinced me both that this is so and that the two camps Carter identifies, "hard" and "soft," are ultimately untenable positions. Roger Salomon is quite correct when he argues that the novel poses a philosophy of history and that "the concept of change" is central to that philosophy (5). Twain struggled with the idea of meliorism, that is, with whether human society could improve over time, progressing materially and spiritually. Salomon believes Twain ultimately embraces a cyclic view of history in which "civilizations rise and fall, [in which] human character *seems* to progress or progresses for a short while" but then falls "back into barbarism" (49). As Jay Martin puts it, "Twain simultaneously entertains the opposite views of history as decline and history as progress" (178). Howard Baetzhold, in his revision of his earlier work, wonders, "Why the change of purpose?" that led Twain's novel to involve more "serious themes" ("Let It Go" 51). Baetzhold provides many reasonable explanations, but the primary and fundamental cause, I believe, was Twain's reading, which revealed to him that human nature does not change, and so for Twain the drama became change itself. The marginalia do not merely indicate Twain's thinking at any particular point; they chart his *changing* thought about *change* as his research into history influenced the composition of *Connecticut Yankee*.[21]

The sources studied here will reveal, however, another complexity of Mark Twain's view of history. Twain has been accused of an "ambivalence" to technology, to history, and to progress. Henry Nash Smith, for example, sees in the book "a conflict within Mark Twain's mind between a conscious endorsement of progress and a latent revulsion against the non-human imperatives of the machine" (*Fable* 105). James L. Johnson also contends that the book "reflects the irresolvable conflicts within Twain himself" (121). He goes so far as to call Hank Morgan a "projection of Twain's own personality" that allows the author to express "contradictory impulses and attitudes" (141). Such ambivalence and contradiction may have existed in Twain's mind but certainly also existed within his historical sources and within history itself. Lecky, Macaulay, and Carlyle, although adherents of the concept of meliorism in its general outlines, were hardly as naive as some have argued. Kim Moreland, for example, characterizes the historians Twain read as offering a "simplistic vision of history as a progressive march through the centuries, an irrevocable movement toward perfection" (30). From them, she argues, Twain received a "teleological perspective" in which the present moment is "the apex of history" (28). A quick dip into any of the histories discussed in this study dispels any assumptions about their allegedly facile explanations of history. The sources of *Connecticut Yankee*, specifically the passages Twain marked in books from the Cranes's library at Quarry Farm during the novel's composition, illustrate that no civilization is ever perfected and that every society, in the process of progressing, will be destroyed by the new one that supplants it.[22]

In fact, while Twain accepts implicitly Hegel's assertion in *Reason in History* that human life "presents to us a universal thought, a category: that of *change* in general," he rejects the philosopher's teleology (88). Even the structure of *Connecticut Yankee* suggests such a rejection, for Twain's method in moving backward in time is analogous to Foucault's "genealogy" that proceeds back in time specifically to avoid teleology. Foucault focuses, as Andrew Thacker points out, not on "an image of progressive unity" but on the "struggle of forces" (34). Foucault states that his genealogy "does not resemble the evolution of a species, and does not map the destiny of a people" (81). This may be difficult for some to accept, but Twain was not the naive carnival barker shilling for progress as some have depicted him. Twain's realism is, in this respect, most definitely not the realism of Lukács, who argues that "knowledge of the facts" and "knowledge of reality" are integrated only when the writer understands them "as aspects of the historical process" (*Class Consciousness* 8). For Lukács the process is a dialectic, a historical materialism, and a teleology. For Twain the "facts" he locates grant him an aesthetic and a philosophy of change, but his study of history made impossible any naive philosophy of progress.

If the history of change is complex, it is also violent, and *Connecticut Yankee* necessarily partakes of that violence. The process of historical change is messy and can hardly legitimately be termed a "march of progress," when, as often as not, it features armies marching in the vanguard. Whereas some critics attribute the violence of the book to the author's turbulent psychology, Hamlin Hill proposes the intriguing idea that the gore in *Connecticut Yankee* owes something to Twain's attempt to appeal to the "blood and thunder" audience he faced with the subscription publication of the book (37–38). Like Hill, Bruce Michelson attributes the grisly aspects of the novel to Twain's narrative strategy: "Like a good piece of platform humour, the novel tries to sustain itself on a sequence of surprises—on no continuity except astonishment and shock" (630). Both explanations recall Raymond Chandler's advice to aspiring writers of detective pulp: "When in doubt have a man come through a door with a gun in his hand" (ix). In reality, as Twain's historical sources show, the grisliest incidents in *Connecticut Yankee* emerge directly from historical precedent that he "found" rather than "invented." Such incidents constitute the compass of fact that kept Twain on course as he wrote his book. Nietzsche, speaking of history, claims in *The Genealogy of Morals* that

> Whenever man has thought it necessary to create a memory for himself, his effort has been attended with torture, blood, sacrifice. The ghastliest sacrifices and pledges, including the sacrifice of the first-born; the most repulsive mutilations, such as castration; the cruelest rituals in every religious cult (and all religions are at bottom systems of cruelty)—all these have their origin in the instinct which divined pain to be the strongest aid to mnemonics. (193)

In the suffering individual, violence is trauma; in suffering humanity, it is history. Copious incidents of intentional and terrific cruelty assault the reader of *Connecticut Yankee,* but the examples emerge directly from Twain's sources and ultimately from the master text of history itself. Paul Ricouer's sentiment is noble and true: "The whole history of suffering cries out for vengeance and calls for narrative" (75). Realism, ever contrary in its relation to the reality it attempts to portray, actually censors history in the act of portraying it. For good reason does Katharine

Kearns argue that realism is based on an "economy of pain," for the realist must actually *limit* the intrusion of reality lest readers become "paralyzed or enraged" (21). Speaking of *Connecticut Yankee* and Twain's work generally, Clark Griffith contends, "To reject reality is to have the head filled with nonsense and become a ludicrous figure. To accept reality is to strew catastrophes everywhere and become a ludicrous figure" (85). Kenneth Burke's vocabulary sums up the progression from "*reflections* of reality" to "*selections* of reality" and finally to a "*deflection* of reality" (59). Twain found his facts in history, and his sources demonstrate that his book contains less horror than the histories he consulted while he wrote it. The grisliest violence in *Connecticut Yankee* is perpetrated by history on the humans existing within its onslaught; history in *Connecticut Yankee* is what we remember precisely because it is what we would most like to forget.[23]

The violence in *Connecticut Yankee* results from the concept of change that holds the inevitable destruction of two civilizations, the one supplanted and the one victorious, whose defeat is latent even in its victory. Hank, then, cannot represent anything so limited as "industrial capitalism," as Smith contends (*Fable* 104). Change as dialectic, as trauma, as history is central to Twain's novel. History, not Hank Morgan, is the protagonist of *Connecticut Yankee*. Thus, Smith's observation that Twain "could not hope to represent the Yankee's undertaking as permanently successful" because he chose Arthurian Britain as the setting (*Fable* 105), although perhaps true, begs the issue: Twain learned from his historical research that no human achievement is permanently successful. Auerbach, too, in his study of realism comments, "Imitation of reality is imitation of the sensory experience of life on earth—among the most essential characteristics of which would seem to be its possessing a history, its changing and developing. Whatever degree of freedom the imitating artist may be granted in his work, he cannot be allowed to deprive reality of this characteristic, which is its very essence" (191). For Auerbach, as for Twain, the equation is simple: Realism = History = Change.

Amy Kaplan asserts in *The Social Construction of American Realism* that central to the realist practice is a "direct confrontation with the elusive process of social change" (9). That is more obviously true of those novelists she treats, who focused on contemporary conditions. But Twain's concern, too, is social change, although on a larger scale, in its way, even than Tolstoy's *War and Peace;* Twain limns our ability to sense the passing of time and the changes large and small that are central to what it means to be human. This might cause us to reinterpret Twain's assertion that we hate the past because "It's so damned humiliating" ("MMT" 274). With "change" as the preeminent, and perhaps sole, historical truth, history humiliates us because no ultimate success in any human endeavor is possible. Even those who win are ultimately defeated. Hank wins the "Battle of the Sand-Belt" at the novel's conclusion, but his loss is imminent even as he destroys his opposition. The marginalia Twain left in the works of history he consulted during the novel's composition are replete with examples of this fundamental paradigm.

The marginalia, along with Twain's writing notebooks, illustrate, too, that he believed a revolution had already occurred. Twain's violation of historical chronology adheres to the fundamental truth of history as Americans of the nineteenth century experienced it and as people at all times experience it: history as rapid change. Bruce Michelson discusses the "anomaly of 'moral, realistic fiction'—of a far-fetched tale about a long-ago, never-was place" (611), and Edgar Branch similarly refers to Twain's Camelot as a "never-never land" (63). In reality Twain's Camelot is the "always-was" place, an "ever-ever" land, one might say. In each of his prefaces, including the one finally adopted, Twain proclaims that the laws and incidents he depicts may not have occurred during Arthur's reign but did occur within human history. Throughout the fictional history of his novel Twain compresses over a thousand years of human history so that he can discuss how and in what ways the cause of humanity has been advanced and how humans have reacted to change.

Gregg Camfield sees Twain as "always struggling toward conscious understanding" of the difficulties inherent to modernity (21). But Connecticut Yankee is Twain's great, conscious experiment; Connecticut Yankee is one of his most researched and planned novels. In his penultimate preface, written after the summer of 1888, Twain asserted, "Human liberty—for white people—may fairly be said to be one hundred years old this year."[24] He may have done violence to chronology, then, but he certainly did no violence to history, for he chronicles the accelerated progress that occurred at a given time and place within a very short period of time. Lawrence Howe is quite correct when he discusses Twain's "repeatedly bumping up against history" in his works but incorrect, I think, when he sees in Connecticut Yankee Twain's attempt "to circumvent history entirely" (154). Rather the contrary is the case, and Twain sought to create a synchronic space containing and exploring change. Twain was interested in ascertaining whether an accelerated progress could be peaceful and lasting and what the effects would be on the people who found themselves experiencing the "accelerated grimace," as Pound called it (383). Writing about Chinese history and aesthetics, Ban Wang notes the "shock-effects" (5) that literature retrieves and records. Those emotions are central sense experiences that are often overlooked by those discussing realism, but they are, as John Dewey contends, part of the overarching purpose of mimesis: "For the doctrine did not signify that art was a literal copying of objects, but that it reflected the emotions and ideas that are associated with the chief institutions of social life" (7). Those institutions are in constant flux, as are the emotional responses they provoke. Twain proclaimed in 1880 that "we do live in an age compared to which all other ages are dull and eventless," but reading *Connecticut Yankee* one recalls the sharper-edged proverbial curse, "May you live in interesting times" (quoted in Lauber 35).

Although Mark Twain fooled even those who knew him best, and managed to conceal the depth of his reading, he could not conceal his genius. George Washington Cable, his fellow "twin of genius," observed at a memorial service that "it was the rigor of his art, an art which was able to carry the added burden beyond the burden of all other men's art, the burden of absolutely concealing itself and of making him appear, whenever he appeared, as slipshod in his mind as he was in his gait" (Turner 133). This study delves behind the margins of that purposefully "slipshod" exterior to reveal some of the deeper sources of *Connecticut Yankee* and of Mark Twain's composing process. After Twain finished writing his novel in 1889, he wrote his friend William Dean Howells: "Well, my book is written—let it go. But if it were only to write over again there wouldn't be so many things left out. They burn in me; & they keep multiplying & multiplying; but now they can't ever be said. And besides, they would require a library—& a pen warmed-up in hell" (*MTHL* 2:613). As is so often the case with Twain, there is a double meaning to this passage. He may have meant that if he included everything he wanted to in his book, it would expand to such an extent it would require a library to house. Usually the passage is interpreted this way, and many critics share Everett Emerson's contention that such "comments suggest an author not fully in control of his material" (166). But Twain may also have meant that he would require a library to do the research for the book, and the comment would then evidence control over his material, not a lack of control. In fact, *Connecticut Yankee* did require a library for Twain to write. Unlike most of his library at Hartford, which was scattered to the four winds, important works that he consulted for *Connecticut Yankee*—complete with his marginalia—still exist at Quarry Farm.[25] His notations in these volumes reveal his composing process more eloquently and more truthfully than he himself did. There is a Mark Twain in the margins whose actual methods of composition were anything but haphazard or slipshod as he wrote in his octagonal study at "Do as you Please Hall."

2

Twain's "Cloud of Witnesses"

The 1885 and 1887 Marginalia in Lecky's *Spirit of Rationalism*

> I am plotting out a new book, & am full of it.
> —Mark Twain to Charles Webster,
> December 16, 1885 (*MTBus* 343)

> Mark Twain is spending the summer at his country home near
> Elmira, N.Y., and is busily engaged on a new book. He is rich,
> but he wants more money. He does not work for fun.
> —Announcement in the *St. Louis Post-Dispatch*,
> July 18, 1887 (*MTPD* 216)

Among the volumes Mark Twain consulted and wrote in while summering at Quarry Farm was William Edward Hartpole Lecky's *History of the Rise and Influence of the Spirit of Rationalism*. One of at least three sets of Lecky's works owned by the Cranes, this work bears marginalia written by Twain on two different occasions. This find is particularly notable, for Lecky was one of Twain's favorite writers, and he had without question the most significant impact on Twain's philosophy of morality and history. Twain may have read Lecky's *History of European Morals from Augustus to Charlemagne* as early as 1874, but he certainly reread the book many times in the years to come and even borrowed and wrote in a copy belonging to Susan Crane in 1903 (Gribben, *Library*, 1:400–401).[1] Twain did not read Lecky passively but actively engaged with his thought, often writing his own opinions in the book's margins. From Lecky Twain acquired the concept of environmental determinism, with which he would wrestle for many years. According to Howard Baetzhold, Twain rejected Lecky's view that "moral choices are governed by an innate sense" and leaned toward the belief that "it is external forces rather than intuitive perceptions of good and evil which determine moral choices" (*MT&JB* 55). These "external forces" are a crucial function of history because they change over time, and from Lecky Twain arrived at a conundrum that would occupy him all his life: what relation do the mutability of character and environment share, and how do they produce the evolution through history of moral ideas and behavior?

This question, already singularly complex, becomes particularly knotty when one considers that the marginalia discovered at Quarry Farm in Lecky's *Spirit of Rationalism* were made during the composition of *A Connecticut Yankee in King Arthur's Court*, Twain's "historical novel." One might then view Hank Morgan as a vehicle for testing the idea of moral and material progress. By introducing Hank Morgan into Camelot, Twain infuses nineteenth-century ideas into a sixth-century world to ascertain how the mutability of character and environment relate. The book is in this sense an inquiry into the process of change over time that we call history. Will Hank's ideas reconstitute a nineteenth-century environment in the sixth century, thus effecting positive change in the character of the inhabitants, or will the sixth-century environment dominate Hank, converting his character? The central assumption of *Connecticut Yankee* that character and morality are temporal conceits is largely as unspoken as it is revolutionary. Twain lined the margin of a passage in Lecky's *Spirit of Rationalism* derisive of the idea that moral ideas are static. Lecky asserts that although the "insect whose existence is but for a moment" might see such ideas as "eternal," they actually "shift and vary with each changing breeze" (1:182). Similarly, when discussing "inherited ideas" in chapter 8, Hank characterizes the attitude of the aristocracy toward their subjects as toward "creatures of no more consideration than so many animals, bugs, insects" (111). Morgan's great program is the altering of inherited ideas by his own words and deeds, transforming thereby the environment that engenders words and deeds. To adopt Lecky's metaphor, Hank seeks to educate the "insect" about the nature of history and morality.

Indeed, although Harold Aspiz, in his outline of Lecky's influence on Twain, asserts that Hank seeks "to *create* a nineteenth-century milieu" and thus to create people with nineteenth-century ideas, the program seems far more circular than that ("Lecky's" 18). Louis Althusser's discussion of how people, ideas, and environment relate gives a better idea of the complexity: "I shall therefore say that, where only a single subject (such and such an individual) is concerned, the existence of the ideas of his belief is material in that *his ideas are his material actions inserted into material practices governed by material rituals*" (169, emphasis in original). Hank's ideas are his only "material." These ideas, after all, constitute the baggage he takes with him. But there exists a complicity of material, particularly on the plane of character. For Hank, who would be Boss, there is little distinction between idea and action; Hank *embodies* the environment that produced him. His material is really the entire bundle of nineteenth-century material: ideas, actions, practices, and rituals. These materials are what he injects into the sixth century, and they become material to that culture. Hank's tools are both his nineteenth-century ideas and his nineteenth-century environment in the form of modern technological improvements; his adversaries are both sixth-century ideas and the sixth-century environment. Hank hopes to revolutionize the environment that will in turn revolutionize the minds of its inhabitants, but when the centuries and their material ideas and rituals collide, words like *progress* and *civilization* suffer an erosion of meaning. The violence that ensues grants them new, negative connotations. Many critics have suggested that Twain had difficulty ending his novel, a problem typical of realistic novels. As Amy Kaplan points out, "Realistic novels have trouble ending because they pose problems they cannot solve, problems that stem from their attempt to imagine and contain social change" (160). Twain, however, composed his "fictional history" to vivify the sense of change as experienced by human beings living through time, not to "contain" change. His ending of victory and defeat and violence seems perfectly consonant with the reality of what happens when different people with different ideas from different worlds collide.

The copy of Lecky's *Spirit of Rationalism* discovered at Quarry Farm contains two distinct types of marginalia, those made in purple pencil and those made in black pencil. Those in purple pencil are easily dated. Mark Twain almost certainly made the purple markings during the summer of 1885, when he and his family stayed with the Cranes from June until September. During that time, Twain wrote more than half of his journal entries, some dated, in purple pencil.[2]

Connecticut Yankee in 1885 was perhaps at its most crucial stage. Twain knew little more than the germ of the story, which he set down in his notebook:

> X Dream of being a knight errant in armor in the middle ages.
> X Have the notions & habits of thought of the present day mixed with the necessities of that. No pockets in the armor. No way to manage certain requirements of nature. Can't scratch. Cold in the head—can't blow—can't get at handkerchief, can't use iron sleeve. Iron gets red hot in the sun—leaks in the rain, gets white with frost & freezes me solid in winter. Suffer from lice & fleas. Make disagreeable clatter when I enter church. Can't dress or undress myself. Always getting struck by lightning. Fall down, can't get up. See Morte Darthur. (*MTN&J* 3:78).[3]

Beyond the structural first cause of mixing the "notions" of the present with the "necessities" of the past, however, the purview of the novel remained nebulous. Still, one can extract from Twain's discussion of the "habits of thought" of the present day and the "necessities" of the past the philosophical problem of environmental determinism that erupts in the novel when Hank's nineteenth-century ideas and Camelot's sixth-century environment collide.

The marginalia offer a privileged insight into Mark Twain's creative process at this very early stage in the novel's composition. Howard Baetzhold's comment that Twain "all but abandoned his writing for most of 1885" is technically accurate but not quite true ("Let It Go" 45). As Twain said later of this early stage, "I began to make notes in my head for a book" (*MTN&J* 3:79). To employ a phrase Twain impressed many times in the margin of Lecky's *Spirit of Rationalism*, these marginalia are the "clouds of witness" that testify to the gestation of the book during that crucial time. The philosophies and ideas that would take form in *Connecticut Yankee* were in the summer of 1885 commingling freely without coalescing. That they would do before the year was out: December 16, 1885, would find Twain writing to his publisher, Charles Webster, "I am plotting out a new book, & am full of it" (*MTBus* 343).

As he read Lecky's *Spirit of Rationalism*, Twain marked in particular many passages dealing with the belief in witches, magic, and the supernatural. In one Lecky asserts that the existence of witchcraft was "admitted by almost all the ablest men in Christendom" (1:93). Throughout the book Lecky outlines a general credulousness and willingness to accept the supernatural as a part of everyday life; Twain marked many of these passages, often imprinting derisive comments in the margin. Fulminating, he wrote, "Another infallible 'Cloud of Witnesses'" next to a passage from Glanvil, who asserted "the attestation of thousands of eye and ear witness" (1:134). Similarly, next to Cudworth's citing of authorities "in all ages" who argued for the existence of witchcraft, Twain responded tersely: "The eternal argument that in the concurrent testimony of a multitude of fools lies proof" (1:136). Like Twain, but in contrast to the inhabitants of Camelot, Hank relies on his own reason because, as he says, "I knew that the testimony of men wouldn't serve—my reason would say they were lunatics, and throw out their evidence" (62–63).

One might say that Hank follows the "compass of fact" to avoid going off course, even as his creator follows historical fact in order to create a realistic portrayal of the inherently unrealistic situation. As he wrote in his draft for the *Princeton Review*, Twain wished his descriptions would "seem realities" (*MTN&J* 3:343). Twain's realism is both a literary and a philosophical stance: it provides a means of achieving fictional verisimilitude, and it poses the question of historical and environmental determinism. If one can identify the facts in a given situation, might one find the means to effect, and benefit from, positive change? Susan Mizruchi terms this notion "the fallacy of historical self-consciousness" (81). Likewise, that knowledge can be so gleaned and so applied is a question left fundamentally unresolved in Twain's thought. As subsequent discussion will show, Hank's occasional ability to master cause and effect is usually overtaken by unexpected impediments and consequences. Twain always hoped and sometimes believed that his writing could change attitudes and, ultimately, history. This belief was the point d'appui of his craft, for without the possibility of effecting positive change through writing, what point was there? Twain was no "joyful nihilist," and even the darker moods that occur in *Connecticut Yankee* articulate the frustration of an author who sought to change the world that had been presented him as a "given." When Hank tries to retrain King Arthur and laments, "But lord, it was only just words, words,—they meant nothing in the world to him . . . words realize nothing, vivify nothing to you, unless you have suffered in your own person the things which the words try to describe," we sense Twain's despair of retraining his own readers (324–25). Twain peppered his own book with the contrast between laudable nineteenth-century reason and lamentable sixth-century credulity in such elements as the court's fear of Merlin, a fear based on the "storms and the lightnings and all the devils that be in hell at his beck and call," and again one senses that Hank's frustration is at times Twain's (71). Similarly, Sandy's insistence that the swine in chapter 20 are really aristocrats enchanted by an evil spell testifies to the willingness of those in the sixth century to ascribe supernatural agency, to violate the compass of fact. Belief in the supernatural produces, and is produced by, the milieu in Camelot.

Although these examples in *Connecticut Yankee* may seem humorous, Twain imprinted marginal lines in Lecky's *Spirit of Rationalism* next to more deleterious results of such beliefs. On page 126 of the first volume, for example, Twain left marginal lines alongside the comment that "in Suffolk sixty persons were hung for witchcraft in a single year." On another page Twain responded to Lecky's description of the execution of witches by commenting in the margin, "All this results from a remark put into God's mouth by the lying Scriptures: 'Thou shall not suffer a witch to live'" (1:85). Twain noted many such passages in Lecky, and the fear of torture pervades *Connecticut Yankee*. In chapter 5, for example, Hank fears he has "waked only just in time to keep from being hanged or drowned or burned, or something" (82). As it turns out, like those accused of witchcraft in Lecky's *Spirit of Rationalism*, Hank is sentenced to be burned at the stake: "As we stepped into the vast enclosed court of the castle I got a shock; for the first thing I saw was the stake, standing in the centre, and near it the piled fagots and a monk" (91). The whole scene recalls the many burnings of witches related by Lecky.

Later scenes in *Connecticut Yankee* recall even more dramatically certain elements of Lecky's descriptions. A woman is accused of communicating with the devil in order to inflict a "strange disease" on local cows, for example, and startles Hank suddenly with "shrieks and yells" after breaking away from her accusers (399). Her flight recalls a passage in Lecky that Twain had scored: "An Earl of Mar (who appears to have been the only person sensible of the inhumanity of the proceedings) tells how, with a piercing yell, some women once broke half-burnt from the slow fire that consumed them, struggled for a few moments with despairing energy among the spectators, but soon with shrieks of blasphemy and wild protestations of innocence sank writhing in agony amid the flames" (1:148). Even the language of "shrieks and yells" in *Connecticut Yankee* seems to emerge from the marked passage in this work, and the unfortunate woman in Twain's description is likewise captured and burned at the stake.

A passage a few pages later also caught Twain's eye, and he underlined these lines: "we have to picture the anguish of the mother, as she imagined that it was in the power of one whom she had offended to blast in a moment every object of her affection" (1:153–54). Twain was always affected by mothers in peril, and he seems to have incorporated these sentiments in the burning of the accused witch in *Connecticut Yankee*. The tormentors pile wood about her and "applied the torch while she shrieked and pleaded and strained her two young daughters to her breast" (400). Lecky's description of the treatment of women led Twain to write in the margin: "The modern claim that Christianity was a blessed boon to poor downtrodden woman seems to be a very pleasant sarcasm" (1:99).

When Hank imagines he has "waked only just in time to keep from being hanged or drowned or burned, or something," the truly horrible fate is left ill-defined as "something" (82). Twain tagged another passage in Lecky's work: "There are opinions that may be traced from age to age by footsteps of blood" (1:149). In reading Lecky's *Spirit of Rationalism* Twain walked in these "footsteps of blood," and, as unbelievable as it sounds, there were worse tortures than being burned at the stake, and they were those practiced by the Scottish clergy. The underlining in the passage is Twain's.

> The three principal that were habitually applied, were the penny-winkis, the boots, and the caschielawis. The first was a kind of thumb-screw; the second was a frame in which the leg was inserted, and in which it was broken by wedges, driven in by a hammer; the third was also an iron frame for the leg, which was from time to time heated over a brazier. Fire-matches were sometimes applied to the body of the victim. We read, in a contemporary legal register, of one man who was kept for forty-eight hours in "vehement tortour" in the caschielawis; and of another who remained in the same frightful machine for eleven days and eleven nights, whose legs were broken daily for fourteen days in the boots, and who was so scourged that the whole skin was torn from his body. (1:147)

The passage recalls Nietzsche's claim in *The Genealogy of Morals* that "torture, blood, sacrifice" typify the attempt by organized religion to "create a memory" (193). The clergy in *Connecticut Yankee* use pain as an "aid to mnemonics," to employ Nietzsche's phrase, and so create within their societies a history of morality based on torture (193). Katharine Kearns perceptively discusses the "economy of pain" in realism, noting that realists had to limit the intrusion of reality or their readers would be "paralyzed" through vicarious "suffering" (21). Twain may have left the pennywinkis, the boots, and the caschielawis ill-defined as "something" to limit the horror in a book that tried to craft comedy out of tragic materials.

The scenes of such cruelty that emerge in Twain's book arise neither from an appeal to the "blood and thunder" audience as Hill claims (37–38) nor from the less-reasonable psychological causation dispensed with in the first chapter. Rather, these scenes emerge directly from the compass of fact that has seared the memory of such morality in history. Although *Connecticut Yankee* contains no direct references to "the pennywinkis," "the boots," or "the caschielawis," the description of the rack in Morgan le Fay's dungeon in chapter 17 resembles the "frightful machine" in some significant respects. Hank is made aware of the rack by the "muffled shriek" that makes his "flesh crawl" (199). The man, Morgan le Fay tells him, "is truly a stubborn soul, and endureth long," refusing to confess his crime. Much like the man in Lecky's description, the "young giant" of Hank's description is tortured at great length on a "machine," with each turn of the windlass producing waves of pain and gales of shrieking (201).

Next to his underlining in the passage from Lecky quoted above, Twain commented laconically, "These are Scotch, not Iroquois." Hank at several points in the earliest portions of the novel refers to the inhabitants of Camelot as Indians. In chapter 2, catching sight of the other prisoners, Hank notes that they were "maimed, hacked, carved, in a frightful way" and yet remained without "a moan or a groan"; he then refers to them as "white Indians" (66). When the king confers on Hank the honor of escorting Sandy to the enchanted castle, Hank is "as glad as a person is when he is scalped" (136). Later, too, Hank labels the inhabitants of Camelot "merely modified savages" (154). Still later, he condemns the whole court as "a sort of polished-up court of Comanches" (176). Twain converted what he knew of American society to the English situation. With Hank Morgan Twain can present English history through American eyes, and with words like *scalped* he can use American language to express an attitude toward that history from the very beginning. The concept of "change" is also an issue, for Twain imagined the equation Realism = History = Change, an equation within which even the Americanisms are markers. As Megan Stitt observes, a "character's speech, then, could be seen to proclaim individuality, while placing him or her into a 'drama' of changing language" (7). The Americanisms in *Connecticut Yankee* and Twain's marginal comment function in this way and indicate historical change; both make manifest change that is otherwise hidden. "Scotch" behavior, in particular, has changed over time. What was typical behavior for the Scots in an earlier time becomes, in the nineteenth century, typical behavior for North American aboriginal tribes.[4]

Twain's tack here might seem strange, but it was actually quite common in the nineteenth century to compare Scots and Indians and to use Scotland as a proving ground for theories about progress. Anthropologist David Richards explains the reason for such comparisons:

> Since the European "past" could be seen in the lives of contemporary primitives who lived nonetheless in a "previous" epoch of human development, travel to those peoples involved not only a geographical journey, but a voyage in time. . . . The Highlands are to be seen as a historical test case for a world "experiment" with history which can subsequently become the structuring principles of narrative. (125–29)

Much has been made of Twain's use of modern historians and the anachronisms that result in *Connecticut Yankee*, but such disturbing details create not anachronism but synchronism. Modern Scottish history provided the example for Twain of a primitive culture undergoing a test with the effects of civilization. In his analysis of the development of realism, Mikhail Bakhtin notes that in Scotland, Sir Walter Scott "could see time in space" (53). Lecky's history, one might say, provided Twain with a synchronic panorama wherein were depicted the struggles of all humanity to rise through fits and starts from barbarism to civilization, although in the process those terms undergo scrutiny. The historical perspective Twain gained from reading Scottish history of the eighteenth century was one of violent domination by the clergy that evolved into the more enlightened practices witnessed occasionally in the contemporary world.

As a result, in several of the scenes in *Connecticut Yankee* that involve torture, the Church is directly involved and implicated. When the young man is broken on the rack, and Hank tells us that a "priest bent over him on each side" (201), one recalls Lecky's assertion that "in every prison the crucifix and the rack stood side by side" (1:332–33). Presumably the priests attend because the young man may need extreme unction at any moment, but their passive acquiescence to his torture makes them accomplices to the crime. The Church is even more directly involved when Hank himself is slated to be burned at the stake. When Hank first sees the stake, he catches sight of "the piled fagots and a monk" (91). Just as the bundles of sticks are torched, the monk lifts his "eyes toward the blue sky, and began some words in Latin" (92–93). Again, although the monk may attend so that he can perform the last rites, one cannot avoid the conclusion that his presence in some sense consecrates the event. Many of the passages marked in Lecky chronicle the tortures inflicted by the Scottish clergy on the Scottish people. Lecky condemns them for it roundly but criticizes as well the passivity of the Church when it errs by doing nothing. Twain impressed a line next to Lecky's stern condemnation of the behavior of the Scottish clergy under circumstances similar to those in Camelot: "One word from them might have arrested the tortures, but that word was never spoken" (1:149). Gleaned from his research into British history, this idea must have seared itself in Twain's memory, for it emerges many times in *Connecticut Yankee*.

One of the most significant contributions of the *Spirit of Rationalism* to *Connecticut Yankee* consists precisely in Lecky's criticism of the Church for failing to use its great power for equally great ends. Hank, speaking of himself and King Arthur, declares that "there was another power that was a trifle stronger than both of us put together. That was the Church" (109). Throughout *Connecticut Yankee* the Church establishes itself as the major source of repression in Camelot. Hank even associates the Church with slavery, saying that the people have less reason to honor the Church and royalty than "a slave has to love and honor the lash" (110). Later he becomes more explicit, branding the "Established Church" an "established slavepen" (185–86). "The Church has never started a good work," Twain wrote next to a discussion of the Church's continued insistence on the existence of witchcraft, "& has always been the last to relinquish an evil one. American slavery's last & stubbornest friend & champion in the North was the church" (1:141). Besides indicating his continued focus on the interplay of morality and history, and that he was thinking synchronically, Twain's response indicates he connected at an early stage his thinking about actual slavery in Camelot with what Lecky, in his later *History of England in the Eighteenth Century*, calls "slavery of the mind" (2:96). Many nineteenth-century writers spoke of such slavery. John Stuart Mill discussed "mental slavery" in *On Liberty* (125), and William Blake in "London" criticized the "mind-forg'd manacles" that limited human imagination and freedom (64). Ann Jefferson explains this in *Reading Realism in Stendhal* by observing that between 1780 and 1825 there was "a complete transformation of mental habits, of the way that people perceived the world" (6). Twain pondered the mental habits of those living in such an age and wrote in the margin of Lecky's *Spirit of Rationalism*, "Think a moment—weigh well the meaning of those eight lines. They mean that the *entire world* wise & simple, believed for ages in a thing—sorcery—which had absolutely *no existence*" (2:113). The shift from mental slavery to freedom as a mental habit governed Lecky's thought and history, and it governed Mark Twain's thought through the three and a half years it would take him to complete his novel.

Equally pernicious, then, is the effect of the Church's dogma on the imagination. Twain marked passages in *Spirit of Rationalism* that berate the Church's influence in this respect. The Church, Lecky contends, "cursed the human intellect by cursing the doubts that are the necessary consequence of its exercise" (1:72). Likewise, Twain imprinted a triple marginal line next to Lecky's observation that "The single employment of the reason was to develop and expand premises that were furnished by the Church" (1:88). These sentiments erupt in Hank's disparaging of the people of Camelot as "poor-spirited" (111) and later even as a "mistaught herd of human sheep" (160). The culprit, Hank notes, is a "united church" that spells "death to human liberty, and paralysis to human thought" (127). The Church substitutes a prescriptive and mistaken "compass of dogma" for the realist's compass of fact, causing those it dominates to confuse truth with lies.

Hank's solution to the Church's domination of the human mind, the "paralysis" of thought, is a reformation. In passages Twain lined Lecky illustrates that the Reformation was preeminently a revolution of the mind that produced a "general secularisation of the European intellect, which is such a marked characteristic of modern civilisation" (1:79). Twain responded as well to Lecky's description of the "mental servitude" enjoined by the Scottish ministers by writing in the margin: "There are people, even in this day, who long for a 'united church.' There never was a united church which did not usurp the privileges of hell" (1:143). Hank tries to end such usurpations and the "paralysis to human thought" by introducing "a complete variety of Protestant congregations" (127). Hank, then, tries to impose his character onto the environment and so, as Harold Aspiz has said, "*create* a nineteenth-century milieu" that will in turn beget people with nineteenth-century characters ("Lecky's" 18). At this early stage in the novel's composition Twain still hoped that, even though environment creates character, strong-willed people following the compass of fact might effect change on the matrix that engenders character; their ideas might enter the world of material reality. Twain wrote this comment in the margin of Lecky's book: "There were a million evidences that witchcraft did exist; & only one solitary argument that it didn't—namely, its improbability; & that one argument proved stronger than the million proofs in the end" (1:135). The probability of a thing existing concerns Twain both as a writer of realism and as a person searching for ways to locate moral truths; probability is the compass of fact that conflates Twain's ethics and aesthetics. Soon, however, Twain would discover historical examples proving the truth of Marx's assertion that people cannot make history "just as they please" and that the "tradition of all the dead generations weighs like a nightmare on the brain of the living" (15).

The black marginalia in Lecky's *Spirit of Rationalism* are more difficult to date. The interspersing of the markings in black and purple pencil suggests they were made at different times, probably different summers. It is important to clarify at this point that the purple and black markings are truly interspersed. The purple markings *do not* all occur within one block, to be succeeded later by black markings. Were that the case it would be likely Twain began marking the book in purple and then finished his reading with another pencil. That is what we would expect to find if the markings were made in the same summer. Just the opposite is the case. The markings go back and forth from one to the other, suggesting at the very least different readings and perhaps, as I shall attempt to show, in different summers. That the black-pencil marginalia were written after the purple is also supported by Twain's editing of his own comment on page 143 of the first volume. Twain originally wrote, "There never was a united church which did not usurp the privileges of hell" in purple. Later, however, he scratched out *hell*, using his black pencil to substitute *tyranny*.

Although 1886 saw little work done on the novel, Twain continued his study of English history through the summer of 1887. Internal references point toward this year as the summer Twain reread Lecky's *Spirit of Rationalism*. For example, the *Connecticut Yankee* manuscript version of chapter 20 contains a discussion of infant damnation that owes much to a multiplicity of marked passages in Lecky's treating of the subject. Twain's passage, later excised, has Hank declaring that he "had only recently sloughed off the Roman-Catholic-Presbyterian belief" that unbaptized infants would suffer "in hellfire forever and ever because of that omission."[5] Twain marked a total of five passages—and in two cases the entire page—surveying such beliefs in Lecky's *Spirit of Rationalism*. One passage features the opinion of St. Fulgentius—written, like Hank's manuscript, in the sixth century—that even stillborn children "must be punished by the eternal torture of undying fire" (1:362). One imagines Twain was so struck and horrified by the assertion that he marked it with the intent of including it in his book. If Baetzhold's chronology is correct, and chapter 20 was written *before* July 1888, when Twain arrived at Quarry Farm, he must then have read and marked this passage and its fellows in Lecky's *Spirit of Rationalism* the previous summer during his stay at Quarry Farm.

Although the infant damnation passages strongly suggest that the marginalia in black pencil were written in 1887, they also provoke some intriguing questions, among them, why did Twain strike the passage from his novel? We can never know for certain, but I believe the phrase "Roman-Catholic-Presbyterian belief" holds the key to this mystery. Twain used Lecky as the source for the tortures practiced in previous ages, but many of these, if not most, were tortures tolerated or enjoined not by Roman Catholicism but by Scottish Presbyterianism or in some cases English Anglicanism. One might argue that Twain made Roman Catholicism his villain in order to preserve historicity because Presbyterianism did not exist prior to the Reformation. One could also argue with some justification that Twain was biased and simply did not approve of Catholicism and that he did not wish to offend an audience that, like himself, would prefer a Catholic villain: why alienate one's readership by associating Catholicism and Presbyterianism in the same sentence? Twain himself was Presbyterian. Whatever the vagaries of his Christianity—and they were many—Twain grew up in the Presbyterian Church and remained a Presbyterian throughout his life. Before his burial at Woodlawn Cemetery in Elmira, his funeral was held at Brick Presbyterian Church in New York City. In short, Twain faced the dilemma that his source provided evidence that the Reformation was no panacea and that the worst abuses continued well after the Catholic Church no longer dominated Britain. The plurality of these problems led Twain, I believe, to strike the passage referring to the "Roman-Catholic-Presbyterian belief" of infant damnation. Aside from the vexing question of his personal religious beliefs, to couple Roman Catholicism with Presbyterianism would complicate his thesis that a reformation would solve the problem of the Church's abuse of power. Even at this relatively early stage, the skies of the cause and effect universe were growing cloudy. As a result of his reading, Twain struck the reference and took care throughout the book to have Hank discuss the established or united Church instead of vilifying only Roman Catholicism.[6]

As with the 1885 marginalia, many of the 1887 marginalia relate to Twain's concern for the established Church's tyranny. Many of the passages deal with the Church's reliance on torture as a means of enforcing doctrine, and Twain underlined, for example, Lecky's assertion, "Terror is everywhere the beginning of religion" (1:40). As with the 1885 marginalia, the later marked passages suggest this terror impedes the imagination by diverting it from freethinking to fearful obedience to authority. Thus, Twain tagged a passage in which Lecky quotes Gregory XVI, who rejected "liberty of conscience" (2:74).

The Church's tyranny extended, however, to politics as well. Twain impressed lines on a page that discusses the Spanish Inquisition as "the special expression of a national religion" in which the burning of Jews and heretics is both "religious ceremony" and "public amusement" (2:116). The passage highlights the danger of a national religion, whose torture is accomplished to advance religious and political agendas. Nowhere is this complicity revealed so clearly as in the passages Twain lined discussing the Anglican Church's doctrine of nonresistance. He marked, for example, a passage in Lecky discussing the Anglican Church flinging "herself on every occasion into the arms of the civil power" (2:174). Below this passage Twain marked the footnote containing a passage from a church document that states, "Heaven is the place of good obedient subjects, and hell the prison and dungeon of rebels against God and their prince" (2:174). Similarly, Twain marked three more passages in subsequent pages that flatly assert those who oppose civil authority oppose the will of God (2:175, 176, 184).

Twain's antagonism to the Church on precisely these grounds emerges at several points in *Connecticut Yankee*. Hank explains the process by which the Church manipulates the people to accept the divine right of kings. He blames the Church for inventing the concept and propping it up "brick by brick, with the Beatitudes" (113). Hank himself is anything but meek and takes exception to the very idea of a king and, most particularly, to the notion of "non-resistance under oppression" taught by the Church (113). Later, in chapter 13, Hank again derides the concept, tracing its lineage to the priests who instructed their parishioners "that this ironical state of things was ordained of God" (156). Considering the consequences to those who rebel against civil or religious authority in Lecky's Britain or Twain's Camelot, little wonder it is that most people accepted the ordination without question.

Hank responds by suggesting, on the contrary, that one has a duty to resist tyranny. Hank attempts to introduce this nineteenth-century idea into the sixth-century mind by questioning beliefs inculcated into the people by training. Hank tries to awaken them to the compass of fact by asking them whether, if every person had a vote, they would elect one family to "reign over them forever" (158). Sam Girgus interprets Hank's reformation as an attempt to create "an individual sense of conscience compatible with the Protestant work ethic" (555), and here he does try to retrain the people into free agents. Again, one sees the circularity of Hank's project, for he here tries to create a nineteenth-century environment by infusing his ideas into the sixth-century mind. That mind would then bring its environment up to date. Hank's concept of disloyalty emerges from Twain's study of history, as his research at Quarry Farm uncovered the many ways people have been manipulated and coerced into supporting those opposed to their interests. Hank calls "disloyalty" a "gospel" that redefines the idea of loyalty; Hank asserts that it is the "duty" of the citizens to resist tyranny and that one is disloyal if one *fails* to "agitate" for an end to it (159–60).

Hank utilizes a variety of animal metaphors to describe the passivity of the people. In chapter 13 he refers to them as "clams," indicating in particular their disinclination to speak up for their rights. Twain placed a marginal line along much of a section in Lecky discussing Etienne de la Boetie's treatise called by either of the two titles *La Servitude Volun-taire* (On voluntary servitude) or *Le Contre Un* (Against one man) (1574–76). A contemporary and friend of Montaigne, who wrote of their friendship in the essay "Of Friendship," La Boetie, like Hank, is faced by a people who have been trained to accept a variety of indignities: "'Wretched and insensate people,' writes the author, 'enamoured of your misery and blind to your interests, you suffer your property to be pil-laged, your fields devastated, your houses stripped of goods, and all this by one whom you have yourselves raised to power, and whose dignity you maintain with your lives!'" (2:199). Similarly, Hank decries the tolerance of the peasants of Camelot who "smother their anger when his hunting parties [gallop] through their fields" and who then watch as the king and Church take their portion of the remaining crop (156).

Hank's lengthy diatribe probably derives mainly from Twain's reading of Taine's *L'Ancien Regime*, as Rodney Rogers establishes. Rogers, how-ever, asserts that although Twain built on Taine's ideas, the passage also witnesses a "rejection of certain of Taine's attitudes," in particular his antagonism toward the French Revolution (441). The passage, Rogers argues, is really an amalgam of facts derived from Taine's *L'Ancien Re-gime* and Lecky's *History of European Morals;* the passage also includes, it seems to me, La Boetie's tone of moral outrage at the aristocracy and, more particularly, indignation at those oppressed people who allow themselves to be so abused. Even his title, *On Voluntary Servitude*, asserts that the people are themselves to blame for tolerating the state of affairs. As Lecky chronicles in *Spirit of Rationalism,* La Boetie attacks the sub-jects of a king as tolerating "indignities that the beasts themselves would not endure" when they could end their oppression in a simple manner: "Resolve to serve no more, and you are free" (2:200). Like Hank, La Boetie identifies the source of the oppression as the complicity of the people with their oppressor. Both would probably agree with Steven Biko's assertion that "the most potent weapon in the hands of the op-pressor is the mind of the oppressed." Hank's reformation becomes, at its most basic level, an attempt to reorganize society by reorganizing the minds that serve the oppressors.[7]

Twain may well have seen in La Boetie a type of Hank. Like Hank, La Boetie espoused a belief in political liberty and stressed the duty of individuals to fight for their rights. La Boetie's ideas were, like Hank's, anachronistic; both La Boetie and Hank are men "before their time." Although La Boetie wrote in the mid-1500s, his writing recalls, says Lecky, "the declamations of the revolutionists of the eighteenth century" (2:199). Montaigne said of his friend, "He had a mind shaped to the pattern of other ages than this" (73). In La Boetie Twain found the rage of a person frustrated by history, the rage of one whose ideas are sound but at variance with the time. The preeminent fact, though, is that La Boetie did exist, did have ideas "ahead of his time," and so one has to question the idea that Twain is supposed to have violated historicity by placing an American democrat in Camelot. La Boetie's existence, along with Twain's awareness of it, undermines the argument that one cannot escape the chains of one's historical moment. Such transcendence is possible, as La Boetie attests, and as I believe Twain illustrates, by taking one's bearings from the compass of fact. This, at least, was Twain's hope when he wrote such satires as *Adventures of Huckleberry Finn* and *Connecticut Yankee*. One could argue that Hank's ideas rightly belong in the sixth century because that is where they can do the most good; precisely because the environment is inimical to engendering and nurturing revolutionary ideas, the historical context requires them. Still, as Marx notes when discussing the "tradition of all the dead generations," history tends toward conservatism (15). La Boetie may have been a forerunner of later "revolutionists," as Lecky says, but he led, in fact, no revolution. The disjuncture between Hank's ideas and the age he tries to convert will eventually cause the death of twenty-five thousand knights and precipitate his own return to the nineteenth century through the agency of sixth-century magic.

Susan Crane's copy of Lecky's *Spirit of Rationalism* discovered at Quarry Farm allows us to observe Mark Twain in the process of composing one of his masterworks. Bearing Twain's comments and interlinings, Lecky's work itself stands as tangible "witness" to Twain's creative process and testifies to the conscious artistry of that process. Those, like Robinson, Bell, or Bridgman, who would marginalize Twain's conscious aesthetics bear the responsibility of examining Twain's marginalia and manuscripts and not just Twain's conscious misrepresentations. Lecky's book is, in some sense, the real "site" of creative activity, for although Twain occupied the octagonal study at Quarry Farm, the books he consulted for his research and in which he wrote served as the locus of composition where he weighed and considered the ideas his Yankee would espouse. One cannot help but conjecture that Twain thought of himself when he marked a passage lauding Montaigne, a writer who could "contemplate the systems of the past, without being dazzled by the reverence that surrounded them" (1:113).

3
Macaulay's "Stately Sentences"

Twain's 1885 and 1887 Marginalia in *The History of England*

> You see, I went back and read my 350 pages of MS through,
> yesterday, and found out that I am making an uncommonly bully
> book—and am swelled up accordingly.
> > —Mark Twain to Fred J. Hall and Charles L. Webster,
> > August 15, 1887 (*MTLP* 224)

Although William Lecky and Thomas Carlyle undoubtedly had the greatest influence on Mark Twain's thought during the composition of *Connecticut Yankee,* or indeed at any other time, Thomas Babington Macaulay also had a decided impact. Over the years Twain's family owned as many as four sets of Macaulay's *History of England from the Accession of James II.* Early in his career Twain particularly admired Macaulay's literary craftsmanship, referring in *The Innocents Abroad* to "the march of his stately sentences" (2:220). Years later, in a passage excised from *Following the Equator,* Twain again commended Macaulay's vigorous prose, exclaiming, "I have read that History a number of times, & I believe it has no dull places in it."[1]

Given Twain's extensive reading of Macaulay's work, one might expect equally extensive marginalia, but in fact few such marginalia exist.[2] Recently, however, several previously unknown sets of Macaulay's work have been discovered in the Cranes's collection in their home at Quarry Farm, among them a copy of Macaulay's *History of England* that Mark Twain consulted at least twice during the composition of *Connecticut Yankee.* This find is particularly significant because of the impact on *Connecticut Yankee* of what Sydney Krause terms the "Macaulayan

Method" (229). Macaulay aimed at an almost fiction-like "vivification of history," coupled with a realism based on "a sensory awareness of the passage of man through time" (Krause 232). Twain's concern as he wrote his novel with the concept of change and of being within all history at one time mirrors the Macaulayan Method, which was to have a momentous impact on *Connecticut Yankee.* Just as Macaulay used literary technique to vivify history, Twain adopted a historical approach to ground his fiction in the "real." In Aristotle's terms Twain united "poetry" and "history" as part of a realist agenda.

As with Lecky's *Spirit of Rationalism,* the marginalia in Susan Crane's copy of Macaulay's *History of England* are in two different colored pencils, one purple and one black; the two colors of marginalia are again alternating and interspersed. Hence, it is very likely that Twain read both books during the same two summers that he read Lecky's work, 1885 and 1887.

Mark Twain evidently did not read Macaulay's *History of England* extensively in the summer of 1885, and he made only three markings in purple, all of them in the first volume. The first marking occurs on page 7, where Twain struck through *entombed* from the line "great works of ancient power and wisdom lay entombed," substituting *engulfed*† in his distinctive handwriting. Twain often subjected books he read to this kind of revision, even the histories of his beloved Lecky. However "stately" Macaulay's sentences, Twain apparently felt he could improve them. The remaining purple marginalia chart Twain's crescive anti-Catholicism. On page 19 of the first volume he underlined the phrase "except her own" in a passage lauding the Church's enfranchising of bondmen. Throughout *Connecticut Yankee* Twain exposes the complicity of the Church with slavery. In chapter 8, for example, Hank Morgan says the English "were slaves, pure and simple," whose primary responsibility was to "grovel before king and Church and noble; to slave for them" (111). Twain also evinces concern about the Church's impact on the psychology of its communicants. On page 37 of *History of England* Twain drew a marginal line along a passage where Macaulay states that "during the last three centuries, to stunt the growth of the human mind has been her chief object." "Her" in this passage refers to the Church of Rome. Similarly, Hank rails against the Roman Catholic Church because it had, he says, "converted a nation of men to a nation of worms" (113). Twain describes the process of conversion as a "subtle" one whereby freedom of thought is checked by "inherited ideas" (112–13). Twain vented his anti-Catholicism years *engulfed*

. These
mpt from
were, in
ages, and
ry of the
ty of the
however
restraints
of muscle
e fiercest
ndman, a
more re-
ts.
mpt with
ak of the
monastic
hen were
or by the
nt of the
than that
as and un-
when life
from ty-
f a shrine
that there
tiousness.
extensive
an nations
the Holy
rwhelmed
may, at a
lence and
in an age
isters and
cultivated,
nd an asy-
transcrib-
g the Ana-
art might
which he
ke experi-
Had not
ig the huts

of a miserable peasantry, and the castles of a ferocious aristocracy, European society would have consisted merely of beasts of burden and beasts of prey. The church has many times been compared by divines to that ark, of which we read in the Book of Genesis; but never was the resemblance more perfect than during that evil time when she alone rode, amidst darkness and tempest, on the deluge beneath which all the great works of ancient power and wisdom lay entombed, bearing within her that feeble germ from which a second and more glorious civilization was to spring.

Even the spiritual supremacy arrogated by the pope was, in the dark ages, productive of far more good than evil. Its effect was to unite the nations of Western Europe in one great commonwealth. What the Olympian chariot course and the Pythian oracle were to all the Greek cities, from Trebizond to Marseilles, Rome and her bishop were to all Christians of the Latin communion, from Calabria to the Hebrides. Thus grew up sentiments of enlarged benevolence. Races separated from each other by seas and mountains acknowledged a fraternal tie and a common code of public law. Even in war, the cruelty of the conqueror was not seldom mitigated by the recollection that he and his vanquished enemies were all members of one great federation.

Into this federation the Anglo-Saxons were now admitted. A regular communication was opened between our shores and that part of Europe in which the traces of ancient power and policy were yet discernible. Many noble monuments which have since been destroyed or defaced, still retained their pristine magnificence; and travellers, to whom Livy and Sallust were unintelligible, might gain from the Roman aqueducts and temples some faint notion of Roman history. The dome of Agrippa, still glittering with bronze, the mausoleum of Adrian, not yet deprived of its columns and statues, the Flavian amphitheatre, not yet degraded into a quarry, told to the Mercian and Northumbrian pilgrims some part of the story of that great civilized world which had passed away. The islanders returned, with awe deeply impressed on their half-opened minds, and told the wondering inhabitants of the hovels of London and York that, near the grave of Saint Peter, a mighty race, now extinct, had piled up buildings which would never be dissolved till the judgment day. Learning followed in the train of Christianity. The poetry and eloquence of the Augustan age was assiduously studied in the

1. A page featuring Twain's revision of Macaulay's prose. Courtesy Mark Twain Archives, Elmira College.

earlier in *The Prince and the Pauper* but softened his criticism with the presence of Father John, who befriends Tom Canty. There are few such characters in *Connecticut Yankee,* however, and the criticism grows uglier. One senses even in these marginalia "mental notes" that emerge in the finished novel.[3]

The markings in black pencil are more difficult to date. Intermixed with the purple markings, the marks in black pencil were probably not inscribed during the same reading. The Cranes acquired Macaulay's *History of England* in 1870, but of the books Twain wrote in the seventies and early eighties only *A Tramp Abroad* contains references to Macaulay and then only to his use of "doubled-up haves" (203). The summer of 1886 witnessed almost no creative work by Twain at Quarry Farm because he had decided to "loaf all summer," as he told an interviewer, and Twain is unlikely to have returned to Macaulay's book in 1889, after having completed *Connecticut Yankee.* Most probably the markings in Macaulay correspond to the black pencilings Twain inscribed in Lecky's *Spirit of Rationalism* during the summer of 1887.[4]

I suspect that Twain returned to Macaulay's *History of England* while simmering with resentment at Matthew Arnold's criticisms of General Grant. Arnold antagonized Twain early in that year with criticisms in his *Murray's Magazine* review of General Grant's *Memoirs.* On April 27, 1887, Twain defended Grant in a speech to the Army and Navy Club in Hartford and turned the tables on Arnold, offering him "a *lofty* place in that illustrious list of delinquents" who abuse the language ("General" 135). In the *Connecticut Yankee* manuscript Twain even satirized Arnold's insistence on the distinction between *shall* and *will.* In a passage written in the summer of 1887, but later cancelled, Twain ridiculed the distinction by having Hank correct Sandy: "Not shall—*will* tell you. I know it's human to mix the shalls and wills, but it's a curable defect."[5] Arnold's broadside against all American civilization in April of the following year would move Twain to consider countering the Englishman's "Civilization in the United States" with his own book, *English Criticism on America, Letters to an English Friend.* Although he never completed his book, Twain was angry at Arnold even in 1887 for his earlier insults and had increased his note taking, mental and otherwise, by studying historical works that would provide appropriate ammunition. Perhaps his anger at Arnold's first jibe in 1887 led Twain to reread Macaulay's *History of England,* leaving as evidence marginalia in black pencil, just as in 1885 he had annotated the work in purple pencil.

By midsummer Twain found his novel stagnating and himself harassed by business and financial woes that were intruding uncharacteristically on the serenity of Quarry Farm. On August 3, 1887, he wrote to Charles L. Webster, his publisher:

If the canvassing book can with *certainty* be gotten ready and distributed by the 12th or 15th of September, let me know, for I want relief of mind; the fun, which was abounding in the Yankee at Arthur's Court up to three days ago, has slumped into funereal seriousness, and this will not do—it will not answer at all. The very title of the book requires fun, and it must be furnished. But it can't be done, I see, while this cloud hangs over the workshop.

I work seven hours a day, and am in such a taut-strung and excitable condition that everything that *can* worry me, does it; and I get up and spend from 1 o'clock till 3 A.M. pretty regularly every night, thinking—not pleasantly. (*MTLP* 221–222)

Twain left Hartford the summer of 1887, but Hartford didn't leave Twain. Despite business concerns and artistic quandaries, however, the letter testifies to the freedom Twain enjoyed to pursue his creative work. According to his own calculations, he was spending seven hours each day working on his novel. Within two weeks Twain would cheer up and write again to his publisher, this time with better news: "This present book (I mean the 'Yankee at King Arthur's Court,') will be finished by the end of the year" (*MTLP* 224).

A comparison between the marginalia and the composition history of *Connecticut Yankee* strengthens 1887 as a candidate for the second reading of Macaulay's *History of England*. The marginalia recall specific incidents in sections of *Connecticut Yankee* that were written during and after that summer. Most notable are the many marked passages that treat the Reformation. On page 36 of volume 1, for example, Twain underlined "Council of Constance" in a sentence discussing the Reformation. A few pages later, on page 39, Twain marked words in sentences dealing with aspects of the Reformation, as he did on page 40 when he underlined "Thomas Cranmer" and "Calvin." Throughout the *History of England* Twain marked such topics either by underlining individual words or phrases or by marking entire passages. It seems likely that Twain's antipathy to Catholicism was exacerbated by Macaulay's continually negative characterizations of it in contrast to his positive characterizations of Protestantism. Twain underlined part of a sentence in which Macaulay refers to the "enlightened and temperate Protestant," for example (1:35). Hank Morgan, it should be recalled, seeks to introduce the Protestant faith into Camelot as part of his overall reform movement. In chapter 10, written in 1888 at Quarry Farm, Hank declares that a "united church . . . means death to human liberty, and paralysis to human thought" (127). In chapter 40 Hank specifically links the "two schemes" of destroying the Catholic Church and introducing free elections: "You see, I had two schemes in my head, which were the vastest of all my projects. The one was, to overthrow the Catholic Church and set up the Protestant faith on its ruins—not as an Established Church, but a go-as-you-please one; and the other project was, to get a decree issued by and by, command-ing that upon Arthur's death unlimited suffrage should be introduced" (444). Macaulay, too, connects religious and political freedom in several marked passages, including those describing the reticence of some Prot-estants to own the authority of the newly formed Anglican Church, whose head was the British monarch. Twain underlined the word *Vati-can*, for example, in a sentence where Macaulay justifies the Protestants' not transferring "to an upstart authority the homage which they had withdrawn from the Vatican" (46). "To their hatred of the Church," Macaulay observes, making the connection between religious and politi-cal tyranny explicit, "was now added hatred of the crown" (46). Twain also imprinted a double line in the margin adjoining Macaulay's discus-sion of the Church's refusal to countenance resistance to tyranny (2:317). In chapter 18 of *Connecticut Yankee* Hank exclaims that "the Established Church is only a political machine" (207), and throughout the novel the Church sides always with monarchy. Religious and political liberty inter-digitate in the historical Reformation and in Hank's intended reforma-tion of sixth-century England.

Twain also marked two passages in Macaulay's work that indicate his preoccupation with class structure. Both concern the status of a curate in the Anglican Church and whom he might marry. In the first case the curate is to take a wife who "had ordinarily been in the patron's service, and it was well if she was not suspected of standing too high in the patron's favor. Indeed, the nature of the matrimonial connections which the clergymen of that age were in the habit of forming is the most cer-tain indication of the place which the order held in the social system" (1:256). Note how Macaulay carefully locates a curate's standing by mar-riage. On the page that follows, too, Twain has marked a passage that states "the chaplain was the resource of a lady's maid whose character had been blown upon, and who was therefore forced to give up hopes of catching the steward" (257). In *Connecticut Yankee* Hank comments on the class structure of Camelot, noting in chapter 31 the "nice and exact subdivision of caste" (348): "Toward the shaven monk who trudged along with his cowl tilted back and the sweat washing down his fat jowls, the coal burner was deeply reverent; to the gentleman he was abject; with the small farmer and free mechanic he was cordial and gossipy; and when a slave passed by with countenance respectfully lowered, this chap's nose was in the air—he couldn't even see him" (348).

Although the aforementioned passages Twain marked in Macaulay do not seem to directly contribute to events in *Connecticut Yankee*, Hank's critique, like Macaulay's description, illustrates the social dynamic of the class structure in action. Twain's treatment suggests that class position is a crucial element of one's character because it has bearing on how one treats others, how one is treated by them, and indeed how one identifies oneself. Moreover, Twain did initially include a passage that derived directly from Macaulay's description. Twain struck out a lengthy passage treating Arthur's "private chaplain" who married "one of the chambermaids," a practice "which was to retain its popularity in England for eleven or twelve centuries yet."[6] Chapter 17, in which this passage originally appeared, was composed in 1887, according to Baetzhold's chronology, thus lending credence to my assertion that Twain reread Macaulay's *History of England* in 1887.

Occupying the pinnacle of the class system is the king, whose quasi-divine influence is so powerful the inhabitants of Camelot believe he can cure by touching the afflicted. Arthur's touching of the scrofulous in chapter 26 of *Connecticut Yankee* has long been attributed to Twain's reading of Lecky's *History of European Morals*. James Williams believes Twain gleaned the information for the chapter from "Lecky's description of that ceremony, which was in turn based on Macaulay."[7] Although it is true that Lecky cites Macaulay by volume and page, there is no reason to suppose that Twain did not consult Macaulay's *History of England* directly. Indeed, Twain's reading of the passage in Lecky's *History of European Morals* may have prompted a closer consultation of Macaulay's *History of England*. The passage in Theodore Crane's copy of the book is not marked, but Twain may have made note of it mentally as he proceeded with the writing of his book.

Of greater import is Twain's patterning of Hank Morgan after two dominant personalities in Macaulay's *History of England*. As Hank's scheme for the reorganization of society unravels, his plight resembles that of King James II, who, in a story related by Macaulay and marked by Twain, sends Queen Mary and their child to France for safety (2:427). The king's concern for his son mirrors Hank's concern for his daughter. Hank and Sandy remove with Hello-Central to France for her health, but Hank's absence precipitates a political crisis as disturbing as that facing King James. In Hank's absence civil war breaks out followed by the Church's interdict. Hank's concern is aroused when he looks out from the French coast toward England and sees no ships at all, "just a dead and empty solitude" (455). Perhaps it is worth noting that in the same chapter of Macaulay, "The Flight of King James," Twain drew six lines in black pencil back to back alongside lines 3–9, which describe a battle at sea, writing next to them "25 miles apart"† in his distinctive hand, referring to the French and English shores, Calais and Dover (2:374). In this passage Macaulay notes that the "flourish of trumpets, the clash of cymbals, and the rolling of drums were distinctly heard at once on the English and French shores" (2:374). In contrast to the noise of Macaulay's description, Hank is struck by the lack of ships and the silence. Twain knew Hank could have seen and heard the bustling of his recently industrialized isle even from the French shore. The marked text may have functioned as Twain's way of reminding himself that Hank could gaze back at Camelot.

If the passages Twain marked recall the general outline of the crisis facing James and his reaction to it, they also recall several other incidents in *Connecticut Yankee* in which mothers care for their children. Twain underlined part of this sentence describing Queen Mary's escape: "She remained with her child, cowering for shelter from the storm under the tower of Lambeth Church, and distracted by terror whenever the ostler approached her with his lantern" (2:427). Such a scene would have had an emotional impact on Twain, and he often created tableaux featuring mothers and infants in perilous situations. Macaulay's description of Queen Mary's escape is the perfect example of what Sydney Krause calls "the Macaulayan theory that history should provide an imaginative vivification of the past" (229) and doubtless illustrates why Macaulay was one of Twain's favorite authors. Macaulay himself wrote that "a truly great historian would reclaim those materials which the novelist has appropriated" ("History" 236).

Macaulay's attempt to reclaim aesthetics for history corresponds to Twain's attempt to reclaim history for aesthetics by following the "com-

pass of fact": each constitutes a kind of literary realism that would produce "fictional history." Perhaps it was Macaulay's practice of vivifying history that Twain referred to in *Innocents Abroad* when contrasting
Macaulay to the ancient writers. Twain lauded those who enjoyed the
"faculty of sinking themselves entirely out of sight of the reader and
making the narrative stand out alone and seem to tell itself," but at
the same time he commended Macaulay, who "is present when we follow the march of his stately sentences" (2:220). Twain followed Macaulay's lead, and when William Dean Howells reviewed *Connecticut Yankee*
in the "Editor's Study" for January 1890, he made note of this aspect of
the book:

> Mr. Clemens, we call him, rather than Mark Twain, because we
> feel that in this book our arch-humorist imparts more of his per-
> sonal quality than in anything else he has done. Here he is to the
> full the humorist, as we know him; but he is very much more, and
> his strong, indignant, often infuriate hate of injustice, and his love
> of equality, burn hot through the manifold adventures and experi-
> ences of the tale. What he thought about prescriptive right and
> wrong, we had partly learned in *The Prince and the Pauper*, and in
> *Huckleberry Finn*, but it is this last book which gives his whole
> mind. (319)

In truth, whether we call the writer Mr. Clemens or Mark Twain, there
is a greater authorial presence in *Connecticut Yankee* than in many of
Twain's works. Hank's voice often betrays the author's presence, and one
even senses at times Twain in the background, pounding a clenched fist
on his writing table in the octagonal study. Still, Twain is not Hank any
more than Macaulay is History.

Macaulay's *History of England* served as a model of historiography
and literary technique that Twain drew on for *Connecticut Yankee* and
later for *Personal Recollections of Joan of Arc*. Whereas Macaulay employed
literary techniques to vivify history, Twain used history as the matrix for
his imaginative writing. Hayden White discusses in *Metahistory* the
"*transformation of chronicle into story*" practiced by historians (5). This is
a trait Macaulay and Twain share; they begin with historical fact and
then organize, arrange, and embellish it into art. For example, in chapter
35 of *Connecticut Yankee* Hank describes a young mother who is condemned to be hanged: "After his prayer they put the noose around the

young girl's neck, and they had great trouble to adjust the knot under her ear, because she was devouring the baby all the time, wildly kissing it, and snatching it back to her face and her breast, and drenching it with tears, and half moaning half shrieking all the while, and the baby crowing, and laughing, and kicking its feet with delight over what it took for romp and play" (403). Similarly, despite the harrowing circumstance of the queen's flight, the infant prince in Macaulay's *History of England* remains oblivious and "uttered not a single cry" (2:427). In each case the incongruity of the infant's behavior highlights the desperate straits, and perhaps the helplessness, of the parents. Both writers develop bare, historical fact into a narrative calculated to elicit an emotional response from the reader.

Although Hank's *plight* bears parallels to that of King James, Hank's *reaction* to the thwarting of his plan parallels the reaction of the Master of Stair to the rejection of his plan to bring "civilization" to the Scottish Highlands. Initially, the British plan was simply to transform Scotland, as historian Marianne McLean explains, "into a modern commercial society modeled on that of southern Britain" (42). Like many such ventures, however, the means became brutal, and even the ends have been called into question. Anthropologist David Richards notes that the Highlands were a "test case for a world 'experiment' with history" (129). This is one reason Bakhtin argues that Scott could "see time in space" in Scotland; so much progress and history occurred in such a short span of time that Scotland seemed to encapsulate all human history, which must include the history of brutality. Forced modernization disrupted entire ways of life, and viewing it as an "experiment," as the English did, dehumanized and objectified the Scots. Tragedy, under such circumstances, was inevitable. John Dalrymple, Master of Stair, was adviser to King William during the crisis of British rule in Scotland that followed the removal of James II. The Master of Stair is still infamous in Scotland for orchestrating the massacre at Glencoe.

We know from a letter Twain wrote to his daughter Susy on July 16, 1889, that this section of Macaulay's *History of England* held a special appeal for the writer: "For forty years Macaulay's England has been a fascinator of mine, from the stately opening sentence to the massacre at Glencoe. I am glad you are reading it. And I hope it is aloud, to Mamma."[8] Several pages in this section of the Cranes's copy of the book are marked, either by actual penciling or by bent pages and, in one case, with a piece of yellowed envelope. The pages describe the state of Scottish civilization at the time, in particular the system of clans and the "revenge rule," whereby whole clans were held responsible for the act of an individual member. Macaulay lavishes much attention on such horrific acts as the burning of men, women, and children alive; beheadings; mutilations of corpses; and a variety of other choice brutalities (4:158). As Macaulay says in a passage Twain scored, "There was scarcely any excess of ferocity for which a precedent could not be found in Celtic tradition" (4:158). Twain, to employ again White's terminology, did not "invent" these elements; he "found" them in history. Although he certainly embellished his material, the "found" elements emerge in his book not as a marketing strategy, as some have suggested, but as evidence of the "fanatic striving" Lukács identifies as the hallmark of realism (*Studies* 11). Twain "finds" in the Scottish example personalities and events that he consciously employed to make his own fictional history "real." As early as Macaulay's first volume, Twain showed an interest in Irish and Scottish civilization, writing in large letters "Celts"† at the top of a page weighing the relative virtues of Celtic and Anglo-Saxon cultures (1:51). The Welsh, of course, have always claimed King Arthur, and he was part of the Celtic remnant that survived the encroachments by the Angles, Saxons, and Jutes. Certainly, it is worth pointing out that Macaulay wrote of the seventeenth century and Twain of the sixth; however, Highland society of the seventeenth century resembles Camelot society of the sixth century in many respects beyond the Celtic connection. Richards points out that Scotland of the eighteenth century "offers the reader an alternative vision of a society untouched by the corrosive effects of commercial civilisation, social mobility and demographic change affecting civilised Britain" (131). Or the civilized United States, one hastens to add, for the Scotland Twain grew familiar with by reading Macaulay's work was very much like the static, pastoral, noncommercial world of Camelot and contrasted with Gilded Age America. Still, Scotland of the eighteenth century was not a peaceful world, as Macaulay illustrates. The brutality of the Scottish chieftains, who were, like King Arthur, absolute monarchs, provided a model for Camelot and for the behavior of characters like Morgan le Fay, whose tortures, as we saw in the previous chapter, were based on those practiced by the Scottish clergy. Twain based the world of *Connecticut Yankee* not on Malory's tales of sixth-century Camelot but on the history of eighteenth-century Scotland. In particular, the modernization suffered by Scotland parallels Hank Morgan's attempts to civilize Camelot. As Avrom Fleishman contends, "One of the reasons . . . the historical novel begins with Scott is that the tension between tradition and modernity first achieved its definitive form in Scotland" (38). Ironically, Twain followed in the footsteps of his nemesis Scott in this regard.

Just as Hank Morgan enters Camelot with a will to reform it, so too does the Master of Stair resolve to reform the social structure in the Highlands. Like Hank Morgan, the Master of Stair finds his will thwarted. Initially, his plan had been to achieve a "great social revolution" for the good of all the people, Macaulay tells us on the page marked with a piece of envelope, but when those he would help stand in his way, he gives the infamous orders to his soldiers: "Your troops will destroy entirely the country of Lochaber, Lochiel's lands, Keppoch's, Glengarry's and Glencoe's. Your power shall be large enough. I hope the soldiers will not trouble the government with prisoners" (4:162). To achieve his object, the Master of Stair instructed his soldiers to appear in Glencoe as if on the routine business of the king and to seek accommodations in the homes of the Mac Ian clan. Macaulay describes how the men dossed with the families, for more than a week enjoying Highland hospitality, knowing all the while that on a given night they would rise and execute all Scots under seventy in their slumber.

Perhaps it is too much to say that Hank acts out this kind of treachery; he does, however, live and love with the aristocracy of Camelot, and one wonders at his ability then to slaughter them in "The Battle of the Sand-belt." Even before that, Hank engraves on a brass plate words that convey his promise to stand "*against the massed chivalry of the whole earth and destroy it*" (443). Sewell correctly sees Morgan as an "avatar of Columbus, Cortes, and General Custer" (32), citing Hank's statement "While one of these men remains alive, our task is not finished, the war is not ended. We will kill them all" as evidence (479). Certainly there are legitimate parallels to be made, just as Chadwick Hansen compares Hank to Hitler (66–67) and Robert Wiggins likens him to "Der Fuhrer or Il Duce" (79). But, if anything, Hank Morgan is an avatar of John Bull, and in his character, behavior, and language he is closely patterned after the Master of Stair. Hank's language recalls Macaulay's description, on a page Twain marked, of the Master of Stair's desire that "the Camerons, the Macleans, and all the branches of the race of Macdonald, should be rooted out" (4:162). Twain "found" in history both the Master of Stair and his fiat "should be rooted out" and then dramatized the scene even more than Macaulay, changing the Master's language to the more forceful, "We will kill them all" (479). Speaking of Scott's Highland novels, David Richards contends that what they record "borders on genocide" (133). Similarly, many critics have struggled to unravel Hank's motivation and Twain's attitude toward it. At the very least, the parallels between Hank and the Master of Stair cause one to question Everett Carter's assertion that the book on the whole concerns "a Yankee's praiseworthy attempt to make a better world" (419). Reflecting on Hank's actions, we recall, in another passage Twain marked, Macaulay's assessment of the Master of Stair, who "hardens his heart against the most touching spectacles of misery, by repeating to himself that his intentions are pure, that his objects are noble, that he is doing a little evil for the sake of a great good" (4:159–60). Hank serves himself precisely this cold comfort, and in this he is supported by many literary apologists.

With the marginalia we can see Twain consciously crafting his novel, and one wonders if the attributions of unconscious motivations in *Connecticut Yankee* must now be qualified or even put aside altogether. James L. Johnson, for example, contends that

> Hank's ambivalent character, his contrary bursts of sympathy and cruelty, are not simply the result of Twain's failure in artistic control, or of a carefully considered plan to "mask" a monster with a transparent veneer of fraudulent humanity which we are expected to penetrate. His is rather a vent for Twain's own contradictory impulses and attitudes. In his compassion for humanity, in his often sickly sweet sentimentality, and in his terrifyingly casual violence and cruelty, Hank Morgan is the picture of his creator. (141)

And yet evidence now exists demonstrating that Twain "found" his character within history, through the Master of Stair and other examples, and then built up the fact gleaned from history to produce Hank Morgan. Twain wrote, in Paine's phrase, a fictional history. The significance of the Master of Stair is twofold: as I have already suggested, his contribution to Hank's language and character casts doubts on the Yankee's motivation, but equally profound is how this source of Hank's character alters our view of Twain. Twain's manipulation of the historical material, the compass of fact, reveals him as an artist much more in control of his craft than many critics have granted. Despite the attempts by many critics to marginalize Twain's conscious artistry, the writer's motivation emerges here as a conscious one. Change is *Connecticut Yankee*'s protagonist, and Twain's story is, in some sense, a lament, a coronach, so to speak, for the suffering of humanity undergoing the throes of historical change. Hank, like the Master of Stair, is an agent of change who, finding his will to aid others thwarted, settles on killing those he would assist. The paradigm, as critics David Sewell, John Carlos Rowe, and others have noted, is the imperialist experience. Hank is the forerunner of Twain's later diatribes against King Leopold, U.S. involvement in the Philippines, and so on. Macaulay's story of the Master of Stair provided Twain with profound insight into the character and motivation of the imperialist in all ages.

During research trips to Quarry Farm, I also discovered two other works by and about Thomas Babington Macaulay that contain Twain's marginalia: *The Life and Letters of Lord Macaulay* and *Selections from the Writings of Lord Macaulay*. Twain is known to have read the first of these books on a number of occasions, having first read it in 1876, the year of its publication. Twain based his speech "Life of Lord Macaulay" (for the Hartford Saturday Club) on that reading. Twain also read the book in April 1885 and made comments on it in his journal.[9] Twain was not previously known to have read *Selections from the Writings of Lord Macaulay* but did read widely in Macaulay's writings other than the famous *History of England*. These books occupy a unique position in the holdings at Elmira College's Center for Mark Twain Studies in that they are among a handful of volumes bearing Twain marginalia that belonged to Olivia's parents. Nearly all of the books bearing Twain marginalia at Elmira College belonged originally to the Cranes.

The marginalia in these volumes are not dated, and it is difficult to assign even a year with any precision. Neither the medium of transmission nor the numbered bookplates from the Langdon library establish when the marginalia were inscribed.[10] It was unusual for Twain to write in any of the Langdon books, and the marginalia are spare and very light, perhaps because he feared censure. That he did so at all might indicate a protracted stay at the Langdon home in Elmira. Of course, given their brevity, they could have resulted from a brief visit with the attendant desultory reading. In any case the marginalia seem less research oriented than the pencilings in Macaulay's *History of England*. Several of them indicate Twain's dislike of Macaulay's use of "doubled-up haves." That bothered him at least as early as 1880, when in *A Tramp Abroad* he criticized their use by Macaulay, saying that "milk-teeth are commoner in men's mouths than those 'doubled-up haves'" (203). Although the infrequent marginalia in these volumes offer little from which to deduce even a tentative date, they testify to Mark Twain's perennial interest in English history, again reminding us that he prepared to write his own books by reading—and writing in—those written by others.

Twain gained much from Macaulay. By following the Macaulayan Method in his own book Twain vivifies history and telescopes all history into a very short period of time. Sydney Krause argues that the Macaulayan Method grants one "the feeling of having seen the fatality of human experience, and of having encompassed the whole moral gamut" (244). Twain, too, follows the compass of fact but is not a slave to chronology. By patterning events in his novel after actual historical incidents, Twain ensures that he does not violate human nature and creates a vivid sense of realism even in the patently unreal situation of an American mechanic leading a revolution in Camelot.

Despite the troubles that insinuated themselves into the peace and repose of Quarry Farm, Twain ended the summer of 1887 optimistic about finishing his book:

> This present book (I mean the 'Yankee at King Arthur's Court,') will be finished by the end of the year; I allow myself time enough, because when we leave for Hartford I shall have but 500 pages of MS finished—just ⅓ of the book—and in H. I shall not have the uninterrupted rush that I secure to myself here. But it may never go to press; for it is a 100,000-copy book, if Huck Finn was a 50,000-copy book, and I shall wait until I see at least an 80,000-copy sale ahead before I publish. (You see, I went back and read my 350 pages of MS through, yesterday, and found out that I am making an uncommonly bully book—and am swelled up accordingly.) (*MTLP* 224)

Although Twain's forecast for the completion date was too sanguine by more than a year, his assessment of the quality of the work he was doing in 1887 was right on target, as was his prediction that once in Hartford, work on *Connecticut Yankee* would stall. In fact, during the summer of

1887 Twain wrote chapters 4–9 and 11–19; after leaving Elmira and Quarry Farm, he wrote only chapter 20 and the first paragraph of chapter 21 during the winter in Hartford that followed. The next summer he would return to "Do-as-You-Please Hall" and enjoy one of his most productive summers at Quarry Farm.

4
"The Men of Old Ideas Must Die Off"

Mark Twain and Lecky's *England in the Eighteenth Century*

I am just burying myself as well as I can in a book.
> —Mark Twain to Orion Clemens, July 2, 1888
> (*MTN&J* 3:394)

To some Mark Twain might seem less than an ideal guest. The Cranes, however, tolerated and even encouraged his eccentricities, including the disfiguring of many books from their library. Perhaps Twain meant to atone for his deficiencies, for as he prepared to leave Quarry Farm at the end of the summer of 1887, he presented Theodore Crane with the newly published *A History of England in the Eighteenth Century* by William Lecky. To make amends for past misdeeds, to commemorate the many long conversations about English history they had enjoyed that summer, and certainly to thank Theodore Crane for his hospitality, Twain inscribed the flyleaf of the sixth volume, "T.W. Crane / Quarry Farm, / Go-as-You-Please Hall / Rest-&-be-Thankful / East Hill / Elmira, N.Y. / Sept. 1887." Twain's gift of these volumes to the Cranes would exert a profound influence on the composition of *Connecticut Yankee*, for the following summer would find the guest from Hartford writing throughout these same gift volumes.[1]

   Scholars have long been aware that Twain consulted William Lecky's *History of England in the Eighteenth Century* during the composition of *Connecticut Yankee*. His notebooks are sprinkled with references, most of them brief: "584 vol 3—18th cent." is a typical example (*MTN&J* 3:417). A few entries record more developed responses to certain passages in

Lecky's *England in the Eighteenth Century*. Howard Baetzhold has discussed some of these and has suggested other passages that probably caught the author's eye (*MT&JB* 152–53, 351–52 nn. 35, 38). But none of the earlier researchers had access to Mark Twain's annotations in the books at Quarry Farm. Many contemporary researchers who do have access seem more interested in relegating Twain's aesthetics and conscious research to the margins than in examining the writer's marginal comments.

The summer of 1888 was a watershed in the composition of *Connecticut Yankee*. Twain made great strides in his book, and the marginalia in Lecky's volumes show a writer fully engaged with his material and document the extent of his research that summer. One must therefore question the validity of Sherwood Cummings's argument that at that time "the author only wanted to end his novel" (168). Moreover, during this period Mark Twain reached several crucial, though hardly happy, conclusions about historical change and progress. Twain came to believe that progress dictates "the men of old ideas must die off," a realization that had serious implications for his book (*MTN&J* 3:415). An entry in volume 6—"True to-day. 1888."—appears next to Lecky's discussion that although it was once a disgrace for women to be seen in bars, it had become common by the mid-eighteenth century. This entry clearly establishes the date of Mark Twain's reading (6:263). On previous occasions when he consulted Lecky, he selected either the two-volume *History of European Morals* or the two-volume *Spirit of Rationalism*. Walter Blair explains that Lecky's *History of European Morals* held such appeal for Twain, in part, because "it covers great spans of time" (135).

Lecky's theme in *A History of England in the Eighteenth Century* is, as always, the theme of change; however, the purview of this work is much more specific and focused, and therein resides its influence. In his previous works Lecky charts change throughout the world over the course of centuries, with examples from history varying widely by century and by location. In contrast, *A History of England in the Eighteenth Century* treats only England, Scotland, and Ireland and is limited to a discussion of change and growth in the British Isles during the eighteenth century. The change in focus is notable. Because the book deals exclusively with British history, it provided Twain with the kind of ammunition he sought for his book, in some sense an extended diatribe against England and specifically Matthew Arnold.

Lecky's focus on a specific time and place is significant for another important reason and has to do with the question of what *Connecticut Yankee* "means": is the book a satire of England or America? Lecky studies the changes that occurred in a specific location over the course of a very short period, so one might see in the source proof that Twain was engaged in satirizing England. But as specific as the information Twain gleaned is, it is in another sense very general. For example, Twain underlined a passage that characterizes the sense of progress: "One of the most remarkable features of the first sixty years of the eighteenth century is the great number of new powers or influences that were then called into action of which the full significance was only perceived long afterwards" (1:624). This idea dominated Twain's thinking during his final push to complete the novel, but the idea itself involves the concepts of change, progress, and historicity, not English civilization versus American. Twain marked a number of passages where Lecky discusses this feature of his study, including this discussion about dueling: "No revolution of public sentiment has been more remarkable than that which in the space of little more than a generation has banished from England, and in a great measure from Europe, this evil custom which had so long defied the condemnation both of the Church and of the law" (6:267). Twain marked the passage both with a marginal line and with the underlining that I have indicated. Although he placed a line in the margin along a lengthy passage, Twain underlined only the phrase "little more than a generation." Hence, it seems that his central concern was the time factor. Hank, after all, seeks to accomplish a great deal in a very short period of time.

Some of the scorings in the second volume of Lecky's work speak to this issue. In the fifth chapter, "The Colonies and Scotland," Lecky outlines the "Effects of Legislation on Character," using Scotland as a microcosm to illustrate what can be done in a very short time. There Twain marked a long passage in which Lecky summarizes the raison d'etre for such a narrowly focused study:

There are very few instances on record in which a nation passed in so short a time from a state of barbarism to a state of civilization, in which the tendencies and leading features of the national character were so profoundly modified, and in which the separate causes of the change are so clearly discernible. . . . The character of large bodies of men depends in the main upon the circumstances in which they have been placed, the laws by which they have been governed, the principles they have been taught. When these are changed the character will alter too, and the alteration, though it is very slow, may in the end be very deep. (2:79)

I believe that Twain noted this passage for a particular reason: Lecky provides here an outline for the entire structure of *Connecticut Yankee.* After all, Hank hopes to apply outside pressures on Camelot so that it will pass "in so short a time from a state of barbarism to a state of civilization." Camelot becomes Twain's experimental landscape, just as Scotland had served in that capacity for Lecky's England. Twain turned once more to the question of character and environment in terms provided by Lecky and explored whether character influences environment or environment determines character. The "tradition of all the dead generations" Marx identifies as a conservative force do weigh on Hank as he attempts to radicalize the society (15), but Twain began to explore how quickly substantive change might be achieved, if in fact it were possible to direct the course of history. The best description of Twain's mind at this point is hopeful but not naive. Twain's realism was always ethically charged and motivated; he wanted to change society by changing lives. As with Lecky's analysis of England in the 1700s, Twain trusts that the factors that cause the changes in Camelot will be visible. Trying to master cause and effect, Hank plans each change himself and consciously sets out to cause a revolution in the environment that will revolutionize character.

Hank, though, is less patient than Lecky: Lecky *describes* change while Hank *prescribes* change. As a historian Lecky recognized that a century is a short period for any notable change in national character to be effected. Thus, although Lecky uses the phrase "in so short a time" to indicate the eighteenth century, he understood that any alteration in character "though it is very slow, may in the end be very deep" (2:79). In contrast, when Hank first arrives in Camelot, he vows to "boss the whole country inside of three months" and begins an aggressive campaign to reform individual and social character based on his nineteenth-century knowledge (63). This attempt to accelerate progress and modernize a country in such a short period has happened rarely in world history, most notably in Third World countries subjected to the rigors of imperialism and in Russia and the Soviet Union under Stalin. And it has never occurred without significant hardship and crushing repression. Lecky's primary example is Scotland.

Despite the aggressiveness inherent in Hank's character, his initial plan to accelerate the material and moral progress of Camelot is peaceful. He sees himself as "just another Robinson Crusoe cast away on an uninhabited island," who must "invent, contrive, create; reorganize things" (100). Like Crusoe Hank is on an island—England—and like Crusoe he plans to create a new society. Despite the many instances in which Hank violates his plan for peaceful progress, his plan for reorganization remains essentially pacific until near the end of the book. In chapter 40, probably written near the end of 1888, Hank still declares that he desires "a rounded and complete governmental revolution without bloodshed" (445). In a passage Twain scored, Lecky had asserted that the great watersheds of human history, such as the end of slavery, the Reformation, and the spread of Christianity, were really "the result of a long series of religious, social, political, economical, and intellectual causes, extending over many generations" (1:15). Two pages later Twain would similarly mark Lecky's belief that the lasting effects of the French Revolution would have been far more profound if they had "been effected peacefully, legally, and gradually" (1:17).

The question of whether the rate of social progress can be significantly accelerated without bloodshed dominates *Connecticut Yankee*. For the greater part of the book Hank suggests that such an acceleration is possible. At some point, however, Twain returned to the earlier portion of the manuscript and excised one of several passages in which Hank advocates a peaceful revolution. Part of the canceled passage finds Hank saying that "the convulsion I was gropingly projecting, had no blood in it; I intended it should be peaceful, and had no very serious doubt that I could work it out on that line."[2] According to Howard Baetzhold's chronology, Twain revised his manuscript in 1888, and it seems plausible that, along with the other changes, he struck this line because under the influence of Lecky's *England in the Eighteenth Century* Twain came to recognize that a peaceful revolution of the magnitude planned by Hank was simply not possible.[3] The excising of this passage suggests Twain followed the "compass of fact" in particulars and in the more general truths offered by history.

Many entries Mark Twain made in his writing journal for the second half of the novel (chapters 10 and 21–36) support this contention. One of the notes actually announces a plan for a revolution without bloodshed:

I make a <u>peaceful</u> revolution & introduce advanced civilization. The Church overthrows it with a 6 year interdict.

A revolution cannot be established under 30 years—the men of old ideas must die off. (*MTN&J* 3:415)

This entry shows Twain grappling with the central question posed by *Connecticut Yankee,* a question that becomes urgent as the novel proceeds: can radical change occur in a very short time, and can that change be both lasting and peaceful? I believe that Twain's underlining of *peaceful* indicates his recognition that a peaceful revolution would be unique and suggests that he may have no confidence in the viability of such a revolution. As Hank says, this would be "the first of its kind in the history of the world—a rounded and complete governmental revolution without bloodshed" (445).

Even as he planned to have Hank establish a peaceful revolution, Twain hypothesized that it could not last because conservative forces like the Church would reverse the changes. Just as significant, however, is Twain's epiphany that a true revolution cannot occur as rapidly as Hank hopes and that at least "30 years" are required. Here, then, nestled among the various disparate journal entries, is the germ of the great destructive ending, "The Battle of the Sand-Belt." From his intensive study of history Twain realized that substantive change requires that the men of old ideas must die off. This implies that character contributes to environment in a complex way. Individuals bearing ideas inherited from the environment exert a conservative influence that preserves the very matrix that created their character. For Twain's protagonist, Hank Morgan, this fact of historical process confirms his latent tendency to kill those who oppose him. Rather than wait for the "men of old ideas" to die natural deaths, Hank decides that a peaceful acceleration of lasting progress is impossible; he therefore decides, like the Master of Stair described by Macaulay, to kill those he would help.

Despite the "men of old ideas," Hank accomplishes quite a good deal within the first nineteen chapters of the book. Lecky had noted that the aristocracy "perpetuates and honours the memories of the past," thus supporting the national institutions and their own power (1:194). "It is very true," Twain agreed in the margin, "where the people are ignorant" (1:194). Twain knew, then, that the problem was to alter the character of the environment by establishing educational facilities, so altering the character of the people; he would exorcise the "old ideas" from society. Hank introduces "all sorts of industries" but also founds a teaching college that he calls a "teacher-factory" and secretly opens other schools that train people "in every sort of handiwork and scientific calling" (127). Much of chapter 10, written in the summer of 1888, was very likely based on a single paragraph that Twain marked in Lecky's *England in the Eighteenth Century:*

> The great legislative changes that were effected at the Revolution—the immobility of judges, the reform of the trials for treason, the liberty of the press, the more efficient control of the income of the sovereign, the excision from the oath of allegiance of the clause which, in direct contradiction to the great charter, asserted that under no pretence whatever might subjects take up arms against their king; the establishment of Presbyterianism in Scotland, and the partial toleration of Dissenters in England, have all been justified by history as measures of real and unquestionable progress. (1:14)

Twain underlined the phrase, "liberty of the press" when he read Lecky's work in 1888, and then wrote chapter 10 to insert as a list of achievements accomplished in Hank's first four years. Later in Lecky's work Twain also imprinted a double marginal line next to Lecky's comment that, "Before the close of the eighteenth century there were already more than seventy provincial newspapers in England" (6:168). Twain then wrote, "70 provincial papers. What kind?" Clearly, as a former journalist Twain understood the important role newspapers play in the democratization of society. In chapter 10 Hank discusses Camelot's first newspaper, which was indeed "provincial." Shortly after its establishment, "it was already up to the back-settlement Alabama mark, and couldn't be told from the editorial output of that region either by matter or flavor" (130). High praise, indeed!

Hank's discussion in chapter 10 of how he "systemized" the "royal revenues" for the good of both sovereign and subject seems to have emerged directly from the passage marked in Lecky (130). Even his declaration that "I could have given my own sect the preference and made everybody a Presbyterian" reflects Lecky's paragraph. Twain did not allow his protagonist to do this, however, because just the summer before he had read Lecky's *Spirit of Rationalism* and Macaulay's *History of England* and marked many passages outlining the terrible tortures encouraged or even inflicted by the Presbyterian ministers. Twain could hardly count "the establishment of Presbyterianism in Scotland" as chief among the benefits of the English Revolution. Instead, Hank institutes Protestantism but not, he says, "an Established Church, but a go-as-you-please one" (444). One wonders if Hank's "go-as-you-please" religion was a private joke intended for Susan Crane, a devout Christian but by all accounts a nondogmatic one, who teased Twain about his lack of faith. The hostess of "Go-as-You-Please Hall" called him "Holy Samuel"; he called her "Saint Sue" (*MFMT* 59–60).

Lecky's discussion of the English Revolution contributed much to Twain's discussion of revolution through his character Hank Morgan. If much of the progress in England during the eighteenth century was a result of the Revolution, Hank's "peaceful" revolution also produces positive results. Hank makes progress in Camelot, just as progress was made in England during the eighteenth century, but he faces similar impediments. Over the course of a dozen pages, Lecky, in passages Twain marked, sketches the provinciality of the British countryside, stating, "A journey into the country was then considered almost as great an undertaking as a voyage to the Indies" (6:169). Continuing, Lecky credits the "improvements of roads" for the "transformation of manners" that occurred in the eighteenth century (6:173). Twain reserved triple marginal lines for Lecky's discussion of how the rural inhabitants responded to attempts to improve their lot. "The improvement in traveling," Lecky asserts, "advanced very slowly. The new turnpike roads were extremely unpopular, and fierce mobs—sometimes taking for their rallying cry the words of the prophet, 'Stand ye in the ways, and see, and ask for the old paths'—frequently attacked and destroyed the turnpikes" (6:174). Twain may have inscribed three marginal lines to indicate the degree to which people resist change or perhaps to indicate the Church's power as a conservative force. Hank makes it clear throughout *Connecticut Yankee*, but particularly in chapter 10, written during the summer of 1888, that his primary antagonist is the Church. He keeps his educational endeavors secret because "I should have had the Established Roman Catholic Church on my back in a minute" (83). Writing in his notebook during this summer, Twain left notes for an incident for possible inclusion in *Connecticut Yankee:* "Cathedral struck by lightning—they had just removed my thunder-rod, a mob led by priests" (*MTN&J* 3:416). Both passages illustrate a popular resistance to Hank's revolution that is compounded by the Church's influence.

Whereas the triple marginal lines indicate the passage had a significant impact on him, Twain used capital *C*s throughout Lecky's *England in the Eighteenth Century* as a convenient way to note incidents that illustrate specifically how pernicious an established church could be. The capital *C* used by Twain probably refers to *any* established church or Christianity in general, although it often refers specifically to Catholicism—"CATHOLIC WITH A BIG C," as John Irving's Owen Meany puts it (110). Still, as Howard Baetzhold observes, "It was not only the Roman Catholic Church that was under fire" in Mark Twain's book ("Let It Go" 56). The capital *C* doubtless represents an amalgam of all established churches and was used most often to express a complicity of the religious structures of the society with the political and social structures. It probably served as a kind of shorthand that allowed Twain to locate quickly passages he had marked.

A notable exception to Twain's anti-Catholicism is the incident in *Connecticut Yankee* in which a young mother is hanged for theft after her husband's impressment. Twain placed marginal lines along several pages in which Lecky discusses how press gangs roved through England, seizing men to serve in the Royal Navy. Among the marked pages is this passage:

> The breadwinner being gone, his goods were seized for an old debt, and his wife was driven into the streets to beg. At last, in despair she stole a piece of coarse linen from a linen draper's shop. Her defence, which was fully corroborated, was that "she had lived in credit and wanted for nothing till a press-gang came and stole her husband from her, but since then she had no bed to lie on, nothing to give her children to eat, and they were almost naked. She might have done something wrong, for she hardly knew what she did." The lawyers declared that shop-lifting being a common offence, she must be executed, and she was driven to Tyburn with a child still suckling at her breast. (3:583)

Other passages Twain read involving mothers and children in peril, such as Queen Mary's escape described by Macaulay in chapter 3 of this study, probably contributed, but Lecky is the immediate and obvious source of this incident in *Connecticut Yankee:*

> A little while ago this young thing, this child of eighteen years, was as happy a wife and mother as any in England; and her lips were

Georgia there was an express stipulation for the religious instruction of the slaves; it is said that those in or about Savannah have always been noted in America for their piety,[1] and the advantage of bringing negroes within the range of the Gospel teaching was a common argument in favour of the slave trade. The Protestants from Salzburg for a time had scruples, but they were reassured by a message from Germany : ' If you take slaves in faith,' it was said, ' and with intent of conducting them to Christ, the action will not be a sin but may prove a benediction.' [2] In truth, however, but little zeal was shown in the work of conversion. Many who cordially approved of the slavery of pagans questioned whether it was right to hold Christians in bondage ; there was a popular belief that baptism would invalidate the legal title of the master to his slave,[3] and there was a strong and general fear lest any form of education should so brace the energies of the negro as to make him revolt against his lot. Of the extent to which this latter feeling was carried, one extraordinary instance of a later period may be given. The Society for the Propagation of the Gospel sent missionaries to convert the free negroes in Guinea, on the Gold Coast, and in Sierra Leone; but it was itself a large slave-owner, possessing numerous slaves on an estate in Barbadoes. In 1783 Bishop Porteus strongly urged upon the managers of the Society the duty of at least giving Christian instruction to these slaves; but, after a full discussion, the recommendation was absolutely declined.[4]

In the American States slavery speedily gravitated to the South. The climate of the Southern provinces was eminently favourable to the negroes ; and the crops, and especially the rice crop—which had been introduced into South Carolina from

[1] Hildreth, ii. 417–419.
[2] Ibid.
[3] See Hildreth's *Hist. of the United States*, ii. 426. Bancroft, iii. 409. South Carolina, Virginia, and Maryland passed laws expressly asserting that baptism made no change in the legal position of the negro ; an opinion of Yorke and Talbot, the English law officers, to the same effect was circulated in the Colonies; and Gibson, the Bishop of London, declared that ' Christianity and the embracing of the Gospel does not make the least alteration in civil property.'
[4] Hodgson's *Life of Porteus*, pp. 86–88.

2. A page showing Twain's use of the capital *C* as a shorthand for "Church" or "Christianity" in Lecky's *History of England in the Eighteenth Century*. Courtesy Mark Twain Archives, Elmira College.

blithe with song, which is the native speech of glad and innocent hearts. Her young husband was as happy as she; for he was doing his whole duty, he worked early and late at his handicraft, his bread was honest bread well and fairly earned, he was prospering, he was furnishing shelter and sustenance to his family, he was adding his mite to the wealth of the nation. By consent of a treacherous law, instant destruction fell upon this holy home and swept it away! That young husband was waylaid and impressed, and sent to sea. The wife knew nothing of it. She sought him everywhere, she moved the hardest hearts with the supplications of her tears, the broken eloquence of her despair. Weeks dragged by, she watching, waiting, hoping, her mind going slowly to wreck under the burden of her misery. Little by little all her small possessions went for food. When she could no longer pay her rent, they turned her out of doors. She begged, while she had strength; when she was starving, at last, and her milk failing, she stole a piece of linen cloth of the value of a fourth part of a cent, thinking to sell it and save her child. (401–2)

Twain conflates this incident with a later one Lecky discusses in which "a girl of twenty-two was hanged for receiving a piece of check from an accomplice who had stolen it" (6:251). Like Twain's judge, who goes mad and kills himself with remorse, the prosecutor in Lecky's *England in the Eighteenth Century* "was driven almost distracted by remorse, and did not long survive the shock." As in Lecky's description, the woman's "mind was so disordered of late" that "she knew nothing rightly" and she is led to the gallows with a baby at her breast (402). The many similarities between Lecky's description and Twain's are obvious; the similarities provide the compass of fact. For Twain, though, the compass of fact keeps him to his course, it does not limit him. He uses the incident described by Lecky as the outline of an extended story in *Connecticut Yankee* but enlivens the historical treatment with the artistic imagination, writing a "fictional history." We experience the gradual day-by-day economic and psychological impact the husband's disappearance had on the young mother, and Twain's style in this section, with the alternation of sentence types and lengths, grows almost liturgical as he discusses the wrecking of the "holy home" (401). Although Lecky provides the facts for the incident, one senses the Macaulayan Method with its vivification of history behind Twain's treatment.

The passage is remarkable for another reason. The woman's tale is related by a "good priest," who ends his telling with a diatribe against those who are "guilty of thy ruin and death" (403). Not only does the priest criticize the law, the government, and the entire status quo, he also promises the mother he will adopt the child as his own.[4] The child, she says, "has no father, no friend, no mother—," to which he vows, "It has them all. . . . All these will I be to it till I die" (403). Perhaps Twain thought the incident too painful to be left the way Lecky told it, without any hope that the child would survive the mother's premature death. Coming as it does, too, in the section where Arthur and Hank are traveling as slaves, the priest's criticism and compassion contribute to the King's education.

Still, despite occasional glimmerings of compassion exhibited by its priests, the established Church loomed large in Twain's mind because of its overwhelming influence on all aspects of life. The Church had nearly unlimited power. The most effective power it wielded was the threat of excommunication, which, Lecky observes in a passage marked by Twain, "might be imposed by them for many offences" (3:536). The threat of excommunication was so effective because of its consequences: "An excommunicate person in England was placed almost wholly beyond the protection of the law. He could not be a witness or a juryman. He could not bring an action to secure or recover his property. If he died without the removal of his sentence he had no right to Christian burial" (3:536). The "Church's curse" and all it entails is most obvious in the chapters "The Small-Pox Hut" and "The Tragedy of the Manor House." The unfortunate woman dying in the hut tells Hank and Arthur to save themselves by not helping her, for if anyone were to see them providing succor to one under the Church's ban, the authorities would target them as well. The Church's ban exiles those under it to a place beyond human society and demands that no one interact with them. "Since that day, we are avoided, shunned with horror," the dying woman tells Hank and Arthur (334). The next chapter begins with a somber observation: all of the inhabitants of the hut dead, "Their home must be these people's grave, for they could not have Christian burial" (336).

The effect Church doctrine had on the minds of the inhabitants of eighteenth-century England piqued Twain the most. He marked many passages in Lecky treating the Church's complicity with slavery (see especially 2:14, 17, 19), most often in connection with what Lecky called, in a passage Twain marked, the "slavery of the mind" (2:96). Twain, for example, placed marginal lines next to many passages in which Lecky discusses how Christian churches legitimated slavery, including this passage treating the issue of slavery in the Georgia colony: "In Georgia there was an express stipulation for the religious instruction of the slaves; it is said that those in or about Savannah have always been noted in America for their piety, and the advantage of bringing negroes within the range of the Gospel teaching was a common argument in favour of the slave trade" (2:18). On the very next page Lecky details some of the "travel, play, and work on the Lord's day" that were prohibited by law in Massachusetts (2:19). Next to this, Twain writes, "This is one tribe of Christians straining at a gnat; on page 18 you see their brothers swallowing a camel without difficulty" (2:19). One recalls that in the slave-driver episode, a bevy of pilgrims continues on its pilgrimage undisturbed by the presence of the slaves. Such episodes in *Connecticut Yankee* come from a variety of sources and contribute to the synchronic effect of the narrative.

The "slavery of the mind" dominating these "men of old ideas" recalls the marked passages in Macaulay's *History of England* about "mental servitude" and the *Contre Un* of La Boetie. It similarly translates into a lack of clear thinking one needs for reasoned convictions and into a lack of will to act on them; the slavery of the mind alienates one from the compass of fact. Realism, for Twain, is an aesthetic concern with an ethical motivation; realism is an aesthetic quantity whose ethical value is most obvious in its absence. Based on superstition, the slavery of the mind engenders other superstitions, among them a belief in witches. Like his *Spirit of Rationalism,* Lecky's *England in the Eighteenth Century* chronicles the horrendous abuses that resulted from a belief in witchcraft. Twain marked many of these in *England in the Eighteenth Century,* and one in particular contributes to a passage in *Connecticut Yankee* involving a woman accused of witchcraft: "This poor woman had been stoned until she hardly looked human, she was so battered and bloody. The mob wanted to burn her" (399). Twain gets several specific details from Lecky. Lecky, for example, refers to the crowd's "three hours' sport" (2:89), a phrase Twain underlined and then revised to *diversion* for his own book (399). Both reveal one element of the crowd's motivation, and both are implicitly critical. Twain's use of *diversion* accentuates the irony that the crowd's anger and energy are "diverted" from their real manipulators in the Church toward the innocent scapegoat. Moreover, Twain has the woman being burned strain "her two young daughters to her breast" (400), whereas Lecky relates that the "two daughters rushed in and fell upon their knees before the mob" (2:89). Throughout Lecky's discussion of witchcraft Twain penned comments indicating that the contrast of civilizations he began formulating four years earlier was still in his mind: "Within 15 yr of Salem—that they find so much fault with—where *nobody* was burnt" (2:88), "34 yrs after Salem," "43 yrs after" (2:90).

Along with the church, men of old ideas inhabited the ranks of the aristocracy, and the two supported each other. Twain was most offended by the Church's official policy of nonresistance to tyranny. Twain underlined Lecky's discussion of the Anglican Church, which taught the doctrine of nonresistance "enrolled by great Anglican casuists among the leading tenets of Christianity, and persistently enforced from the pulpit" (1:9). The underlining is Twain's, and he also inscribed capital *C*s in the margin. Lecky includes the actual oath of allegiance, which states that "it is not lawful *upon any pretence whatever* to take up arms against the king," and Twain wrote underneath it "Non-resistance" (1:9). Twain criticizes the Church for its associations with slavery, as we have seen, but he also directly connects the aristocratic form of government with slavery both in his marginalia and in his finished book. As Lecky continues his discussion of the doctrine of nonresistance and its assertion of the "absolute sinfulness of resistance," Twain scribbled in the margin "slavery" and an exclamation point (1:12). From Lecky, then, Twain acquired a sense of the complicity of the Church and the government that he likens to slavery.

Provoking the objections of Louis J. Budd, who criticizes the anachronism of Hank's accusing "the church of not only failing to oppose slavery but spreading a slave mentality," Twain equated aristocratic societies and slaveholding societies (*Social* 128). The aristocrat and the slaveholder share, Hank says in chapter 25, "the old and inbred custom of regarding himself as a superior being" (285). Hank asserts that "a privileged class, an aristocracy, is but a band of slaveholders under another name" (285). In addition to the earlier passages in Lecky Twain may have arrived at this connection while reading about the Scottish Highlanders' reverence for their chief, whose "word was the only law they respected" and who commanded "complete devotion" and "absolute obedience" (2:24). The chief could, at his whim, kill his vassals with impunity. Twain inscribed a marginal line the length of the long discussion and then wrote "some more slavery" next to them, clearly connecting the aristocratic form of government with a slaveholding society. Lest the "hard" critics, à la Carter's dichotomy, seize on this as an example of Twain's satirizing aristocratic society alone, the writer also commented, "Slavery during greater part of 18th century" next to Lecky's discussion of "colliers and labourers in the salt works" being bound to their place of employment, and bought and sold with it (2:81). Twain also marked this passage: "a gang of these children was put up for sale among a bankrupt's effects, and publicly advertised as part of the property" (6:225). The former were examples of aristocratic slavery, the latter of capitalistic, industrial slavery. The marginalia suggest that Twain *knew* he was satirizing *both* societies and illustrate again the synchronic quality of *Connecticut Yankee*.

Budd is not alone in criticizing this high-handed way with historical chronology, but Twain's connecting of aristocratic and slaveholding societies is valid and adheres to the concept of the compass of fact that concerned him. Indeed, Twain's object was to achieve a "synchronic moment" in which all time locates itself in a specific place so that the causes and effects of human progress would be all the more visible. It makes perfect sense, then, that in each of his prefaces, including the one finally adopted, Twain proclaims that the laws and incidents he depicts may not have occurred during Arthur's reign but did occur within human history. True, some of the examples Twain provides seem contrived. Hank's discussion of the way money was raised to build the "Mansion House" by taxing dissenters is completely anachronistic, except that he claims to have read about it "in my youth"—in other words, "back" in the nineteenth century (286). That passage comes directly from a paragraph Twain marked in the third volume of Lecky's *England in the Eighteenth Century* (3:538) and which he later entered into his notebook (see *MTN&J* 3:416).

More-general laws work quite effectively in Twain's book. Twain underlined and marginally lined a lengthy passage where Lecky discusses the restrictions on hunting and fishing; he then wrote in the margin, "English liberty was for gentlemen only" (6:262). Twain later copied this sentence with some revision into his notebook, even referring by volume and page to the passage he had marked in Lecky: "What was called English 'liberty' was for gentlemen only. See vol 6; 262" (*MTN&J* 3:423). His revision makes the comment more derisive, using the passive voice to indicate a subtle disagreement on his part and then placing quotation marks around *liberty* to make his disapproval more explicit. In the published book this democratic sentiment is all pervasive but is present particularly in the passages written during the summer of 1888. One example occurs when the dying woman in the smallpox hut refers to the "prowling animals that be scared and must not be hurt by any of our sort" (334).

At the heart of the question of democratic versus aristocratic societies was a disagreement between Twain and Lecky. Lecky enjoyed no disciple in Twain, and the American responded vociferously to the Irishman's assertion that an aristocratic government might, in some respects, be superior to a democratic one. Lecky held that an aristocratic form of government at least avoids "government by speculators, adventurers, and demagogues"; Twain reacted by writing, "He talks as if this had not been the rule throughout English history" (1:190). Twain rejected with greater vigor Lecky's opinion that "when other things are equal, the class which has most to lose and least to gain by dishonesty will exhibit the highest level of integrity." Twain penned a terse rejection in the margin: "It is all pure rot" (1:192).

In contrast, Mark Twain argued that individuals in a democracy must look out for their own interests and that no class can rely on members of a different class to deal fairly with them. In a similar vein he marked many passages in Lecky regarding sumptuary laws, the banning of unions, and the controlling of wages. These, along with Lecky's discussion of Scottish philosopher Dugald Stewart's *Lectures on Political Economy* (1855), enumerate the many ways the aristocracy protected its privilege.[5] Twain arrived at a simple solution and wrote "Universal suffrage would have broken that up promptly" next to Lecky's description of the many laws that proscribed the lower orders from engaging in certain occupations if their "parents did not possess a certain fortune." Similar schemes were devised to "fix the wages of all kinds of labourers and workmen" (6:233). Twain reworded his own comment slightly when entering it into his notebook: "233 vol 6. Elizabeth's law regulating occupations. Universal suffrage would have annulled it instantly" (*MTN&J* 3:422). These ideas emerge in chapters 31–33 of *Connecticut Yankee*, particularly chapter 33, "Sixth-Century Political Economy." Twain responded to Lecky's description of the tyrannical laws by writing in his journal, "The first thing I want to teach is *disloyalty* till they get used to disusing that word *loyalty* as representing a virtue" (*MTN&J* 3:415). Twain's research into the variety of ways the aristocracy preserved its power produced Hank's comment that the upper class will always favor their own, just as "the average mother" would favor her own children "in famine-time" (285). The men of old ideas are those chained by mental slavery but chiefly those who benefit from the old ideas—the aristocracy and gentry.

Throughout the novel Twain compressed over a thousand years of human history so that he could discuss how and in what ways the cause of humanity has been advanced and so that he could vivify, in Martha Banta's words, "what it feels like to experience 'old times,' 'modern times,' and 'future times' simultaneously" (490). For Twain, as for Auerbach, Realism = History = Change. In his penultimate preface, written after the summer of 1888, Twain asserted that "Human liberty—for white people—may fairly be said to be one hundred years old this year."[6] In 1890 Twain attacked Matthew Arnold once more in his speech "On Foreign Critics." He posed this question: "If you grant these terms, one may then consider this conundrum: How old is real civilization? The answer is easy and unassailable. A century ago it had not appeared anywhere in the world during a single instant since the world was made" (942). Likewise, Twain marginally noted, "100 yr ago." next to Lecky's discussion of Scotland's backwardness when compared to England and how quickly, once planted, progress flowered in Scotland (2:84). In another place Twain wrote, "Slavery during greater part of 18th century. Up to 1775. Ceased only 100 yr ago" (2:81). Twain developed these facts in his journal, writing, "For any man or woman not rich or of noble rank, there was but an imaginary difference between England & hell 100 years ago" (*MTN&J* 3:423). History is more than chronology, and although Twain may have done violence to chronology, he certainly did no violence to history; for like Lecky he chronicles the accelerated progress that occurred at a given time and place within a very short period. I am certain it is no coincidence that Twain viewed "Human liberty" as a hundred years old, for Lecky maintains precisely this attitude throughout *England in the Eighteenth Century*.

Much evidence exists to suggest that Twain viewed civilization itself as a thin veneer separating humanity from barbarism. As I have mentioned earlier, Hank refers to the inhabitants of Camelot as "Indians" on several occasions. The reason for this has been clearly explained by James McNutt, who says that "Twain utilized the Indian as a metaphor for violence and a symbol of uncivilized behavior" (240). And yet Twain's marginalia in Lecky's *England in the Eighteenth Century* complicate matters considerably. Twain wrote the word *Civilization* next to Lecky's discussion of Lauderdale's use of eight thousand Scottish Highlanders on behalf of the English government to punish the "western counties" by employing rape, pillage, and torture of every description (2:26). Twain then penned the word *Indians* directly below, next to a description of the Highlanders, among whom "Manual labor was looked upon with contempt" and who "devoted themselves to robbing or begging" (2:26).

The comparison Twain drew between civilized behavior and uncivilized behavior is ironic, suggesting that the dichotomy marks a distinction without much difference. The contrast between civilization and barbarism seems to be that civilization brings an orderly, more destructive waging of war, whereas barbarism operates according to a more individual rapacity. Philip Leon observes that Hank's use of the phrase the "last stand of chivalry of England," in connection with his "Battle of the Sand-Belt," in which twenty-five thousand knights are killed, is "an inverted allusion to the 'last stand' of ill-fated West Pointer George Armstrong Custer and his famously unsuccessful defense against overwhelming odds" (94–95). Richard Slotkin, despite his generally insightful interpretation of Twain's work, misreads the allusion to Custer's Last Stand. Slotkin calls Morgan "a civilizer among savages" (525) and refers to Hank as "Custer" and chivalry as "Sitting Bull" (530). In fact, it is chivalry's "last stand," and the inversion identifies Hank as an Indian and hence as an uncivilized "man of old ideas," not the "new man" he proclaims himself to be when first landing in Camelot (93). If Hank represents change and progress, or even something so limited as "industrial capitalism," as Henry Nash Smith argues (*Fable* 11), he obviously holds the seeds of destruction within himself. That is, Twain rejects teleology, and Hank is really *both* Custer and Sitting Bull in a history with no ultimate winners. Hank poses the horrendous riddle that history itself would ask: how can the barbarism of Lauderdale, or of Hank, or, going back to chapter 3, the Master of Stair, coexist with the advancement of civilization? More to the point, how can barbarism and civilization coexist within one society and even one personality? In the century that followed the publication of *Connecticut Yankee,* many would ask that question.

Hank's "peaceful revolution" mutates into something much darker, so much so that many have come to question even his initial motives. In part, his failure results from the "petrified" training of the inhabitants of Camelot, to the dominating presence of Church and state, and to the "men of old ideas" who benefit from the status quo. The traditions of the past that prevent humans from making history "just as they please," as Marx says, are embodied in the recalcitrance of people and institutions (15). Perhaps this is why Twain wrote in the Cranes's copy of Lecky's *England in the Eighteenth Century,* "Both the American & French Revolutions were precipitated by accidents—& so, indeed, was the English Rev." (1:15). Somehow, to think of these revolutions as unpremeditated events preserves their purity; Hank's revolution lost its innocence even as he planned to "boss the whole country inside of three months" (63). The contribution of Lecky's *England in the Eighteenth Century* to the completed novel cannot be overstated. Although Hank's failure is registered earlier, Twain's research in Lecky's *England in the Eighteenth Century* led him to conclude that rapid, sustained, and peaceful progress was not possible. The changes in Hank's plans are attributable not, as many critics have suggested, to Twain's unconscious motivations but to his conscious attempts to find answers to the questions his historical research provoked. The changes in the *Connecticut Yankee* manuscript testify to Twain's conscious artistry. Twain still had no answer to the circular conundrum of environment and character, but at least a tentative response to this problem is to be found in the marginalia Twain inscribed in another volume from the Cranes's library during the summer of 1888, Thomas Carlyle's *The French Revolution.*

5
Thomas Carlyle's "Bucket of Blood"

Twain's Rereading of *The French Revolution*

> I am finishing a book begun three years ago. I see land ahead. If I
> stick to the oar without intermission I shall be at anchor in thirty
> days; if I stop to moisten my hands I am gone.
> —Mark Twain to W. D. Foulke, October 3, 1888
> (*MTN&J* 3:395)

Along with William Edward Hartpole Lecky's three historical surveys,
Thomas Carlyle's *The French Revolution* had a most significant impact
on Mark Twain's aesthetics. Portions of *Tom Sawyer, The Prince and the
Pauper, Adventures of Huckleberry Finn, Connecticut Yankee,* and other
works are enlivened by references to Carlyle's history and inspired by its
philosophy. Walter Blair, for example, credits *The French Revolution* for
the oaths in *Tom Sawyer* and for the mob scenes in both *The Prince and
the Pauper* and *Adventures of Huckleberry Finn* (117, 310–13). Twain evidently first read *The French Revolution* in 1871. Later, in "My First Lie
and How I Got Out of It" (1899), he declared, "I have a reverent affection
for Carlyle's books, and have read his *Revolution* eight times" (167).
Howard Baetzhold reports that Twain even returned to the book in 1910
during the last few minutes of his life (*MT&JB* 87). Scholars have long
known that Twain had the book at hand during the composition of *Connecticut Yankee* because on August 22, 1887, he wrote William Dean Howells of his changing response after rereading it at Quarry Farm:

> How stunning are the changes which age makes in a man while he
> sleeps. When I finished Carlyle's *French Revolution* in 1871, I was a

Girondin; every time I have read it since, I have read it differently—being influenced & changed, little by little, by life & environment (& Taine, & St. Simon): & now I lay the book down once more, & recognize that I am a Sansculotte!—And not a pale, characterless Sansculotte, but a Marat. Carlyle teaches no such gospel: so the change is in me—in my vision of the evidences. (*MTHL* 2: 595)

This is a remarkable passage but only because Twain's reading has been so marginalized.

Twain's classing of books with the environment that forms character hardly strikes one as a revolutionary claim. Given the tendency of critics to disregard that reading, it resonates with greater power. The change in Twain's "vision of the evidences" probably owes more to the intensive study of history he embarked on during the composition of *Connecticut Yankee* than to any other single factor. In addition to Taine, St. Simon, and other historical works, Twain's opinions were altered by his reading of Lecky, Macaulay, and certainly by his rereading of Carlyle's work itself. James Williams surmises that Twain read *The French Revolution* "at least once during the composition" of *Connecticut Yankee* ("History" 106). Twain's letter to Howells and the edition of *The French Revolution* discovered at Quarry Farm prove that Twain read the book at least *twice* during the composition of *Connecticut Yankee*.[1]

Sometime during the summer of 1888 Mark Twain sauntered into the library at Quarry Farm and removed Susan Crane's newly acquired copy of Carlyle's *The French Revolution* from the bookshelves, perhaps taking it to the famous octagonal study where he composed many of his novels. Although one cannot be certain when he started rereading the book—probably not earlier than July—the date he finished is easily determined, for on the last page of volume 2 he wrote "Finish Sept. 10th .88" in heavy black pencil.

Howard Baetzhold has identified several passages in *Connecticut Yankee* that probably derive from Twain's pre-1888 readings of *The French Revolution*. Among these is the destruction of Merlin's tower, which has close parallels to Carlyle's book 8, "The Feast of Pikes" (*MT&JB* 146–47). Twain also adopted—and adapted, Baetzhold notes—Carlyle's metaphor of government and clothing in producing Hank Morgan's famous statement that "institutions are . . . mere clothing" (*MT&JB* 144–

45). Despite these examples, James Williams's contention that although "one can guess that Carlyle had an important and manifold influence over the composition of the *Yankee* . . . specific borrowing from him was very limited" ("History" 106) has seemed essentially accurate. With the discovery of the Quarry Farm marginalia, however, his assessment needs qualification. Twain's marginalia allow us to ascertain, finally, what some of Carlyle's specific contributions were and to probe with greater certainty the "manifold influence" he had on *Connecticut Yankee*. Among other things, the marginalia make it clear that Hank's hope for a peaceful revolution was, by the end of the summer of 1888, fading fast and becoming bloodier by the moment.

A few of the markings in Susan Crane's copy of *The French Revolution* suggest connections to Mark Twain's work in general. Carlyle's description of the aristocracy laughing over a "word mispronounced" (1:23), for instance, would have appealed to Twain's fascination with the contrast between formal and vernacular languages. Marking the passage during the composition of *Connecticut Yankee*, Twain may have recognized that such a contest/comedy of languages plays a role in his own work when Hank's American vernacular comes into contact with the Camelot aristocracy's Malory-inspired argot. Thus, in chapter 22, written in the summer of 1888, Sandy considers Hank's slang expressions "shut up shop, draw the game, bank the fires" to be "golden phrases of high mystery" and "miracles of speech" (257–58). The specific languages here in conflict are less important than the historicity of the clash; that is, the clash of the two languages illustrates the clash between progressive and conservative values that typifies any kind of change. It also serves Twain's purpose of vivifying what it feels like to experience change, for as Megan Stitt observes, dialect creates "a 'drama' of changing language" (7). Similarly, Twain may have marked Carlyle's paean to "DEMOCRACY" (1:6) as an acknowledgment that Hank, too, represents democracy writ large; like the American Revolution that infects French society, Hank infects English society with American democratic ideas, although ultimately he introduces less praiseworthy traits of the American national character.

Examining Twain's markings, one can also cite several specific elements of *Connecticut Yankee* that may have derived from his reading of Carlyle's work in 1888. According to Howard Baetzhold, Twain wrote chapters 10 and 21–36 during the stay at Elmira in 1888 and completed the book in May of the following year ("Composition" 204–14). Logically, chapter 10 and any of the chapters after 21 may have been influenced by Twain's rereading *The French Revolution* in 1888.

Someone, perhaps Twain, placed a piece of newspaper between pages 274 and 275 in volume 1 of Carlyle's book at the point where the author describes a mob of "Menadic women" and "infuriated men" storming the king's home at Versailles (1:274). If Twain placed the newspaper there, he may have done so to mark a mob scene that contributed to chapters 30 and 34 of *Connecticut Yankee*. In chapter 30, "The Tragedy of the Manor House," for example, the lord's home is set ablaze and the lord himself is discovered "bound, gagged, stabbed in a dozen places" (341). Although the manor house passage owes much to Lecky's *A History of England in the Eighteenth Century,* and also to Charles Dickens's *Tale of Two Cities* (see *MT&JB* 153–54), the description of events in chapter 30 resembles Carlyle's description of the rabble forcing entrance into Louis's palace:

> But glance now, for a moment, from the royal windows! A roaring sea of human heads, inundating both Courts; billowing against all passages: Menadic women; infuriated men, mad with revenge, with love of mischief, love of plunder! Rascality has slipped its muzzle; and now bays, three-throated, like the Dog of Erebus. . . . Whirled down so suddenly to the abyss; as men are, suddenly, by the wide thunder of the Mountain Avalanche, awakened not by *them,* awakened far off by others! (1:274)

Compare this to Twain's description of the scene in England:

> Within the next mile we counted six more hanging forms by the blaze of the lightning, and altogether it was a grisly excursion. That murmur was a murmur no longer, it was a roar; a roar of men's voices. A man came flying by, now, dimly through the darkness, and other men chasing him. They disappeared. Presently another case of the kind occurred, and then another and another. Then a sudden turn of the road brought us in sight of that fire—it was a large manor house, and little or nothing was left of it—and everywhere men were flying and other men raging after them in pursuit. (340)

There are several points of similarity between Carlyle's description and Twain's. In each case, to describe the attack on an aristocrat in his home, the writer couples weather patterns with the actions of a mob.

The mob at Versailles is "billowing," and those attacked are "whirled down" by its actions. Twain, too, uses suggestive words like *flying* throughout chapter 30. And both mobs "roar," again suggesting the sound of wind. Most obviously, Carlyle repeatedly compares the actions and emotions of the crowd to thunder, and Twain sets the action in chapter 30 during a lightning storm. Both writers even employ cumulative sentence structures to convey the feeling of a rushing crowd or the whipping wind; in each case the weather serves as a barometer of the mob's "stormy" emotions.

In Twain's presentation, however, the lord of the manor is murdered by an escaped prisoner who is in turn hunted by the mob. Although the mob scenes of *The French Revolution* serve as the prototype for those in *Connecticut Yankee,* Twain's mob is counterrevolutionary—a "depressing" fact, Hank muses, "to a man with the dream of a republic in his head" (343). Twain ironically twists the paradigm of Carlyle's work again in chapter 34 even while drawing on it, when a mob pursues Hank and King Arthur. Unlike the mob that storms Versailles, this mob is not knowingly antiaristocratic, but it does serve, ironically, a democratic function. Twain again uses weather imagery to describe the mob: "Presently we heard it coming—and coming on the jump, too; yes, and down both sides of the stream. Louder—louder—next minute it swelled swiftly up into a roar of shoutings, barkings, tramplings, and swept by like a cyclone" (386). Here Twain's use of the cyclone simile compares to Carlyle's metaphor of the mountain avalanche that threatens to engulf the onlookers. In addition, Twain includes the barking of dogs in his description and, in a passage that follows, has an aristocrat refer to the entire mob as dogs: "'Lash me these animals to their kennels!'" (389). Carlyle's description of the mob storming Versailles as "the Dog of Erebus" may have suggested the metaphor. Like the dog of the underworld, Twain's mob emerges from the lower depths to harry the damned over the earth. Here and elsewhere we can conclude with the evidence of the manuscript and the marginalia that Twain *consciously* patterned passages after scenes in Carlyle's work, manipulating them to serve his own artistic needs; we witness Twain composing a "fictional history."

Twain also drew a line along Carlyle's description of the terror in the prisons next to these lines: "Rigor grows, stiffens into horrid tyranny; Plot in the Prison getting ever rifer" (2:378). The discussion following the marked passage most obviously recalls Twain's description of Morgan

le Fay's dungeon in *Connecticut Yankee:* "Dear me, for what trifling offences the most of those forty-seven men and women were shut up
there! Indeed some were there for no distinct offence at all, but only to
gratify somebody's spite" (212). Carlyle, too, describes a legal system
based on personal spite, a legal system in which "indictments are drawn
out in blank" (2:378). Hank's visit to Morgan le Fay's dungeon occurs in
chapter 18 and so probably derives from Twain's earlier reading(s) of the
book. Accounts of the slaves in chapters 21 and 34, on the other hand,
owe much to Twain's 1888 reading of Carlyle's passages depicting the
Reign of Terror. Howard Baetzhold identifies George Kennan's articles
on the Russian penal system, which appeared in the May, June, and July
1888 issues of the *Century,* as a probable source of the chapters ("Composition" 209). Twain's reading of Charles Ball's *Slavery in the United
States* was likewise significant (*MT&JB* 151, 349–50 n. 33, 352 n. 39). As
we now know, Twain also relied on Lecky's *History of England in the
Eighteenth Century* for the compass of fact that kept him on course in
this section. Twain reread *The French Revolution* during that summer,
and although Baetzhold correctly cites Kennan and Ball as sources,
Twain's portrayal of slaves in chains may derive from Carlyle's description of the prisoners during the Reign of Terror:

> Nightly come his Tumbrils to the Luxembourg, with the fatal Roll-
> call; list of the *Fournee* of tomorrow. Men rush toward the Grate;
> listen, if their name be in it? One deep-drawn breath, when the
> name is not in; we live still one day! And yet some score or scores
> of names were in. Quick these, they clasp their loved ones to their
> heart, one last time; with brief adieu, wet-eyed, they mount, and are
> away. . . . Chained two and two they march; in exasperated mo-
> ments singing their *Marseillaise. . . . Vive la Republique* rises from
> them in all streets of towns: they rest by night in unutterable noi-
> some dens, crowded to choking; one or two dead on the morrow.
> (2:378–79)

There are several specific parallels between such passages in *The French
Revolution* and passages treating slaves in *Connecticut Yankee.* Twain's description of the bereaved families separated by the system of slavery, for
example, resembles Carlyle's description of such separations. Carlyle has
his prisoners led off one by one over the course of several days as their
names appear on the roll. Similarly, Twain's band of prisoners dissolves

as the men and women are separated and sold, one by one. In each case the prisoners' fates are revealed with a horrifying regularity, and the families wait anxiously, knowing they will be separated but not knowing when. In both Camelot and Paris husbands and wives attempt to prolong the final moments, but the partings are as brief as they are emotional.

The physical conditions of the slaves and prisoners in the two works also correspond. In chapters 21 and 34 of *Connecticut Yankee*, the slaves are chained two by two and in a line. Baetzhold identifies Kennan as a source for these chapters because Twain's slave driver uses the same method of chaining his wards that the Russian jailers use; however, these methods are the same ones used by the Sansculottes in *The French Revolution*. Likewise, the slaves in chapter 21 of *Connecticut Yankee*, whose "irons had chafed the skin from their ankles and made sores which were ulcerated and wormy" (244), are no worse off than Carlyle's shipboard prisoners who are "wasted to shadows." These prisoners devour "their unclean ration on deck, circularly, in parties of a dozen, with finger and thumb" and sleep in "horrible miasmata, closed under hatches, seventy of them in a berth," some surviving the nights, others not (2:379). In chapter 34 of *Connecticut Yankee* Hank and Arthur survive the night, whereas nine of their number perish (400).

In the same vein Twain probably gleaned from chapter 5 of *The French Revolution* a poignant example of children learning to terrorize others. Shortly after the passage Twain marked, Carlyle describes young people who "'act the Guillotine' by way of pastime. In fantastic mummery, with towel-turbans, blanket-ermine, a mock Sanhedrin of Judges sits, a mock Tinville pleads; a culprit is doomed, is guillotined by the oversetting of two chairs" (2:378–79). Twain appropriated this scene, reworking it into the mock hanging in chapter 31 of *Connecticut Yankee*. Hank and King Arthur rush to aid children who "had hanged a little fellow with a bark rope" (349). Hank moralizes that the children were simply "imitating their elders" and "playing mob" (349).

Here Twain again uses the compass of fact to provide a specific incident that could occur at any time in any society. The children of a community exist as a microcosm of that community, reproducing—in Althusserian terms—the ideology that governs it. This is one reason Hank's program of peaceful progress is so very difficult. What Hank calls "petrified training" governs the behavior of people and results from the negative aspects of human nature accentuated by the institutions of society (201). The children of Camelot were trained from a very early age to accept their environment and to conform their behavior to it.

Perhaps Twain's single greatest debt from his 1888 reading of *The French Revolution* is the near hanging of King Arthur, which derives from Carlyle's description of the guillotining of Louis in book 4, "Regicide." Although there are no markings in this section, the corner of page 215 has been turned down and creased. On this page begins Carlyle's description of Louis's execution. Despite the obvious dissimilarities (Arthur faces hanging, whereas Louis faces the guillotine; Arthur escapes execution, whereas Louis does not), the execution scenes reveal several parallels.

Both Louis and Arthur, for example, face execution alone, even as they appear before vast crowds. Carlyle estimates eighty thousand spectators but also observes that "King Louis's friends are feeble and far" (2:214). Similarly, Twain's Yankee wryly comments that the "multitude was prodigious and far reaching; and yet we sixteen poor devils hadn't a friend in it" (422). Technically Arthur is not "alone," but Twain stresses his sense of isolation and abandonment. Both writers dramatize the solitary nature of the execution by contrasting the vast crowds in the street with the individuals on the scaffold.

If both Arthur and Louis find themselves the cynosure of all eyes, their ordeals corroborate Carlyle's observation that a "King dying by such violence appeals impressively to the imagination" (2:215–16). The nature of kingship piques both writers, and both use the execution scenes to reflect on the ways that a king is a political entity and the ways that a king is a man. Carlyle asserts, "And yet at bottom it is not the King dying, but the man! Kingship is a coat: the grand loss is of the skin" (2:216). Seemingly, Carlyle makes the distinction to gain sympathy for Louis the man, for he then proceeds to discuss the emotional parting between the king and his wife and son. Nevertheless, Carlyle endows Louis the man with virtues that make him appear kingly. When the time arrives for the execution, Louis, still wearing the "coat" of kingship, stamps his foot and delivers one last order to his jailers: "*Partons*, Let us go" (2:218). He endures his fate "in sorrow, in indignation, in resignation struggling to be resigned" while on the scaffold (2:219). As a final kingly gesture he "spurns" those who would bind his hands (2:219). Louis the man and Louis the king, taken together, embody the Carlylean hero, the exceptional man worthy of study and emulation.

Arthur holds similar sway on Hank's imagination. Despite his opposition to aristocratic government, Hank is enthralled by Arthur's regal nature as he faces hanging. Initially, he "proclaimed himself Arthur, king of Britain" only to suffer a "vast roar of laughter" (423). His dignity wounded, Arthur refuses to subject himself to further baiting by the crowd. He falls silent, but Hank remarks, "He put on all his majesty and sat under this rain of contempt and insult unmoved. He certainly was great, in his way" (423).

Grudgingly, at first, Hank grants that Arthur has noble traits. Earlier he had reflected on the duality of kingship, musing that "a king's feelings, like the impulses of an automatic doll, are mere artificialities; but as a man, he is a reality" (397). After the execution is averted, however, Hank endorses Arthur's character as a king enthusiastically, saying "as he stood apart, there, receiving this homage in his rags, I thought to myself, well really there *is* something peculiarly grand about the gait and bearing of a king, after all" (426). Interestingly, Hank phrases his observations in general terms; it is not specifically Arthur's bearing but a king's bearing that strikes Hank as "peculiarly grand." Louis Budd laments Twain's "sneaking taste for chivalric froth" (*Social* 123) at this and other junctures, but Hank's respect for Arthur parallels Carlyle's attraction to the "hero" who can impose himself on history. Hank resembles those at King Louis's execution who respond to a man whose politics they scorn and whom they blame for society's ills but whose noble bearing in the face of *personal* disaster forgives his politics. Twain patterns the execution scene in *Connecticut Yankee* after Carlyle's description of Louis's death because it presents in bold relief the conundrum that although kingship itself is ignoble, its practitioners can behave nobly. Head of an unjust society, Arthur exhibits nobility even while facing execution. Like Louis he emerges through his ordeal as a man worthy of respect, even if unworthy of a crown.

Hank's grudging respect may actually contribute to the violence of the "Battle of the Sand-Belt." Resisting his attraction to Arthur as monarch, demanding of himself obedience to the cause of democracy, Hank violently asserts his belief in revolution. That revolution cannot be a peaceful one, ostensibly because of the dogmatic conservatism of the Church, but perhaps the increasing violence is also due to Hank's inner turmoil. Many critics would credit Twain's inner turmoil, and some see the conclusion to *Connecticut Yankee* as Twain's attack on himself. James Cox interprets the violence of the ending as "symbolically a crippling of the inventive imagination, as if Mark Twain were driven to maim himself in an effort to survive" (210). Twain's response to the conclusion of *The French Revolution,* and to the underlying theoretical position of what Carlyle called the "Chaos of Being," provokes some other intriguing possibilities.

Twain's "specific borrowings" from Carlyle, then, were not as limited as previously thought, and they were certainly consciously obtained and elaborated. One recalls Twain's comment in the draft for the *Princeton Review* that each fact is "an acorn, a root" (*MTN&J* 3:343). Moreover, one can learn from Twain's written response to a book that contributed to the composition of his own. Most obviously, one can discern parallels between Hank's remarks in *Connecticut Yankee* and Twain's robust assessment of Carlyle's achievement that he wrote on the last pages of Susan Crane's copy of *The French Revolution:*

Finish Sept. 10th .88

This is a picture of the French Revolution, but in only a limited way, a history of it. It is as if one gave you a picture [scratched out word] of God manufacturing by tedious & long processes, Hair, Bones, Flesh, Nails, Nerves, Muscles, Tendons, & piling them in separate piles, & adding a bucket of Blood—& stopping there: with the [scratched out word] remark, "Such was the process of the Creation of Man." Now what use were that, except he set up man & let us look at him & see if he was better or worse than this chaos & rubbish he was made out of?

The Revolution had a result—a superb, a stupendous, a most noble & sublime result—to wit, French Liberty, & in a degree, Human Liberty—& was worth a million times what it cost, of blood, & terror, & various suffering, & titanic labor. And this fair & shapely creation was not worth Carlyle's pains to paint. Nothing but the Process interested him—the Result was matter of indifference. He should have given a chapter showing what the French laws were, before the Revolution, & what they were when the Revolution's work was finished.

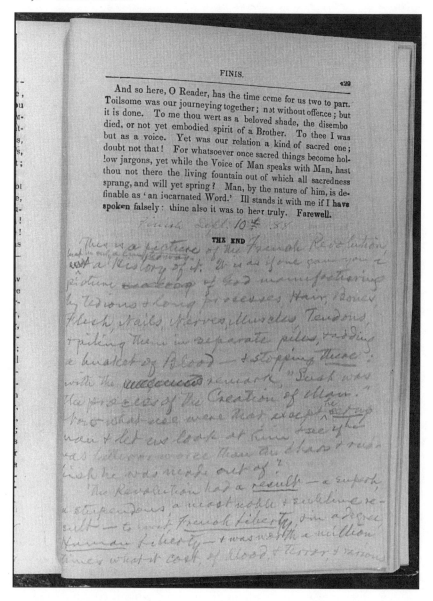

3. and 4. Twain's vigorous response to Carlyle's *French Revolution*. Courtesy Mark Twain Archives, Elmira College.

Twain's final response recalls in particular the Yankee's spirited defense of the "Terror" that occurred during the revolution, where he states that life in Camelot "was like reading about France and the French, before the ever-memorable and blessed Revolution, which swept a thousand suffering, & Titanic labor. And this faint & shapely creation was not worth Carlyle's pains to paint. Nothing but the Process interested him — the Result was matter of indifference. He should have given a chapter showing what the French laws were, before the Revolution, & what they were when the Revolution's work was finished.

years of such villainy away in one swift tidal wave of blood" (157). Twain added Hank's famous elaboration at an unknown, later date:

> There were two "Reigns of Terror," if we would but remember it and consider it: the one wrought murder in hot passion, the other

in heartless cold blood; the one lasted mere months, the other had lasted a thousand years; the one inflicted death upon ten thousand persons, the other upon a hundred millions; but our shudders are all for the "horrors" of the minor Terror, the momentary Terror, so to speak; whereas, what is the horror of swift death by the axe, compared with life-long death from hunger, cold, insult, cruelty and heart-break? What is swift death by lightning, compared with death by slow fire at the stake? A city cemetery could contain the coffins filled by that brief Terror which but all France could hardly contain the coffins filled by that older and real Terror—that unspeakably bitter and awful Terror which none of us has been taught to see in its vastness or pity as it deserves. (157–58)[2]

Howard Baetzhold hypothesizes that Twain may have added this paragraph after his 1887 reading of *The French Revolution,* around the time of his letter to Howells ("Composition" 202). Prior to the discovery of Susan Crane's copy of the book, this argument seemed plausible. But Twain is known to have revised his manuscript in 1888, the following summer. It seems more likely, then, that Twain added this paragraph under the influence of his 1888 reading of Carlyle's book, amending the manuscript to strengthen a sansculottism adopted earlier but confirmed by yet another reading of *The French Revolution.* More significantly, when Twain added this paragraph lauding the French Revolution, he also struck out several lines from the text that I discussed in the previous chapter. Part of the canceled passage finds Hank saying that "the convulsion I was gropingly projecting, had no blood in it; I intended it should be peaceful, and had no very serious doubt that I could work it out on that line." Twain did have his doubts, however, and canceled the passage and added his praise of the Revolution at the same time, I believe, because his study of history convinced him that a bloodless revolution was simply not possible.[3]

Perhaps, then, Carlyle's greatest contribution to *Connecticut Yankee* was as an antagonist who helped Twain to define his own views. In his marginalia Twain compares the Revolution to the "Creation of Man," criticizing Carlyle for focusing on the "process" at the expense of the "noble & sublime result." One might speculate that Twain saw himself as writing the unfinished chapter to Carlyle's book. The character Hank Morgan in *Connecticut Yankee* offered Twain a chance to "set up man &

let us look at him & see if he was better or worse than this chaos & rubbish he was made out of," as he suggested in his marginalia. Twain presents, after all, one person, Hank Morgan, as representing revolution, historicity, historical materialism, and change. By "setting up" this character, Twain imagines a way to assay the "Process" and "Result" of a violent revolution against monarchy. Given his concluding comments in Susan Crane's copy of *The French Revolution*, I believe Mark Twain was offering *Connecticut Yankee* as a response to Carlyle's "bucket of Blood" description of the French Revolution. For the American writer the "Result" of the Revolution surmounted the "Process."

Twain's use of the word *chaos*, moreover, resonates with Carlyle's work in its more general, theoretical orientation. Carlyle espoused a philosophy of historiography that he called the "Chaos of Being" and in his essay "On History" defined his position:

> The most gifted man can observe, still more can record, only the *series* of his own impressions: his observation, therefore, to say nothing of its other imperfections, must be *successive*, while the things done were often simultaneous; the things done were not a series, but a group. It is not in acted, as it is in written History: actual events are nowise so simply related to each other as parent and offspring are; every single event is the offspring not of one, but of all other events, prior or contemporaneous, and will in its turn combine with all others to give birth to new: it is an ever-living, ever-working Chaos of Being, wherein shape after shape bodies itself forth from innumerable elements. And this Chaos, boundless as the habitation and duration of man, unfathomable as the soul and destiny of man, is what the historian will depict, and scientifically gauge, we may say, by threading it with single lines of a few ells in length! . . . Narrative is *linear*, action is *solid*. (551)

Sounding very much like the later theorist Foucault, Carlyle asserts that the "real historical Transaction" can never be resurrected because of the chaos that governs history (550). In *Connecticut Yankee* Twain uses Hank Morgan to investigate a culture in the throes of progress; that is, he analyzes the idea of a linear progression punctuated by distinct stages. Critics often assume, as Susan K. Harris has, that Twain wished to escape "the cause-and-effect universe" (*Escape from Time* 4). In fact, however, Hank's experiences in Camelot illustrate an attempt, albeit ill-fated, to exploit the rule of cause and effect to one's own advantage, and one might suppose that Twain himself saw possibilities in such a manipulation of the concept of change. In her book, *The Power of Historical Knowledge: Narrating the Past in Hawthorne, James, and Dreiser*, Susan Mizruchi discusses "the fallacy of historical self-consciousness" that asserts people can change the environment that produces them (81). Of course, this is the issue that dogs Mark Twain throughout his career, and it is certainly the central question posed by *Connecticut Yankee*. Certainly, Twain did hope that the compass of fact could provide a polestar amid the chaos. The point, after all, of his own writing was to provoke thought and ethical rejuvenation among his readers. If at times Twain's humor grew strained, it was because he never relinquished the hope that people could change for the better and that his writing could assist in the enterprise.

This is as close as Twain ever comes to espousing teleology, and Hank, not Twain, is the champion of cause and effect. Twain investigates the compass of fact, wondering whether change might be finessed into serving humanity if harnessed to the dictates of one aware of what Carlyle terms the "chainlets" of cause and effect. According to Carlyle, however, history is chaos and is "solid," so one cannot identify "parent and offspring" or "causes and effects" with anything approaching certainty (550). Carlyle accepts Aristotle's argument in the *Physics* that "there is no such thing as the immediate occasion when a change has begun, because change has no beginning and there is no immediate occasion in time when a changing object began to change" (151). Put another way, Carlyle rejects Twain's realist equation, Realism = History = Change, substituting his own: Narrative = History + Chaos. Carlyle believed that the "real historical Transaction" could never be found and that no one could uncover the "cause and effect" operating within the chaos of being. No narrative could be "real," then, and even a realist like Twain might, despite a passion for the compass of fact, find himself writing lies.

In the end the cause-and-effect universe loses out to chaos, and when compared to what we might call the "Carlylean Assumption," Twain's "gay abjuration of historicity" abjures less than we might have supposed (Aspiz, "Lecky's" 17). In fact, although Twain engages happily in anachronism, his writing stance throughout the composition of *Connecticut Yankee* remained that of Carlyle: Like the Scotsman, he acknowledged the ineffability of the "real historical Transaction," and so he raised as his standard Change itself, the "solidity" of synchronistic, omnihistorical change. That was Twain's fictional history; Carlyle's assumption, however, that historical narrative must necessarily be chaotic is the dark side, as it were, of Twain's belief that Change is the preeminent historical truth. Clearly, Change does not necessarily imply orderly progression, but the American's belief that he could combine the "science" of history with the art of fiction was challenged by Carlyle's beliefs. Carlyle emerges as a preeminent historian admirably wary of the complexities of his craft but whose main assumption suggests history is irredeemably chaotic and that anything written about it is as much a product of the imagination as of history.

Carlyle's concept of the "Chaos of Being" provides the background for Twain's response to *The French Revolution*. In part Twain responded so vehemently, I believe, because Carlyle's assumptions, expressed in "On History" and practiced in *The French Revolution*, contradicted the concept of the compass of fact, which Twain used as a polestar to guide him while writing a book founded on historical Change. If Carlyle correctly defined history as chaos, then Twain's attempt to create a realistic fiction based on it was flawed from its inception, for how could one depict it? Moreover, if the cause and effect of historical change are irretrievably lost in history, then perhaps they really do not exist in the way we think of them. Clark Griffith discusses this aspect of the book, noting, "It is the same merciless, meaningless, place, called by many different names" and that Hank experiences "only *one* continuous horror" (108–9). This is brilliantly put and expresses so much about *Connecticut Yankee* and Twain's thinking. Twain dreaded the chaos wherein history would cease being just "so damned humiliating" and would become nightmare ("MMT" 274). Ironically, Carlyle provided Twain with further assistance, for Twain was more concerned with reconstituting "how it feels & seems" to exist within time and change; ultimately, that is the "real historical Transaction," for humans experience time, history, and change as chaos.

Twain's response to Carlyle's work is violent for the same reason Hank's response to his situation is violent: no identifiable chain of cause and effect links the past to the present and future; no visible overarching motive force of progress shapes change; no perceptible governor exists but the "Chaos of Being" that necessarily produces the "chaos & rubbish" of humankind. Twain hoped that his readers would learn from

Connecticut Yankee; he hoped his writing would not remain "only just words, words" (*CY* 324), but his intensive study of history in the years 1885–1888 provided him with many negative examples. If history is chaos, there is no point in a serious-minded satirist trying to change minds and, through them, history. Despite the outward disagreement with Carlyle, Twain acts out the concept of the chaos of being in the conclusion to *Connecticut Yankee.* The ending battle does not illustrate, as many have supposed, Twain's despair over a universe governed by "cause and effect" but rather his despair at a universe governed by chaos, where the linear cause and effect are lost in "solidity" of history.

One might question, though, whether this entirely accounts for Twain's vivid corporeal references in the marginalia. To some extent the description is nothing new in Twain's writing, as he often uses such expressions. In the review "English as She Is Taught," for example, Twain employs a vivid metaphor that compares forcing children to learn grammar rules and force-feeding children an unwholesome food: "into the restricted stomach of the public-school pupil is shoveled every year the blood, bone, and viscera of a gigantic literature" (251). But Twain's language in the marginalia at the end of *The French Revolution,* admittedly not written for publication, seems more grotesque than usual. If Twain's corporeal language in his response to *The French Revolution* suggests birth and creation, it also unavoidably suggests death and destruction. Even as he criticizes the "picture" that Carlyle paints, Twain sketches a vivid one of his own where human beings become a "chaos & rubbish" of assorted "Hair, Bones, Flesh, Nails, Nerves, Muscles, Tendons" splashed with a "bucket of Blood." Twain's corporeal language surely owes something to the concluding sentences of *The French Revolution.* Carlyle ends by saying "Man, by the nature of him, is definable as 'an incarnated Word.' Ill stands it with me if I have spoken falsely: thine also it was to hear truly. Farewell" (2:429). Despite continuing to admire *The French Revolution,* Twain apparently did think Carlyle spoke falsely; he appropriated Carlyle's language in his response, with the phrase "incarnated Word" providing him with a metaphor for his diatribe on the "Creation of Man," with its attendant carnality.

Twain's corporeal language in the marginalia probably also owes something to events occurring at Quarry Farm while he read Carlyle's book. Just four days before Twain completed his 1888 reading of *The French Revolution,* his brother-in-law, Theodore Crane, experienced the stroke that would paralyze and ultimately kill him by the following summer.[4] Gretchen Sharlow, director of the Elmira College Center for Mark Twain Studies at Quarry Farm, reports that Twain "rescheduled their departure date from September 13th to the 24th" in response to the tragedy ("Crane" 4). Theodore Crane was not simply Twain's brother-in-law but also a gracious host, a boon friend, and a constant reading companion. Twain, says his biographer, "found comfort in the society of Theodore Crane," and they even reclined in "portable-hammock arrangements which they placed side by side on the lawn, and read and discussed through summer afternoons" (Paine, *Biography*, 1:510). Twain may have started reading *The French Revolution* in that hammock next to Theodore, perhaps discussing aspects of it with him. Theodore's stroke ended any such colloquies, and the shock of his sudden demise may well have confronted Twain with a physical, rather than a political, "Terror."

As sudden as the stroke was, Theodore Crane was not to be granted a quick departure. Reversing their usual arrangement, he stayed with Twain and his family in Hartford much of the winter. Twain described the environment at Hartford to Mary Fairbanks in a letter dated December 30, 1888:

> I reckon you would hardly know this place. We are hermits, now, & must doubtless remain so the rest of the winter. Theodore Crane has been here a month or two in a precarious state, because of a stroke of paralysis. Sometimes he picks up a little, & then for a day or two it is a cheerful home; after that, he drops back again, & the gloom & the apprehension return. It is pulling Susie Crane down a good deal, & Livy also, of course. These two women will get sick if this continues. (*MTMF* 262–63)

The whole environment had changed. Gone were the "perfect days" at the farm; forgotten were the long days writing the "uncommonly bully book." Instead, as he prepared to write the final chapters of *Connecticut Yankee* Twain saw in Theodore Crane a very vivid reminder that humankind enjoys no infinite ability to solve its problems, that progress has limits, and that chaos governs the sublunary world. No amount of Yankee know-how could cure the fundamental ill that corporeal nature had bestowed to "the damned human race" ("MMT" 304). For ten months following the stroke Theodore Crane, Twain wrote, "was a half wreck, physically, & suffered a good deal of pain of a bodily sort, together with a mental depression & hopelessness that made him yearn for death every day" (*MTMF* 264). His brother-in-law's illness furnished Twain with another occasion to ponder the question he returned to many times: what exactly was the "process of the Creation of Man" and could humans ever progress beyond the "chaos & rubbish" from which they were made?

One senses in Twain's marginalia and in *Connecticut Yankee* a pervasive tension surrounding revolutionary change as both birth and death. Although Hank may exclaim "I was a new man!" early in his sojourn in Camelot, the story ends with Hank as an old man, pathetically picking at the coverlet (93). And although the Yankee proclaims an end to a Reign of Terror that ruled in "heartless cold blood," Mark Twain's own revolution is, as he wrote of Carlyle's description of the French Revolution, awash in a "bucket of Blood." Hank's "Battle of the Sand-Belt" kills those opposing his program, rendering them by a discreation into "homogeneous protoplasm" (478). Passages Twain excised from the manuscript on the advice of his friends are even more grotesque in their language of discreation. Twain referred, for example, to "some trifle over 4,000,000 pounds of meat" resulting from his war with English knighthood.[5] With the "Battle of the Sand-Belt," Carlyle's "Chaos of Being" reigns triumphant, and Twain's champion of cause and effect, Hank Morgan, is deposed. He began as an agent of progress in a history pregnant with possibility but ends as an agent of chaos; Hank takes the piles of "Hair, Bones, Flesh, Nails, Nerves, Muscles, Tendons" of the French Revolution and tries to fashion something "fair & shapely" but fails in his attempt at creation.

Conclusion

Well, my book is written—let it go. But if it were only to write
over again there wouldn't be so many things left out. They burn
in me; & they keep multiplying & multiplying; but now they can't
ever be said. And besides, they would require a library—& a pen
warmed-up in hell.
                    —Mark Twain to William Dean Howells,
                        September 22, 1889 (*MTHL* 2:613)

At the end of the summer of 1888 Mark Twain sat down with his notebook to calculate what he owed the Cranes:

4323.=$662. T. W. Crane. Sept. 24, '88.
Farm, from June 23 to Sept. 24, 13 weeks & 2 days.
6 persons, $40 per week, ... ($535) $532.
2 ponies, ($3 per week each) 80
Washing, 10 weeks at $5 50
                                            $662.
                    (*MTN&J* 3:424)

Although this is by no means the household budget, and Twain undoubtedly spent money on various odds and ends, as well as on the occasional draught at Klapproth's Saloon in Elmira proper, the list conveys
the simplicity of life at Quarry Farm.

But of course, Mark Twain owed the Cranes a debt far greater than
he tabulated in his notebook, for they fostered the "go-as-you-please"
attitude that allowed him the creative space he required to write his

books. Only at Quarry Farm could he retreat to a private space—the octagonal study—and remain in that "charming sort of Peter Pan house," as Clara called it, from 10 A.M. to 5 P.M. each day (*MFMT* 60–61). By the end of the summer of 1888 Twain had written the first thirty-six chapters of *Connecticut Yankee* and had accomplished enough research to see him through to the finish. As important as the marginalia he left behind are those things he took with him: the vigor gained from the circumstances of creativity and the tangible "compass of fact" the research afforded. As we interpret Twain's marginalia, and as we gain further insight into the composing process that he claimed to know nothing about and yet talked about so frequently, we see a Twain who did not write his books unconsciously or solely on "personal experience," as is so often argued.

Rather, while writing *Connecticut Yankee,* Twain relied on the compass of fact provided by his historical research to keep him on course. His study of history was not desultory, as some have claimed, but was a deep engagement with the authors whose works he studied. If, as Aristotle decrees in the *Poetics,* "the distinction between the historian and the poet . . . consists really in this, that the one describes the thing that has been, and the other a kind of thing that might be" (637), it is clear that Mark Twain's realism violated the usual dichotomies of fiction and history. In *Connecticut Yankee* Twain used the compass of fact to treat both the "thing that has been" and the "thing that might be," subsuming them into a synchronic exploration of history as humans experience it. Twain wrote "fictional history," and nowhere is this so obvious as in his composing of *Connecticut Yankee.* A full understanding of Twain as a researcher, of Twain as a writer following the compass of fact, of Twain as *both* historian and conscious artist must emerge from the margins and take its place alongside our understanding of Twain as a writer from experience. And Quarry Farm, too, must take its place alongside Hannibal and Hartford.

Twain's composing process—despite misrepresentations—stood him in good stead, and by the next summer he was correcting copy. By August of 1889 he was reviewing Dan Beard's illustrations for the book.[1] In December of 1889 *Connecticut Yankee* appeared in time for the Christmas market. Among the first reviewers was Twain's friend, William Dean Howells. There was nothing lukewarm about Howells's endorsement of *Connecticut Yankee.* Writing in the "Editor's Study" in January 1890,

Howells likened *Connecticut Yankee* to *Don Quixote* and its author to Cervantes (320).

He specifically lauded incidents in *Connecticut Yankee* that Twain had not created from personal experience but from his research, like the scaffold scene with mother and child that Twain obtained from Lecky. Howells noted, too, the synchronic quality of the narrative. "There are incidents in this wonder-book," Howells advised, "which wring the heart for what has been of cruelty and wrong in the past, and leave it burning with shame and hate for the conditions which are of like effect in the present" (321). With the publication of *Connecticut Yankee* it was not just Mark Twain who owed the Cranes a debt of gratitude but the many readers who would find their own thinking influenced by the incidents in this "fictional history."

The magical time at Quarry Farm was largely over. Theodore Crane's death effectively ended the Clemens's habit of spending whole summers at "Go-as-You-Please Hall." Vanished were Ellerslie, the "cat procession," the nightly manuscript readings, and vanished, too, was the toting of books up the hill to the octagonal study. The next few years would witness financial and personal disaster: first with the failure of the Paige typesetter and the Webster Publishing Company, which exhausted the family finances, and later, most tragically, with the death of his daughter Susy.

In his writings Mark Twain continued to follow what he called the compass of fact, particularly in *Personal Recollections of Joan of Arc* and *Following the Equator* but even in the later productions "3,000 Years Among the Microbes" (1905) and "The Secret History of Eddypus" (1907). However, neither his life nor his work would be the same. After Theodore's death, and the virtual end of the Quarry Farm Circle, Twain would publish no work rivaling *Connecticut Yankee*. As Clara would say years later, "The Langdon home, Quarry Farm, could never be the same again. One volume was closed. Another was about to be opened, but we were a little slow to cut the leaves" (*MFMT* 87).

The metaphor is an apt one, for it highlights the importance of books at Quarry Farm. John Tuckey describes Twain's later work as revolving around ideas of a "homecoming fantasy" (22). But it was not just domestic tranquility that eluded him, and Twain's travels in Europe would find him searching vainly for that creative retreat that would substitute for the study at Quarry Farm.[2]

In July 1903 Twain and Livy returned to Quarry Farm to visit Susan Crane. This was his final trip with Livy to Elmira, and it was filled with bittersweet memories. Their lives and hopes had been blasted, and Quarry Farm would never again be the haven from care it had been. One thing had not changed, however: the Crane home was still "Go-as-You-Please Hall." Twain sauntered into the library once more and removed the latest edition of Lecky's *History of European Morals*. Twain accordingly treated another of Susan Crane's books to his marginal comments.

This rereading of one of his favorite books in the twilight of his career finds Twain still grappling with the tangle of related issues that threaded through his life: change, character, history, meliorism, and determinism. These later marginalia show Twain still searching for the "Compass of Fact" so necessary for his realism; here again we encounter a writer deeply philosophical, engaged in a *conscious attack on ideas* that piqued his interest and sparked his imagination. Just as the marginalia inscribed in the 1880s had important connections to *Connecticut Yankee*, so too do the 1903 notations in Susan Crane's copy of Lecky's *History of European Morals* reveal many connections to the later works—but that is another story.

Appendix 1

MARK TWAIN'S MARGINALIA IN WILLIAM LECKY'S *HISTORY OF THE RISE AND INFLUENCE OF THE SPIRIT OF RATIONALISM IN EUROPE*. 2 VOLS. NEW YORK: D. APPLETON AND COMPANY, 1884. [VOLUME 1 BEARS THE INSCRIPTION "SUSIE L CRANE DEC 1884." VOLUME 2 BEARS THE INSCRIPTION "SUSAN L. CRANE QUARRY FARM 1888."]

Volume 1, Chapter 1: "On the Declining Sense of the Miraculous," subtitled "Magic and Witchcraft"

39.24–28: Twain used a black pencil to revise Lecky's wording from "If we considered witchcraft probable, a hundredth part of the evidence we possess would have placed it beyond the region of doubt. If it were a natural but a very improbable fact, our reluctance to believe it would have been completely stifled by the multiplicity of the proofs." Twain struck out unnecessary *haves*, resulting in the greater clarity of "would place it beyond the region of doubt" and "would be completely stifled."

40.last line: Amid Lecky's discussion of the "universal" belief in witchcraft in primitive societies, Twain underlined in black pencil: "Terror is everywhere the beginning of religion."

57.16–23: Twain inscribed a purple marginal line alongside Lecky's description of executions by the Church for "the most trivial offenses."

72.8–9, 18–22: Purple marginal lines mark this passage: "Europe was beginning to enter into that inexpressibly painful period in which men have learned to doubt, but have not yet learned to regard doubt as innocent." More marginal lines mark this segment: "The Church had cursed the human intellect by cursing the doubts that are the necessary consequence of its exercise. She had cursed even the moral faculty by asserting the guilt of honest error."

78.last line–79.2: Twain indited marginal lines in purple next to this passage: "Doubt was almost universally regarded as criminal, and error as damnable; yet the first was the necessary condition, and the second the probable consequence, of inquiry." Twain added a purple hyphen to the word *Totally*, which was broken by the printer after the first two letters.

79.19, 26–27: A double purple marginal line notes a discussion of the Reformation, which "formed a multitude of churches, in which the spirit of qualified and partial scepticism that had long been a source of anarchy, might expatiate with freedom, and be allied with the spirit of order." Another marginal line in purple saves this line: "It, above all, diminished the prominence of the clergy, and thus prepared the way for that general secularisation of the European intellect, which is such a marked characteristic of modern civilisation."

80.21–23: A purple marginal line marks this passage: "Faith always presented to the mind the idea of an abnormal intellectual condition, of the subversion or suspension of the critical faculties."

85.entire: Responding to Lecky's discussion of the execution of witches, Twain wrote these words in purple: "All this results from a remark put into God's mouth by the lying Scriptures: 'Thou shall not suffer a witch to live.'"

86.1–4, 23–24: Twain scored a double purple marginal line where Lecky describes the effect of a charge of witchcraft and subsequent torture on the accused: "her brain reeled beneath the accumulated suffering, the consciousness of innocence disappeared, and the wretched victim went raving to the flames, convinced that she was about to sink for ever into perdition." Another purple line appears alongside a discussion of treatises on witchcraft that "were once regarded as masterpieces of orthodox theology."

88.23–25: Twain imprinted a triple purple marginal line next to this passage: "the single employment of the reason was to develop and expand premises that were furnished by the Church."

91.27–30: A purple marginal line tags these lines: "Rain seems to have been commonly associated, as it still is in the Church of England, with the intervention of the Deity; but wind and hail were invariably identified with the Devil."

93.6–7: A purple marginal line appears next to the assertion that a belief in witchcraft was "admitted by almost all the ablest men in Christendom."

93.last line–94.7: A purple marginal line marks a passage describing Biblical miracles.

94.31–95.3: Twain inscribed a purple marginal line next to this passage: "That the same portion of matter cannot be in two places at once, is a proposition which rests entirely on the laws of nature; but those laws have no existence for the miraculous; and the miracle of transubstantiation seems to destroy all the improbability of the pluri-presence of a human body. At all events, the Devil might furnish, for the occasion, a duplicate body, in order to baffle the ministers of justice. This latter opinion became extremely popular among theologians; and two famous Catholic miracles were triumphantly quoted in its support."

99: Twain responded to a discussion of medieval misogyny by writing these words in purple: "The modern claim that Christianity was a blessed boon to poor downtrodden woman seems to be a very pleasant sarcasm."

100: Twain imprinted exclamation points in black pencil next to footnote 1 regarding a "counteracting surgical operation" performed by angels. There is also a purple line next to footnote 2, which discusses an occasion on which "The Devil not only assumed the appearance of this holy man, in order to pay his addresses to a lady, but when discovered, crept under a bed, suffered himself to be dragged out, and declared that he was the veritable bishop. Happily, after a time, a miracle was wrought which cleared the reputation of the calumniated prelate." A portion of footnote 3 is underlined in purple and continues on the next page.

103.22–23: Twain imprinted a purple marginal line next to a discussion of the belief in witchcraft: "Its decline marks the rise, and its destruction the first triumph, of the spirit of rationalism in Europe." There is also a purple marginal line next to footnote 1, which discusses the scepticism of Peter of Apano, who "denied the existence of demons and of miracles." The marginal line resumes with the continuation of the footnote on the following page.

104.3–7: A purple marginal line appears alongside this passage: "'Those men,' wrote Gerson, 'should be treated with scorn, and indeed

sternly corrected, who ridicule theologians whenever they speak of demons, or attribute to demons any effects, as if these things were entirely
fabulous. This error has arisen among some learned men, partly through
want of faith, and partly through weakness and imperfection of intellect.'"

105.2–5: Twain scored a purple line in the margin adjoining further
criticism of those opposing the execution of witches: "'Most imprudent,
most undevout, and most unfaithful men will not believe the things they
ought to believe; and what is still more lamentable, they exert all their
influence to obstruct those who are destroying the enemies of Christ.'"

108.13–23: Twain impressed a thick purple marginal line next to this
passage:

> The "Demonomanie des Sorciers" is chiefly an appeal to authority,
> which the author deemed on this subject so unanimous and so con-
> clusive, that it was scarcely possible for any sane man to resist it. He
> appealed to the popular belief in all countries, in all ages, and in all
> religions. He cited the opinions of an immense multitude of the
> greatest writers of pagan antiquity, and of the most illustrious of
> the Fathers. He showed how the laws of all nations recognised the
> existence of witchcraft; and he collected hundreds of cases which
> had been investigated before the tribunals of his own or of other
> countries.

Twain wrote in purple: "How often the argument is flung at our heads
that a thing must be true because a 'cloud of witnesses' & all supreme intellects have for ages believed it!—& what a silly argument it is, after all."

109.5–11: Squiggly purple marginal lines appear next to this passage:
"That a puny doctor should have dared to oppose himself to the authority of all ages; that he should have such a boundless confidence in his
own opinions, and such a supreme contempt for the wisest of mankind,
as to carp and cavil in a sceptical spirit at the evidence of one of the most
notorious of existing facts; this was, in truth, the very climax of human
arrogance, the very acme of human absurdity." Twain underlined in purple "his reputation was sacrificed in the cause" in footnote 1 and commented in purple, "Karl Schurz's fate for exposing the paltry scoundrel
Blaine." Schurz, an early supporter of Lincoln, was a Republican activist
who ardently opposed James G. Blaine in the 1884 presidential election.
The marginalia indicate Twain was thinking omnihistorically.

110.11–13, 21–27: Twain inscribed purple marginal lines next to this passage: "To pardon those whom the law of God condemned to death, was indeed beyond the power of princes." Further purple marginal lines tag Lecky's discussion of Charles IX and his early demise, attributed by contemporaries to his pardoning of a sorcerer: " 'For the word of God is very certain, that he who suffers a man worthy of death to escape, draws the punishment upon himself, as the prophet said to king Ahab, that he should die for having pardoned a man worthy of death. For no one had ever heard of pardon being accorded to sorcerers.' "

111.2–4, 12–15, 26–29: Three separate purple marginal lines span the length of this page amid a discussion of the destruction of the superstitions of the sixteenth century. The first marks this passage: "Such were the opinions which were promulgated towards the close of the sixteenth century, by one of the most advanced intellects of one of the leading nations of Europe; promulgated, too, with a tone of confidence and of triumph, that shows how fully the writer could count upon the sympathies of his readers." The second marks this sentence: "The vast mass of authority which those writers loved to array, and by which they shaped the whole course of their reasoning, is calmly and unhesitatingly discarded." The third scores a quotation from Montaigne: "I do not pretend to unravel them. I often cut them, as Alexander did the knot. After all, it is setting a high value upon our opinions, to roast men alive on account of them."

112.1–6, 23–113.1: Purple marginal lines mark the assertion that "it is far more probable that our senses should deceive us, than that an old woman should be carried up a chimney on a broom stick; and that it is far less astonishing that witnesses should lie, than that witches should perform the acts that were alleged." Twain also underlined lines at the bottom of the page as well as the first line of the next. The passage quotes Bodin: " 'the laws of Plato, of the twelve tables, of the consuls, of the emperors, and of all nations and legislators—Persian, Hebrew, Greek, Latin, German, French, Italian, Spanish, English—had decreed capital penalties against sorcerers;' he knew that 'prophets, theologians, doctors, judges, and magistrates, had elucidated the reality of the crime by many thousand violent presumptions, accusations, testimonies, convictions, repentances and voluntary confessions, persisted in to death.' " In the margin of page 113 Twain wrote in purple, underlining some of his own words: "Think a moment—weigh well the meaning of those eight lines. They mean that the <u>entire world</u> wise & simple, believed for ages in a thing—sorcery—which had absolutely <u>no existence</u>." A further marginal comment, now indecipherable, was written in purple and scribbled out in purple.

113.9–14: A purple marginal line abuts this passage:

> While Catholics, Protestants, and Deists were vying with each other in their adoration of the past; while the ambition of every scholar and of every theologian was to form around his mind an atmosphere of thought that bore no relation to the world that was about him; while knowledge was made the bond-slave of credulity, and those whose intellects were most shackled by prejudice were regarded as the wisest of mankind, it was the merit of Montaigne to rise, by the force of his masculine genius, into the clear world of reality; to judge the opinions of his age with an intellect that was invigorated but not enslaved by knowledge; and to contemplate the systems of the past, without being dazzled by the reverence that had surrounded them.

114.29–32: Twain imprinted a purple marginal line next to this passage: "From the publication of the essays of Montaigne, we may date the influence of that gifted and ever largening rationalistic school, who gradually effected the destruction of the belief in witchcraft, not by refuting or explaining its evidence, but simply by making men more and more sensible of its intrinsic absurdity."

116.9–13: A purple marginal line marks this discussion of magic: "Some great scholars and writers, who were fully sensible of the improbability of the belief, yet regarded the evidence as irresistible, and looked upon the subject with a perplexed and timid suspension of judgment."

118.5–9: A purple marginal line appears alongside this passage: "It was when some of these commutations had been made, that the Parliament of Rouen drew up an extremely remarkable address to the king, protesting in a strain of high religious fervour, against the indulgence as directly contrary to the Word of God, to all the precedents of French law, and to all the traditions of the Christian religion."

123: The marginalia were removed by cutting—see below.

124.10–11: The margin is cut off down the length of the page, with some purple marking still visible. Twain underlined this sentence in purple: "Sir Thomas Browne declared that those who denied the existence of witchcraft were not only infidels, but also, by implication, atheists."

125.12–14: Twain imprinted a purple marginal line next to a discussion of Puritanism in England and the recrudescence of belief in witchcraft: "As soon as Puritanism gained an ascendency in the country, as soon as its ministers succeeded in imparting their gloomy tenets to the governing classes, the superstition assumed a gigantic magnitude."

126.5–10: A purple marginal line marks this passage: "It would have been impossible to take any measure more calculated to stimulate the prosecution, and we accordingly find that in Suffolk sixty persons were hung for witchcraft in a single year. Among others, an Anglican clergyman, named Lowes, who was now verging on eighty, and who for fifty years had been an irreproachable minister of his church, fell under the suspicion." Footnote 2, which gives more detail about the unfortunate clergyman, is also marked.

128: The last three lines are marked with three purple marginal lines: "Scriptures had affirmed so much; and secondly, the wisdom of all nations had provided laws against such persons, which is an argument of their confidence of such a crime." The passage is a quotation from Sir Mathew Hale, a judge who in 1664 ordered two women hanged in Suffolk.

130: The last line of footnote 1 is underlined in purple: "Paley's watch simile is fully developed by Glanvil, in chap. v."

132: Lines 2–3 of footnote 1 are underlined in purple, marking this passage: "He compares the leading scholars of his day to the mariner who returned laden with common pebbles from the Indies, imagining that that must necessarily be rare that came from afar."

133.1–4: A purple marginal line marks this passage: "Penetrated by the sense of human weakness, they were to rebuke the spirit of dogmatic confidence and assertion, and were to teach men that, so far from doubt being criminal, it was the duty of every man 'to suspend his full and resolved assent to the doctrines he had been taught, till he had impartially considered and examined them for himself.'"

134: Using his purple pencil, Twain underlined portions of a footnote quoting Glanvil's evidence for the existence of witchcraft: "All histories are full of the exploits of those instruments of darkness, and the testimony of all ages, not only of the rude and barbarous, but of the most civilised and polished world, brings tidings of their strange performances. We have the attestation of thousands of eye and ear witnesses, and those <u>not of the easily deceivable vulgar only, but of wise and grave discerners,</u> and that when no interest could oblige them to agree together in a common lie." Twain wrote along the margin, "Another infallible 'Cloud of Witnesses.'"

135: Twain continued underlining the footnoted quotation from Glanvil: "Such cases have been often determined with us, <u>by wise and reverend judges,</u> upon clear and constructive evidence; and <u>thousands in our own nation have suffered death for their vile compact with apostate spirits.</u>" Twain wrote his own opinion in purple along the margin: "There were a million evidences that witchcraft did exist; & only one solitary argument that it didn't—namely, its improbability; & that one argument proved stronger than the million proofs in the end." A further comment has been scratched out in black pencil, probably by Twain during his subsequent reading.

136.3–6, 10–12: This page features marginal lines next to further discussion of the universality of belief in witchcraft. Twain underlined part of footnote 3, which quotes Cudworth: "'As for wizards and magicians, persons who associate and confederate themselves with these evil spirits for the gratification of their own revenge, lust, ambition, and other passions; besides the Scriptures, <u>there hath been so full an attestation given to them by persons unconcerned in all ages,</u> that those our so confident exploders of them in this present age can hardly escape the suspicion of having some hankering towards atheism.'" Twain responded with a comment in purple at the bottom of the page: "The eternal argument that in the concurrent testimony of a multitude of fools lies proof."

140.15–23: Twain inscribed purple marginal lines and underlined "but to the suffrage of the wisest and best of men in all ages and nations. They well know . . . that giving up witchcraft is in effect giving up the Bible.'" This quotation is from John Wesley in 1768. Alongside, Twain wrote in purple, "Cloud of witnesses again."

141: The whole of the page concerns belief in witchcraft and is scored with marginal lines, with this passage underlined in purple: "they continued to assert and defend it when the great bulk of educated laymen had abandoned it." Then Twain wrote his comment: "The church has never started a good work, & has always been the last to relinquish an evil one. American slavery's last & stubbornest friend & champion in the North was the church."

143.16–23: Three parallel marginal lines in purple tag this passage: "Supported by public opinion, the Scottish ministers succeeded in over-awing all opposition, in prohibiting the faintest expression of adverse opinions, in prying into and controlling the most private concerns of domestic life; in compelling every one to conform absolutely to all the ecclesiastical regulations they enjoined; and in, at last, directing the whole scope and current of legislation." Next to this Twain wrote, "There are people, even in this day, who long for a 'united church.' There never was a united church which did not usurp the privileges of hell." The original comment is in purple, but Twain later scratched out "hell," substituting "tyranny" in black pencil.

144.1–14, 25–27: Twain inscribed a marginal line alongside passages describing the influence of Scottish ministers in promulgating a belief in witchcraft. A further marginal line in purple tags this passage: "It was produced by the teaching of the clergy, and it was everywhere fostered by their persecution. Eagerly, passionately, with a thirst for blood that knew no mercy, with a zeal that never tired, did they accomplish their task."

145: The entire length of the page is scored with a purple marginal line. Lecky discusses the clergy in Scotland in the seventeenth century and their torturing for witchcraft of "old and feeble and half-doting women."

146: The entire page features a purple marginal line. The page describes Scottish methods of torture including sleep and water deprivation.

147.1–17, 26–28: Twain imprinted a purple marginal line next to this passage:

But other and perhaps worse tortures were in reserve. The three principal that were habitually applied, were the pennywinkis, the boots, and the caschielawis. The first was a kind of thumb-screw; the second was a frame in which the leg was inserted, and in which it was broken by wedges, driven in by a hammer; the third was also an iron frame for the leg, which was from time to time heated over a brazier. Fire-matches were sometimes applied to the body of the victim. We read, in a contemporary legal register, of one man who was kept for forty-eight hours in "vehement tortour" in the caschielawis; and of another who remained in the same frightful machine for eleven days and eleven nights, whose legs were broken daily for fourteen days in the boots, and who was so scourged that the whole skin was torn from his body. This was, it is true, censured as an extreme case, but it was only an excessive application of the common torture.

The underlining is Twain's, and next to it he wrote, still with the purple pencil, "These are Scotch, not Iroquois." A further marginal line marks this sentence: "After these facts, it is scarcely necessary to notice how one traveller casually mentions having seen nine women burning together at Leith in 1664, or how, in 1678, nine others were condemned in a single day."

148: Twain marked Lecky's description of burnings at the stake with purple marginal lines: "An Earl of Mar (who appears to have been the only person sensible of the inhumanity of the proceedings) tells how, with a piercing yell, some women once broke half-burnt from the slow fire that consumed them, struggled for a few moments with despairing energy among the spectators, but soon with shrieks of blasphemy and wild protestations of innocence sank writhing in agony amid the flames." Twain also used his purple pencil to mark footnote 2, which discusses the "affection of many young Scotchmen" for "evil spirits in human form."

149.2–3, 16–20: Purple marginal lines tag this passage: "There are opinions that may be traced from age to age by footsteps of blood." More purple marginal lines note this condemnation of the clergy: "One word from them might have arrested the tortures, but that word was never spoken. Their conduct implies, not merely a mental aberration, but also a callousness of feeling which has rarely been attained in a long career of vice."

150.7–12: Purple marginal lines appear next to this passage: "They were but illustrations of the great truth, that when men have come to regard a certain class of their fellow-creatures as doomed by the Almighty to eternal and excruciating agonies, and when their theology directs their minds with intense and realising earnestness to the contemplation of such agonies, the result will be an indifference to the suffering of those whom they deem the enemies of their God, as absolute as it is perhaps possible for human nature to attain."

151.1–3, 11–13, 20–21, 23–24: The lines on this page are in purple. The first appears next to a discussion of Presbyterianism's "constant contemplation of the massacres at Canaan, and of the provisions of the Levitical code." Further lines mark this statement: "Two things only can, I think, be asserted on the subject with confidence—that the sceptical movement advanced much more slowly in Scotland than it did in England, and that the ministers were among the last to yield to it." Other lines find Lecky contending that belief in the burning of witches "found its most ardent supporters among the Presbyterian ministers." The last line marks this sentence: "As late as 1773, 'the divines of the Associated Presbytery' passed a resolution declaring their belief in witchcraft, and deploring the scepticism that was general."

153–54: Both pages bear purple marginal lines amid Lecky's discussion of the belief in witchcraft and its effect on the family. Twain also underlined portions of the passage at the bottom of 153 and continuing to the next page: "And, besides all this, we have to consider the terrors which the belief must have spread through the people at large; we have to picture the anguish of the mother, as she imagined that it was in the power of one whom she had offended to blast in a moment every object of her affection, we have to conceive, above all, the awful shadow that the dread of accusation must have thrown on the enfeebled faculties of age, and the bitterness it must have added to desertion and to solitude. All these sufferings were the result of a single superstition, which the spirit of rationalism had destroyed." The underlining is Twain's.

Volume 1, Chapter 2: "On the Declining Sense of the Miraculous," subtitled "The Miracles of the Church"

155: The first page of the chapter is folded over.

161: Twain imprinted a purple exclamation next to footnote 1, an explanation from Bishop Spratt that most miracles occur in "dark and ignorant ages" rather than during a state of civilization because in the modern age people are "diligent in the works of His hands."

173.8–12: The page bears a double purple marginal line next to this passage: "It has often been remarked as a singular fact, that almost every great step which has been made by the English intellect in connection with theology, has been made in spite of the earnest and persistent opposition of the University of Oxford."

174.1–6: A purple marginal line demarcates a further discussion of Oxford's theological conservatism: "Its supporters denounced these habits as essentially and fundamentally false. They described the history of English theology for a century and a half as a history of uninterrupted decadence. They believed, in the emphatic words of their great leader, that 'the nation was on its way to give up revealed truth.'"

182.7–20: Lecky derides the conceit that morals do not change, and Twain marginally lined this passage in purple:

> The insect whose existence is but for a moment might well imagine that these were indeed eternal, that their majestic columns could never fail, and that their luminous folds were the very source and centre of light. And yet they shift and vary with each changing breeze; they blend and separate; they assume new forms and exhibit new dimensions; as the sun that is above them waxes more glorious in its power, they are permeated and at last absorbed by its increasing splendour; they recede, and wither, and disappear, and the eye ranges far beyond the sphere they had occupied into the infinity of glory that is above them.

183: Twain left a marginal line in purple to mark footnote 1, part of which follows: "A large section of German theologians, as is well known, even regard the impossibility, or at all events the unreality, of miraculous accounts as axiomatic."

186.5–8: Twain left a purple marginal line next to this passage: "But while Catholicism has been thus convulsed and agitated to its very basis; while the signs of its disintegration are crowding upon us on every side; while the languor and feebleness it exhibits furnish a ready theme for every moralist and a problem for every philosopher, the Protestant sects have gained nothing by the decay of their ancient rival."

200.25–201.entire page: A purple marginal line extends along this passage:

> If it be true Christianity to dive with a passionate charity into the darkest recesses of misery and of vice, to irrigate every quarter of the earth with the fertilising stream of an almost boundless benevolence, and to include all the sections of humanity in the circle of an intense and efficacious sympathy; if it be true Christianity to destroy or weaken the barriers which had separated class from class and nation from nation, to free war from its harshest elements, and to make a consciousness of essential equality and of a genuine fra-

ternity dominate over all accidental differences; if it be, above all, true Christianity to cultivate a love of truth for its own sake, a spirit of candour and of tolerance towards those with whom we differ—if these be the marks of a true and healthy Christianity, then never since the days of the Apostles has it been so vigorous as at present, and the decline of dogmatic systems and of clerical influence has been a measure if not a cause of its advance.

Volume 1, Chapter 3: "Aesthetic, Scientific, and Moral Developments of Rationalism"

291.17–20: Twain imprinted a double purple marginal line next to this passage: "Halley predicted the revolution of comets, and they were at once removed to the domain of law, and one of the most ancient of human superstitions was destroyed."

312.3–21: Purple marginal lines mark this passage:

But the great characteristic of Christianity, and the great moral proof of its divinity, is that it has been the main source of the moral development of Europe, and that it has discharged this office not so much by the inculcation of a system of ethics, however pure, as by the assimilating and attractive influence of a perfect ideal. The moral progress of mankind can never cease to be distinctively and intensely Christian as long as it consists of a gradual approximation to the character of the Christian Founder. There is, indeed, nothing more wonderful in the history of the human race than the way in which that ideal has traversed the lapse of ages, acquiring a new strength and beauty with each advance of civilisation, and infusing its beneficent influence into every sphere of thought and action. At first men sought to grasp by minute dogmatic definitions the divinity they felt.

315: Purple marginal lines mark lines 1–6 of footnote 1: "In France especially the persecution on this ground was frightful. Thus, Bodin tells us that in 1539 the magistrates of Angers burnt alive those who were proved to have eaten meat on Friday if they remained impenitent, and hung them if they repented."

322.1–7: In black pencil Twain scored a marginal line alongside a vivid description of Scotus's vision of hell featuring "every form of ghastly suffering."

323.16–20: A marginal line in black pencil tags these lines: "No other religious teachers had ever proclaimed such tenets, and as long as they were realised intensely, the benevolent precepts and the mild and gentle ideal of the New Testament could not possibly be influential."

328.13–27: A marginal line in black marks another passage detailing visions of hell.

330.2–7: A line in black marks this passage:

> But while the marvellous influence of Christianity in this respect has been acknowledged by all who have mastered the teachings of history, while the religious minds of every land and of every opinion have recognised in its Founder the highest conceivable ideal and embodiment of compassion as of purity, it is a no less incontestable truth that for many centuries the Christian priesthood pursued a policy, at least towards those who differed from their opinions, implying a callousness and absence of the emotional part of humanity which has seldom been paralleled, and perhaps never surpassed.

Volume 1, Chapter 4: "On Persecution," Part 1, subtitled "The Antecedents of Persecution"

358.15–26: These lines are scored in the margin with black pencil:

> For the essence of aristocracy is to transfer the source of honour from the living to the dead, to make the merits of living men depend not so much upon their own character and actions as upon the actions and position of their ancestors; and as a great aristocracy is never insulated, as its ramifications penetrate into many spheres, and its social influence modifies all the relations of society, the minds of men become insensibly habituated to a standard of judgment from which they would otherwise have recoiled.

360.last four: Twain marked this passage in black amid Lecky's discussion that "the whole body of the Fathers without exception or hesitation, pronounced that all infants who died unbaptized were excluded from heaven."

361.1–3, last three: Black marginal lines tag Lecky's discussion of infant baptism: "The learned English historian of Infant Baptism states that, with the exception of a contemporary of St. Augustine, named Vincentius, who speedily recanted his opinion as heretical, he has been unable to discover a single instance of an orthodox member of the Church expressing the opposite opinion before Hinemar, who was Archbishop of Rheims in the ninth century." A subsequent passage is marked in black pencil: "It was on this point that he was most severely pressed by his opponents, and St. Augustine says that he was driven to the somewhat desperate resource of maintaining that baptism was necessary to wash away the guilt of the pettishness of the child!"

362.last eight lines: These lines are marked in black pencil: "'Be assured,' writes the saint, 'and doubt not that not only children who have begun to live in their mothers' womb and have there died, or who, having just been born, have passed away from the world without the sacrament of holy baptism, administered in the name of the Father, Son, and Holy Ghost, must be punished by the eternal torture of undying fire.'"

363: Triple black lines run the length of this page treating the doctrine of infant damnation, in particular the effect on "terror-stricken mothers" who baptized their unborn children, indeed stillborn children.

364: This page is similarly marked with black lines and describes women "who never dreamed of rebelling against the teaching of their clergy, could not acquiesce in the perdition of their offspring, and they vainly attempted to escape from the dilemma by multiplying superstitious practices."

Volume 2, Chapter 4: "On Persecution," Part 2, subtitled "The History of Persecution"

73.16–17: A marginal line in black pencil marks these lines, in which Lecky discusses the murder of Catholic priests occurring "when the very existence of the State was menaced by foreign invaders, and when the bulk of the priesthood were openly conspiring against the liberties of their country."

74.18–20: Black marginal lines mark the sentiment of Gregory XVI, deriding "that form of madness, which declares that liberty of conscience should be asserted and maintained for every one."

Volume 2, Chapter 5: "The Secularisation of Politics"

116: The length of the page is lined with black pencil alongside Lecky's description of the Spanish Inquisition: "In that country the Inquisition was always cherished as the special expression of the national religion and the burning of Jews and heretics was soon regarded in a double light, as a religious ceremony and also as a pageant or public amusement that was eminently congenial to the national taste."

161.3–8: A black-pencil marginal line marks this passage describing the Pope's celebrating the assassination of Henry III: "The Pope publicly pronounced the act to be worthy of ranking with that of Judith; he said that it could only have been accomplished by the special assistance of Providence, and he blasphemously compared it to the Incarnation and to the Resurrection."

174.2–12: A marginal line in black tags these lines: "Endeavouring by the assistance of temporal authority and by the display of worldly pomp to realise in England the same position as Catholicism had occupied in Europe, she naturally flung herself on every occasion into the arms of the civil power. No other Church so uniformly betrayed and trampled on the liberties of her country." Footnote 2 is also marked with a marginal line: "'Eternal damnation is prepared for all impenitent rebels in hell with Satan the first founder of the rebellion.' 'Heaven is the place of good obedient subjects, and hell the prison and dungeon of rebels against God and their prince.' (Homily on *Wilful Rebellion.*)"

175.8–12: Twain inscribed a marginal line in black next to this passage: "St. Paul counselled passive obedience under Caligula, Claudius, and Nero, 'who were not only no Christians but pagans, and also either foolish rulers or cruel tyrants.'"

176.14–18: A black marginal line marks lines that include Jeremy Taylor's opinion that "the powers set over us be what they will, we must suffer it and never right ourselves."

177.1–5, 15–21: Twain inscribed marginal lines in black pencil as Lecky reports that "the Church of England directed the stream, allied herself in the closest union with a court whose vices were the scandal of Christendom, and exhausted her anathemas not upon the hideous corruption that surrounded her, but upon the principles of Hampden and of Milton." A further marginal line in black tags this passage: "But no sooner had William mounted the throne than her policy was reversed, her

whole energies were directed to the subversion of the constitutional liberty that was then firmly established, and it is recorded by the great historians of the Revolution that at least nine-tenths of the clergy were
opposed to the emancipator of England."

178.1–4: A marginal line in black adjoins a discussion of the clergy as
supporters "of the wars against America and against the French Revolution, which have been the most disastrous in which England has ever
engaged. From the first to the last their conduct was the same, and every
triumph of liberty was their defeat."

179.13: In this line Twain again corrected Lecky's writing: "From these
principles we should naturally have supposed" becomes "From these
principles we should naturally suppose."

184.last three: A black marginal line tags a discussion of Bishop Hors-
ley's opinion that "'subjects had nothing to say to the laws except to obey
them.'"

199.19–200.4: Marginal lines in black pencil score Lecky's discussion
of *On Voluntary Servitude* (also called *Against One Man*) of La Boetie:

"Wretched and insensate people," writes the author, "enamoured of
your misery and blind to your interests, you suffer your property to
be pillaged, your fields devastated, your houses stripped of their
goods, and all this by one whom you have yourselves raised to
power, and whose dignity you maintain with your lives! He who
crushes you has but two hands, but one body. All that he has more
than you comes from you. Yours are the many eyes that spy your
acts, the many hands that strike you, the many feet that trample
you in the dust: all the power with which he injures you is your
own. From indignities that the beasts themselves would not endure
you can free yourselves by simply willing it. Resolve to serve no
more, and you are free."

Volume 2, Chapter 6: "The Industrial History of Rationalism"

229: This page contains no markings, but the page is folded over.
Lecky is discussing the manumission of slaves: "But when the fullest
allowance has been made for these influences, it will remain an un-
doubted fact that the reconstruction of society was mainly the work of
Christianity."

Appendix 2

ENTRY A: TWAIN'S MARGINALIA IN MACAULAY'S *THE HISTORY OF ENGLAND FROM THE ACCESSION OF JAMES II.* 5 VOLS. PHILA-DELPHIA: J. B. LIPPINCOTT AND CO., 1869. [VOLUME 3 BEARS THE INSCRIPTION "TW CRANE / 1870." VOLUME 4 BEARS THE INSCRIPTION "SUSAN L CRANE."]

Volume 1, Chapter 1: "Britain Down to the Restoration"

4.26–43: Two black pencil marks tag this passage:

Her shores were, to the polished race which dwelt by the Bosporus, objects of a mysterious horror, such as that with which the Ionians of the age of Homer had regarded the Straits of Scylla and the city of the Laestrygonian cannibals. There was one province of our island in which, as Procopius had been told, the ground was covered with serpents, and the air was such that no man could inhale it and live. To this desolate region the spirits of the departed were ferried over from the land of the Franks at midnight. A strange race of fishermen performed the ghastly office. The speech of the dead was distinctly heard by the boatmen: their weight made the keel sink deep in the water; but their forms were invisible to mortal eye. Such were the marvels which an able historian, the contemporary of Belisarius of Simplicius, and of Tribonian, gravely related in the rich and polite Constantinople, touching the country in which the founder of Constantinople had assumed the imperial purple.

7.9: Twain struck out *entombed* from the line "great works of ancient power and wisdom lay entombed" and drew a line to the top of the page, substituting *engulfed*† in purple pencil to preserve the metaphor. The entire sentence is as follows: "The Church has many times been compared by divines to that ark of which we read in the Book of Genesis: but never was the resemblance more perfect than during that evil time when she alone rode, amidst darkness and tempest, on the deluge beneath which all the great works of ancient power and wisdom lay entombed, bearing within her that feeble germ from which a second and more glorious civilisation was to spring."

19.17–18: This sentence is tagged in purple and features some underlining: "So successfully had the Church used her formidable machinery that, before the Reformation came, she had enfranchised almost all the bondmen in the kingdom except her own, who to do her justice, seem to have been very tenderly treated."

23.27, 29: Using a black pencil Twain underlined *Tory* and *Whig* in this sentence: "No candid Tory will deny that these principles had, five hundred years ago, acquired the authority of fundamental rules. On the other hand, no candid Whig will affirm that they were, till a later period, cleaned from all ambiguity, or followed out to all their consequences."

29.5–7: Twain imprinted a black marginal line and underlined *Roses* and *Comines:* "Even while the Wars of the Roses were actually raging, our country appears to have been in a happier condition than the neighboring realms during years of profound peace. Comines was one of the most enlightened statesmen of his time."

31: Twain underlined *arbitrary* in black pencil in this sentence: "The government of Henry the Seventh, of his son, and of his grandchildren, was, on the whole, more arbitrary than that of the Plantagenets."

35.11, 22: Twain used black pencil to underline *Albigensian* and *Lollards* in sentences on this page.

36.8–9: Twain underlined the phrase "Council of Constance" in black pencil: "About a hundred years after the rising of the Council of Constance, that great change emphatically called the Reformation began."

37.19–27: Twain marked this anti-Catholic passage in purple:

But, during the last three centuries, to stunt the growth of the human mind has been her chief object. Throughout Christendom, whatever advance has been made in knowledge, in freedom, in wealth, and in the arts of life, has been made in spite of her, and has everywhere been in inverse proportion to her power. The loveliest and most fertile provinces of Europe have, under her rule, been sunk in poverty, in political servitude, and in intellectual torpor, while Protestant countries, once proverbial for sterility and barbarism, have been turned by skill and industry into gardens, and can boast of a long list of heroes and statesmen, philosophers and poets.

38.15–16, 18: Using black pencil Twain underlined *amalgamation* and *laity* in this sentence: "For the amalgamation of races and for the abolition of villenage, she is chiefly indebted to the influence which the priesthood in the middle ages exercised over the laity."

39.3, 24: Twain underlined *spoliation* with black pencil in this sentence: "The force of his character, the singularly favourable situation in which he stood with respect to foreign powers, the immense wealth which the spoliation of the abbeys placed at his disposal, and the support of that class which still halted between two opinions, enabled him to bid defiance to both the extreme parties, to burn as heretics those who avowed the tenets of the Reformers, and to hang as traitors those who owned the authority of the Pope." Again using his black pencil, he underlined *Bishop Hooper* in this sentence: "Thus Bishop Hooper, who died manfully at Gloucester for his religion, long refused to wear the episcopal vestments."

40.17, 38: Twain underlined *Thomas Cranmer* and *Calvin* in black pencil.

41.13: Twain underlined *episcopacy* in black pencil.

46.32: Twain underlined *Vatican* in black pencil as it occurs in this passage: "It was not to be expected that they would immediately transfer to an upstart authority the homage which they had withdrawn from the Vatican; that they would be afraid to dissent from teachers who themselves dissented from what had lately been the universal faith of western Christendom."

48.17: Twain underlined *Puritans* in black pencil: "The Puritans, even in the depths of the prisons to which she had sent them, prayed, and with no simulated fervour, that she might be kept from the dagger of the assassin, that rebellion might be put down under her feet, and that her arms might be victorious by sea and land." The passage refers to Queen Elizabeth.

49.last line: Twain marked in black pencil an *X* over the second *the* of the page's last line: "In the year 1603 t̶h̶e̶ great Queen died." The queen referred to is again Queen Elizabeth.

51: The word *Celts†* is written in Twain's hand at the top of the page, again in black pencil. The first sentence of the page states, "In Ireland, on the contrary, the population, with the exception of the small English colony near the coast, was Celtic, and still kept the Celtic speech and manners." The passage compares the level of civilization in Ireland and Scotland.

Volume 1, Chapter 3: "England in 1685"

256.5–10: A marginal line in black tags this passage: "With his cure, he was expected to take a wife. The wife had ordinarily been in the patron's service, and it was well if she was not suspected of standing too high in the patron's favor. Indeed, the nature of the matrimonial connections which the clergymen of that age were in the habit of forming is the most certain indication of the place which the order held in the social system."

257.1–5: Twain left a black line next to this passage: "Even so late as the time of George the Second, the keenest of all observers of life and manners, himself a priest, remarked that, in a great household, the chaplain was the resource of a lady's maid whose character had been blown upon, and who was therefore forced to give up hopes of catching the steward."

Volume 2, Chapter 8: "The Seven Bishops"

236–37: The corner of page 236 is folded over toward page 237. Page 236 begins with the word *deprived* in this sentence: "When Charnock summoned the Demies to perform their academical exercises before him, they answered that they were deprived of their lawful governors and would submit to no usurped authority." The page ends with this sentence: "He absented himself; he was ordered to return into residence: he disobeyed: he was expelled; and the work of spoliation was complete."

264–65: Page 265 is folded over toward page 264. The pages chronicle ongoing disputes between the aristocracy, the courts, and parliament.

Volume 2, Chapter 9: "The Flight of King James"

311.5–9: Using black pencil Twain marked in the margin adjoining this sentence: "There is a frontier where virtue and vice fade into each other. Who has ever been able to define the exact boundary between courage and rashness, between prudence and cowardice, between frugality and avarice, between liberality and prodigality?"

317.36–38: There is a double marginal line in black pencil alongside this discussion: "He went about from divine to divine proposing in general terms hypothetical cases of tyranny, and inquiring whether in such cases resistance would be lawful."

370.31–33: Twain marked with black pencil in the margin during a discussion of the king's discovery of a plot: "His first impulse was to hide the paper from all human eyes. He threw into the fire every copy which had been brought to him, except one; and that one he would scarcely trust out of his own hands."

374.3–9: Twain drew six lines in black pencil alongside this passage: "The men of war on the extreme right and left saluted both fortresses at once. The troops appeared under arms on the decks. The flourish of trumpets, the clash of cymbals, and the rolling of drums were distinctly heard at once on the English and French shores. An innumerable company of gazers blackened the white beach of Kent. Another mighty multitude covered the coast of Picardy." Twain wrote "25 miles apart"† in the margin, referring to Dover and Calais.

375.2–4: A pair of marginal lines in black pencil appears alongside this passage: "When Sunday the fourth of November dawned, the cliffs of the Isle of Wight were full in view of the Dutch armament. That day was the anniversary both of William's birth and of his marriage."

425.21–34: A mark made with black pencil appears alongside these lines:

Of this man it has been said that his life was stranger than the dreams of other people. Early in life he had been the intimate associate of Lewis, and had been encouraged to expect the highest employments under the French crown. Then his fortunes had undergone an eclipse. Lewis had driven from him the friend of his youth with bitter reproaches, and had, it was said, scarcely refrained from adding blows. The fallen favorite had been sent prisoner to a fortress; but he had emerged from his confinement, had again enjoyed the smiles of his master, and had gained the heart of one of the greatest ladies in Europe, Anna Maria, daughter of Gaston, Duke of Orleans, granddaughter of King Henry the Fourth, and heiress of the immense domains of the house of Montpensier.

426.1–14: Two black lines tag this passage:

The portion which the princess brought with her might well have been an object of competition to sovereigns; three great dukedoms, an independent principality with its own mint and with its own tribunals, and an income greatly exceeding the whole revenue of the kingdom of Scotland. But this splendid prospect had been overcast. The match had been broken off. The aspiring suitor had been, during many years, shut up in an Alpine castle. At length, Lewis relented. Lauzun was forbidden to appear in the royal presence, but was allowed to enjoy liberty at a distance from the court. He visited England, and was well received at the palace of James and in the fashionable circles of London; for in that age the gentlemen of France were regarded throughout Europe as models of grace.

427.10–16: Twain impressed a double marginal line in black next to this text: "Lauzun gave his hand to Mary; Saint Victor wrapped up in his warm cloak the ill-fated heir of so many kings. The party stole down the stairs and embarked in an open skiff. It was a miserable voyage. The night was bleak; the rain fell; the wind roared; the waves were rough; at length the boat reached Lambeth; and the fugitives landed near an inn, where a coach and horses were in waiting." Twain underlined portions of this sentence: "She remained with her child, cowering for shelter from the storm under the tower of Lambeth Church, and distracted by terror whenever the ostler approached her with his lantern."

Volume 3, Chapter 1: "The Glorious Revolution"

48.20–37: This page features a black pencil marginal line next to a passage decrying the maladministration rife in England: "Honors and public trusts, peerages, baronetcies, regiments, brigates, embassies, governments, commissionerships, leases of crown lands, contracts for clothing, for provisions, for ammunition, pardons for murder, for robbery, for arson, were sold at Whitehall scarcely less openly than asparagus at Covent Garden or herrings at Billingsgate."

49.1–25: This page features a marginal line in black pencil next to a passage discussing the "progress of the decay" in the British government under Charles, James, and William.

95: Dual marginal lines in black pencil run the length of a footnote containing verse satirizing the monarchy.

Volume 4, Chapter 18: "Marlborough Disgraced"

138.6–23: A line in black pencil marks this passage:

Every person well read in history must have observed that depravity has its temporary modes, which come in and go out like modes of dress and upholstery. It may be doubted whether, in our country, any man ever before the year 1678 invented and related on oath a circumstantial history, altogether fictitious, of a treasonable plot for the purpose of making himself important by destroying men who had given him no provocation. But in the year 1678 this execrable crime became the fashion, and continued to be so during the twenty years which followed. Preachers designated it as our peculiar national sin, and prophesied that it would draw on us some awful national judgment. Legislators proposed new punishments of terrible severity for this new atrocity. It was not, however, found necessary to resort to those punishments. The fashion changed; and during the last century and a half there has perhaps not been a single instance of this particular kind of wickedness.

158.8–34: A marginal line in black pencil adjoins this passage:

Unhappily there was scarcely any excess of ferocity for which a precedent could not be found in Celtic tradition. Among all warlike barbarians revenge is esteemed the most sacred of duties and the most exquisite of pleasures; and so it had long been esteemed among the Highlanders. The History of the clans abound with frightful tales, some perhaps fabulous or exaggerated, some certainly true, of vindictive massacres and assassinations. The Macdonalds of Glengarry, for example, having been affronted by the people of Culloden, surrounded the Culloden church on a Sunday, shut the doors, and burned the whole congregation alive. While the flames were raging, the hereditary musician of the murderers mocked the shrieks of the perishing crowd with the notes of his bagpipe. A band of Macgregors, having cut off the head of an enemy, laid it, the mouth filled with bread and cheese, on his sister's table, and had the satisfaction of seeing her go mad with horror at the sight. They then carried the ghastly trophy in triumph to their chief. The whole clan met under the roof of an ancient church. Every one in turn laid his hand on the dead man's scalp, and vowed to defend the slayers. The inhabitants of Eigg seized some Macleods, bound them hand and foot, and turned them adrift in a boat to be swallowed up by the waves or to perish of hunger. The Macleods retaliated by driving the population of Eigg into a cavern, lighting fire at the entrance, and suffocating the whole race, men, women, and children.

159: No markings appear on this page, but the corner is folded over and creased toward page 158. The page begins with the word *polished* in this sentence: "His polished manners and lively conversation were thought the delight of aristocratical societies; and none who met him in such societies would have thought it possible that he could bear the chief part in any atrocious crime." The passage refers to the Master of Stair. The page ends with *himself* in this sentence: "He silences the remonstrances of conscience, and hardens his heart against the most touching spectacles of misery, by repeating to himself that his intentions are pure, that his objects are noble, that he is doing a little evil for the sake of a great good."

160.38–42: A marginal line in black pencil tags lines chronicling further atrocities: "One of them, who had been concerned in some act of violence or rapine, had given information against his companions. He had been bound to a tree and murdered. The old chief had given the first stab; and scores of dirks had then been plunged into the wretch's body. By the mountaineers such an act was probably regarded as a legitimate exercise of patriarchal jurisdiction."

162–63: No marks appear on these pages, but a piece of envelope holds the place. These pages chronicle further atrocities. Page 162 begins with "that the Camerons" in this sentence: "His project was no less than this, that the whole hill country from sea to sea, and the neighboring islands, should be wasted with fire and sword, that the Camerons, the Macleans, and all the branches of the race of Macdonald, should be rooted out." Page 163 ends with the sentence "William had, in all probability, never heard the Glencoe men mentioned except as banditti."

Volume 5

No marginalia noted in this volume.

ENTRY B: TWAIN'S MARGINALIA IN *THE LIFE AND LETTERS OF LORD MACAULAY.* ED. G. OTTO TREVELYAN. 2 VOLS. NEW YORK: HARPER AND BROTHERS, 1876. [BOOK PLATE: "J. LANGDON'S FAMILY LIBRARY NO. 398."]

Volume 1

55.4–8: Twain marked lines in the margin adjoining this portion of a letter to Tom Macaulay from his mother, Selina Macaulay, sent May 28, 1813: "I have always admired a saying of one of the old heathen philosophers. When a friend was condoling with him that he so well deserved of the gods, and yet that they did not shower their favors on him, as on some others less worthy, he answered, 'I will, however, continue to deserve well of them.'"

106–7: Twain struck the "doubled up haves" from this letter Macaulay wrote to his mother: "I could not have imagined that it would ~~have been~~ be necessary for me to ~~have said~~ say that the execrable trash entitled 'Tears of Sensibility' was merely a burlesque on the style of the magazine verses of the day. I could not suppose that you could ~~have~~ suspected me of *seriously* composing such a farrago of false metaphor and unmeaning epithet."

164: In a biographical sketch written by Trevelyan, alongside a discussion of the increased politeness in Parliament, Twain wrote, "They still wear their hats."†

174.3–6: This page is part of an extract from the journal of Margaret Macaulay, sister of Lord Macaulay. Twain left a line in the margin next to this passage: "After a while, however, I began to remark that he became extremely cold to me, hardly ever spoke to me on circuit, and treated me with marked slight. If I were talking to a man, if he wished to speak to him on politics or anything else that was not in any sense a private matter, he always drew him away from me instead of addressing us both."

190.20–23: A marginal line scores a passage from a letter dated May 28, 1831, from Macaulay to Hannah Moore Macaulay. The marked passage reads as follows: "'Always,' said he, 'establish yourself in the middle of the row against the wall; for, if you sit in the front or next to the edges, you will be forced to give up your seat to the ladies who are standing.'"

325.1–10: Twain imprinted a marginal line in a biographical section written by Trevelyan. The passage concerns Macaulay's experiences in India, and part of the marked passage includes this quotation: "when he came across a military man with a turn for reading, he pronounced him, as Dominie Sampson said of another Indian colonel, 'a man of great erudition, considering his imperfect opportunities.'"

Volume 2

No marginalia noted in this volume.

ENTRY C: TWAIN'S MARGINALIA IN *SELECTIONS FROM THE WRITINGS OF LORD MACAULAY*. ED. G. OTTO TREVELYAN. NEW YORK: HARPER AND BROTHERS, 1877. [BOOKPLATE: "J. LANGDON'S FAMILY LIBRARY. NO. 420."]

162.5: In a chapter that extracts a discussion of Charles II from Macaulay's *History*, Twain marked through the second *have:* "From such a school it might have been expected that a young man who wanted neither abilities nor amiable qualities would ~~have~~ come forth a great and good king."

Appendix 3

MARK TWAIN'S MARGINALIA IN WILLIAM LECKY'S *A HISTORY OF ENGLAND IN THE EIGHTEENTH CENTURY.* 6 VOLS. NEW YORK: D. APPLETON AND COMPANY 1887. [VOLUMES 1, 3, AND 4 BEAR THE INSCRIPTION "TW CRANE QUARRY FARM SEP 1887." VOLUME 2 BEARS THE INSCRIPTION "TW CRANE SEP 1887 QUARRY FARM." VOLUME 6 BEARS THE INSCRIPTION "T.W. CRANE QUARRY FARM, GO-AS-YOU-PLEASE HALL REST-&-BE-THANKFUL EAST HILL ELMIRA, N.Y. SEPT. 1887." ALL INSCRIPTIONS ARE IN TWAIN'S HANDWRITING.]

Volume 1, Chapter 1

8.18–25, 32–35: Twain inscribed a marginal line next to this passage:

The judicial bench has more than once proved the most formidable bulwark against the encroachments of despotism, but in England the judges were removable at pleasure, and had become the mere creatures of the Crown. In no age, and in no country have state trials been conducted with a more flagrant disregard for justice and for decency, and with a more scandalous subserviency to the Crown, than in England under Charles II., and eleven out of the twelve judges gave their sanction to the claim of his successor to dispense with the laws.

Below this marked passage Twain drew a large *C*, the first of many in these volumes, next to this passage: "Hobbes, who was the most influen-

tial freethinker of the Restoration, advocated a system of the most crushing despotism, and the ecclesiastical influences which exercised an overwhelming influence over the great mass of the English people were eminently inimical to freedom."

9: Twain wrote "Great Charter" at the top of the page next to a discussion of the Anglican Church, whose "clergy were almost uniformly
despotic." Twain inscribed the letter C four times in the margin adjoining this passage:

> The doctrine of non-resistance in its extreme form was taught in
> the Homilies of the Church, embodied in the oath of allegiance,[1]
> in the corporation oath of Charles II and in the declaration pre-
> scribed by the Act of Uniformity, enrolled by great Anglican casu-
> ists among the leading tenets of Christianity, and persistently en-
> forced from the pulpit. It had become, as a later bishop truly said,
> "the distinguishing character of the Church of England." At a time
> when the constitution was still unformed, when every institution of
> freedom and every bulwark against despotism was continually as-
> sailed, the authorised religious teachers of the nation were inces-
> santly inculcating this doctrine, and it may probably be said with-
> out exaggeration that it occupied a more prominent position in the
> preaching and the literature of the Anglican Church than any other
> tenet in the whole compass of theology.

The underlining in this passage is Twain's. Twain circled footnote 1 of
page 9, which gives the oath of allegiance: "'I, A B, do declare and believe that it is not lawful *upon any pretence whatever* to take up arms
against the king.'" He then wrote "Non-resistance." under the footnote.

10.2, 11–16, 22–29: Twain printed a capital C next to Lecky's comment
regarding the "absolute unlawfulness of resistance." Further down the
page he printed a marginal line next to this passage: "The immense
popularity which the miracle of the royal touch had acquired, indicated
only too faithfully the blind and passionate loyalty of the time." Twain
wrote the word *Skepticism* in this passage and underlined "atrocious persecution": "The immorality of the court of Charles which shocked the
sober feelings of the middle-class, the contemptible character of the
King, the humiliation which French patronage and Dutch victories imposed upon the nation, the growth of religious scepticism, which at last
weakened the influence of the clergy, the atrocious persecution of Non-
conformists, and the infamy of the State trials, had all considerable ef-

fect, but they operated chiefly upon a small body of enlightened men."
Twain also placed a marginal line next to Lecky's description of the
"dread of Catholicism."

11.14–16, 23–24: Twain inscribed two capital *C*s on this page. The first
spans this passage:

> Most happily for the country, a bigoted Catholic, singularly desti-
> tute both of the tact and sagacity of a statesman, and of the quali-
> ties that win the affection of a people, mounted the throne, devoted
> all the energies of his nature and all the resources of his position to
> extending the religion most hateful to his people, attacked with a
> strange fatuity the very Church on whose teaching the monarchical
> enthusiasm mainly rested, and thus drove the most loyal of his sub-
> jects into violent opposition.

The second *C* marks this passage: "Without the assistance of the Church
and Tory party the Revolution would have been impossible, and it is
certain that the Church would never have led the opposition to the dis-
pensing power had not that power been exerted to remove the disabili-
ties of the Catholics and Dissenters."

12.9–14, 22: Twain inscribed a line in the margin, writing "slavery" and
placing an exclamation point by this passage: "The doctrine of the inde-
feasible right of the legitimate sovereign, and of the absolute sinfulness
of resistance, was in the eyes of the great majority of Englishmen the
cardinal principle of political morality, and a blind, unqualified unques-
tioning loyalty was the strongest and most natural form of political enthusiasm. This was the real danger to English liberty." Below, Twain corrected Lecky's style by striking the second perfective: "would have been
to ~~have~~ retain~~ed~~."

13.30–31: A capital *C* and a marginal line mark this sentence: "Religious liberty was extended probably quite as far as the existing condition
of opinion would allow."

14.16–17: Twain marked this passage, underlining "liberty of the
press":

> The great legislative changes that were effected at the Revolu-
> tion—the immobility of the judges, the reform of the trials for
> treason, the <u>liberty of the press</u>, the more efficient control of the
> income of the sovereign, the excision from the oath of allegiance of
> the clause which, in direct contradiction to the great charter, as-

serted that under no pretence whatever might subjects take up arms against their king; the establishment of Presbyterianism in Scotland, and the partial toleration of Dissenters in England, have all been justified by history as measures of real and unquestionable progress.

15.9–18: Twain wrote at the top of the page: "Both the American & French Revolutions were precipitated by accidents—& so indeed was the English Rev." Below, Twain inscribed a line in the margin alongside this sentence: "Whoever will study the history of the downfall of the Roman Republic; of the triumph of Christianity in the Roman Empire; of the dissolution of that empire; of the mediaeval transition from slavery to serfdom; of the Reformation, or of the French Revolution, may easily convince himself that each of these great changes was the result of a long series of religious, social, political, economical, and intellectual causes, extending over many generations."

17.9–13: A marginal line marks this passage: "Profound and searching changes in the institutions of France were inevitable, but had they been effected peacefully, legally, and gradually, had the shameless scenes of the Regency and of Lewis XV. been avoided, that frenzy of democratic enthusiasm which has been the most distinctive product of the Revolution, and which has passed, almost like a new religion, into European life, might never have arisen, and the whole Napoleonic episode, with its innumerable consequences, would never have occurred."

18.29–32: A marginal line spans a discussion of export figures for 1688–1696.

19.16: Twain wrote "Hated all foreigners except their own Foreign kings" at the top of the page. Further down the page, he underlined this line: "The 'Tory' was originally an Irish Robber."

20.11–15: A line tags the assertion that the English King and "his ministers were suspected with only too good reason of being the paid vassals of the French king."

Volume 1, Chapter 2

184.18: There is a faint stray mark next to the word *more*.

185.28–30: "Great Charter described" is written at the top of the page next to this passage: "The great charter had been won by the barons, but, instead of being confined to a demand for new aristocratical privileges, it guaranteed the legal rights of all freemen, and the ancient customs and liberties of cities, prohibited every kind of arbitrary punishment, compelled the barons to grant their subvassals mitigations of feudal burdens similar to those which they themselves obtained from the King, and even accorded special protection to foreign merchants in England." Further down the page Twain left a line next to this passage: "By its strenuous opposition to the encroachments of the House of Commons it secured for electors in 1704 the all-important right of defending a disputed qualification before an impartial legal tribunal."

186.14–17: Twain inscribed a line in the margin adjoining this sentence: "But in England the interests of the nobles, as a class, have been carefully and indissolubly interwoven with those of the people. They have never claimed for themselves any immunity from taxation."

190.16–30, 34–35: Marginal lines tag this passage:

A structure of society like that of England which brings the upper class into such political prominence that they usually furnish the popular candidates for election, has at least the advantage of saving the nation from that government by speculators, adventurers, and demagogues which is the gravest of all the evils to which representative institutions are liable. When the suffrage is widely extended, a large proportion of electors will always be wholly destitute of political convictions, while every artifice is employed to mislead them.

Twain bracketed Lecky's criticism of wide suffrage because the "supreme management of affairs may pass into the hands of men who are perfectly unprincipled, who seek only for personal" gain. Next to this bracketed passage Twain wrote, "He talks as if this had not been the rule throughout English history."

191.1–16, 32–34: Twain placed a line in the margin, writing "This is all English experience" next to this passage:

It would be difficult to exaggerate the dangers that may result from even a short period of such rule, and they have often driven nations to take refuge from their own representatives in the arms of despotism. The disposal of the national revenue may pass into the hands of mere swindlers, and become the prey of simple malversation. The foreign policy of the country may be directed by men

who seek only for notoriety or for the consolidation of their totter-
ing power, and who with these views plunge the nation into wars
that lead speedily to national ruin. In home politics institutions
which are lost in the twilight of a distant past may, through similar
motives, in a few months be recklessly destroyed. Nearly all great
institutions are the growth of centuries; their first rise is slow, obscure, undemonstrative; they have been again and again modified,
recast, and expanded; their founders leave no reputation, and reap
no harvest from their exertions.

Twain also indited a marginal line at the bottom of the page, writing
"True" under this passage: "A government of gentlemen may be and
often is extremely deficient in intelligence, in energy, in sympathy with
the poorer classes."

192.1–13: Lecky moves toward a sentiment with which Twain dis-
agreed:

It may be shamefully biased by class interests, and guilty of great
corruption in the disposal of patronage, but the standard of honour
common to the class at least secures it from the grosser forms of
malversation, and the interests of its members are indissolubly connected with the permanent well-being of the country. Such men
may be guilty of much misgovernment, and they will certainly, if
uncontrolled by other classes, display much selfishness, but it is
scarcely possible that they should be wholly indifferent to the ultimate consequences of their acts, or should divest themselves of all
sense of responsibility or public duty. When other things are equal,
the class which has most to lose and least to gain by dishonesty will
exhibit the highest level of integrity.

Twain wrote alongside of this passage, "It is all pure rot."

194: In the top half of the margin Twain wrote "It is true—where the
people are ignorant." Lecky comments that "To kindle and sustain the
vital flame of national sentiment is the chief moral end of national institutions, and while it cannot be denied that it has been attained under the
most various forms of government, it is equally certain that an aristocracy which is at once popular and hereditary, which blends and assimi-
lates itself with the general interests of the present, while it perpetuates
and honours the memories of the past, is peculiarly fitted to foster it."
Next to this last line of the page, "Popular election is in this respect

exceedingly worthless," Twain scratched out "exceedingly" and wrote "You can't strengthen it by that addition."

197–98: The corner of page 197 is turned down and bears a marginal line extending from line 3 to the end of the page. The crux of the page follows: "Considered abstractedly, every institution is an evil which teaches men to estimate their fellows not according to their moral and intellectual worth, but by an unreal and factitious standard." Twain continued marking on page 198, leaving the comment "Set a mark there. X We reformed you." next to this passage: "Looking again at the question from a purely historical standing-point, it is certain that the politicians of the Upper House were deeply tainted with the treachery and duplicity common to most English statesmen between the Restoration and the American Revolution."

202–3: These pages are deeply shadowed by a bookmark. They discuss the Reformation and the positive effects on a country's economic and social life.

Volume 1, Chapter 4

608–9: These pages are deeply shadowed by a bookmark. Page 608 bears a pencil mark next to a footnote containing Macaulay's statement that "hundreds of thousands of families scarcely knew the taste of meat." Page 609 describes wage fluctuations: "He states that although in Yorkshire, and generally in the bishopric of Durham, a labourer's weekly wages might be only 4s., yet in Kent and in several of the Southern and Western counties agricultural weekly wages were 7s., 9s., and even 10s."

619: This page bears marginal lines from top to bottom. The page describes the "large sums which had to be distributed among the numerous domestics."

620.6–10: Twain wrote "It is not eradicated" after the paragraph featuring Lecky's discussion of the system of vales: "The grand jury of Northumberland and the grand jury of Wiltshire followed the example, pledging themselves to discourage the system of vales, but many years still elapsed before it was finally eradicated."

621.14–17: A marginal line spans lines discussing the "excessive bleedings" performed by doctors.

623.17–22: Twain inscribed a marginal line and a C next to a passage describing theological and popular resistance to vaccination.

624.21–23: Twain underlined part of this sentence: "One of the most remarkable features of the first sixty years of the eighteenth century is the great number of new powers or influences that were then called into action of which the full significance was only perceived long afterwards."

624.28–25.11: Twain underlined a portion of this passage beginning at the bottom of page 624 and then lined the remaining portion on page 625 in the margin:

It was then that the English Deists promulgated doctrines which led the way to the great movement of European scepticism, that Diderot founded the French Encyclopedia, that Voltaire began his crusade against the dominant religion of Christendom; that a few obscure Quakers began the long struggle for the abolition of slavery; that Wesley sowed the first seeds of religious revival in England. Without any great or salient revolutions the aspect of Europe was slowly changing, and before the middle of the century had arrived both the balance of power and the lines of division and antagonism were profoundly modified. Industrial interests and the commercial spirit had acquired a new preponderance in politics, and theological influence had at least proportionately declined.

Volume 2, Chapter 5: "The Colonies and Scotland"
[All marginalia in volume 2 occur in chapter 5.]

3.18–21: Three parallel marginal lines span this passage: "The history of Salem witchcraft, of the persecution of Quakers in Massachusetts, and of the suppression of religious liberty in Maryland, as well as a crowd of savage or absurd laws regulating it, in the interests of religion, not only the opinions but also the minutest actions of the people, remain to show how far the colonists were from attaining any high general standard of religious freedom."

9: Twain wrote "A Chapter on Protection" at the head of the page.

13.15–19: Next to the history of the English slave trade, Twain inscribed a *C* with lines in the margin above and below: "It is a slight fact, but full of a ghastly significance as illustrating the state of feeling prevailing at the time, that the ship in which Hawkins sailed on his second expedition to open the English slave trade was called 'The Jesus.'"

14: Marginal lines span the length of the page and a capital *C* marks this passage:

The traffic was regulated by a long and elaborate treaty, guarding among other things against any possible scandal to the Roman Catholic religion from the presence of heretical slave-traders, and it provided that in the thirty years from 1714 to 1743 the English should bring into the Spanish West Indies no less than 144,000 negroes, or 4,800 every year, that during the first twenty-five years of the contract they might import a still greater number on paying certain moderate duties, and that they might carry the slave trade into numerous Spanish ports from which it had hitherto been excluded.

15.1–4, 7–9, 21–24: Two marginal lines mark a discussion of the slave trade. Further down the page Twain inscribed a large C next to this passage: "Difference of colour and difference of religion led their masters to look upon them simply as beasts of burden, and the supply of slaves was too abundant to allow the motive of self-interest to be any considerable security for their good treatment."

16.13–16, 21–end: Triple marginal lines mark a description of the "attempt to prohibit or restrict" the slave trade in America that was annulled by England. Below this, marginal lines score a discussion of the colonists' attempt to restrict slavery.

17: This page features four large Cs inscribed in the margin. The first appears next to this passage: "As late as 1775 we find Lord Dartmouth, the Secretary of State for the Colonies and one of the most conspicuous leaders of the English religious world, answering the remonstrance of a colonial agent in these memorable words: 'We cannot allow the colonies to check or discourage in any degree a traffic so beneficial to the nation.'" The second and third Cs appear one after another and, with three marginal lines, mark these lines: "A few isolated protests against slavery based on religious principles were heard, but they had no echo from the leading theologians. Jonathan Edwards, who occupied the first place among those born in America, left among other property, a negro boy." The fourth C adjoins this passage: "The article in the charter of Georgia forbidding slavery, being extremely unpopular among the colonists, was repealed in 1749; and it is melancholy to record that one of the most prominent and influential advocates of the introduction of slavery into the colony was George Whitefield."

18: On a page where Lecky treats Christian apologists for slavery in

America and Europe, Twain inscribed six *C*s. The first marks this passage: "In Georgia there was an express stipulation for the religious instructions of the slaves; it is said that those in or about Savannah have always been noted in America for their piety, and the advantage of bringing negroes within the range of the Gospel teaching was a common argument in favour of the slave trade." The second *C* marks this passage: "The Protestants from Salzburg for a time had scruples, but they were reassured by a message from Germany: 'If you take slaves in faith,' it was said, 'and with intent of conducting them to Christ, the action will not be a sin but may prove a benediction." The third *C* adjoins this passage: "Many who cordially approved of the slavery of pagans questioned whether it was right to hold Christians in bondage; there was a popular belief that baptism would invalidate the legal title of the master to his slave,[3] and there was a strong and general fear lest any form of education should so brace the energies of the negro as to make him revolt against his lot." The fourth and fifth *C*s coincide with a marginal line and a great deal of underlining of Lecky's prose, as indicated in this passage: "The Society for the Propagation of the Gospel sent missionaries to convert the free negroes in Guinea, on the Gold Coast, and in Sierra Leone; but it was itself a large slaveowner, possessing numerous slaves on an estate in Barbadoes. In 1783 Bishop Porteus strongly urged upon the managers of the Society the duty of at least giving Christian instruction to these slaves; but, after a full discussion, the recommendation was absolutely declined." Twain left a sixth *C* at the bottom of the page to mark footnote 3, which contains the following statement: "South Carolina, Virginia, and Maryland passed laws expressly asserting that baptism made no change in the legal position of the negro."

19: Twain left a comment: "This is one tribe of Christians, straining at a gnat; on page 18 you see their brothers swallowing a camel without difficulty." The comment appears alongside these lines:

The old Puritanical fervour and simplicity, strengthened as it was by the influx of many persecuted Protestants, may still be sometimes detected. At the close of the seventeenth century, "travel, play and work on the Lord's day," were prohibited in Massachusetts by law; and injunctions were given to constables "to restrain all persons from swimming in the waters, unnecessary and unreasonable walking in the streets or fields of the town of Boston or other places, keeping open their shops or following their secular occasions or recreations in the evening preceding the Lord's day, or any part of the said day or evening following."

20: Twain corrected Lecky by writing, "Mary Wortley Montague was inoculated there in 1717." Then he writes "No, 1636." to correct Lecky as to the founding of Harvard College.

22.10–15: Twain wrote "Protection." alongside Lecky's discussion: "But the jealousy of the manufacturers at home was soon aroused, and as usual they speedily succeeded in crushing the rival trade. A law passed in 1699 and renewed in 1721, absolutely prohibited under severe penalties the use of all Indian silks, stuffs, and printed or dyed calicos in apparel, household stuffs, or furniture in England."

24: Marginal lines span the length of the page. Next to this passage Twain inscribed the words "Some more slavery":

In the beginning of the eighteenth century the Highlands were almost wholly inaccessible to the traveller. They were for the most part traversed only by rude horse-tracks, without any attempt to diminish the natural difficulties of the country. They were inhabited by a population speaking a language different from that of England, scarcely ever intermarrying with Lowlanders, living habitually with arms in their hands, sunk in the lowest depths of barbarism, and divided into a number of kingdoms, that were practically as distinct and independent as those of the Heptarchy. By law the chief had an hereditary jurisdiction over his vassals extending "to the pit and to the gallows," to the execution of capital punishment by drowning and hanging; but the law was a very feeble and inadequate expression of his real power. It is, indeed, no exaggeration to say that the decision of Parliament and of the tribunals were long absolutely inoperative in the Highlands. The chief could determine what king, what government, what religion his vassals should obey; his word was the only law they respected; a complete devotion to his interests, an absolute obedience to his commands, was the first and almost the single article of their moral code. Combining in his own person the characters of king, general, landlord, and judge, he lived with his vassals on terms of the utmost familiarity, but he ruled them with all the authority of an oriental despot, and he rarely appeared abroad without a retinue of ten or twelve armed men.

25.1–8: This dog-eared page features a marginal line alongside this passage: "Sometimes the chief had a regular executioner in his service, and for the slightest cause he could have those who offended him either deliberately assassinated or executed after a mock trial, conducted by his own followers. Sometimes he would grant the temporary use of his power to his guest, and promise him the pleasure of seeing anyone who had offended him hanging next morning before his window, unless he preferred his head as a memorial of Highland courtesy." Marginal lines also mark footnotes 1 and 5, describing the loaning of executioners and Highland feuds that might last hundreds of years.

26.1–7: Twain wrote Civilization next to this discussion: "Few episodes in British history are more terrible than that which occurred in 1678, when Lauderdale let loose 8,000 Highlanders to punish the obstinate Presbyterianism of the western counties by living in free quarters among them. For three months they committed every variety of atrocity that human malignity could conceive; torturing some with thumbscrews, scorching others before vast fires, tearing children from their mothers, foully abusing women, plundering and devastating everything within their range." Twain connects the peasant with Indians by writing Indians from line 15 up to line 10: "Manual labor was looked upon with contempt. Most forms of field-labour were habitually done by the women, while the husband and the son looked on in idleness, or devoted themselves to robbing or begging. Plunder was the passion, the trade, the romance of the Highlander." Twain also left a marginal line next to footnote 3: "Pennant, when he visited Scotland in 1769 and 1772, noticed the same traits, though in diminished intensity, and especially observed how at Caithness 'the tender sex are the only animals of burden.'"

27.1–4, 9–12: Twain marginally lined a passage discussing Highlanders, who "were precisely in the moral condition of the Germans as described by Caesar." A later mark tags lines asserting that cattle theft had "no sense of immorality and dishonour."

28.17–19, 29–end: Marginal lines mark a passage discussing the "barbarous condition of the North" of Scotland. A further marginal line also tags this sentence: "Iron was hardly known except in the form of weapons."

29: Marginal lines span the page's discussion of "abject poverty" in the Highlands.

30.18–21, 29–31: This page features two Cs. The first marks this passage: "In some of the islands and in several of the remoter valleys of the Highlands the Catholic worship lingered on during the greater part of the eighteenth century, and although the Scotch Kirk gradually extended its empire, it found it much more easy to extirpate the worship and the dogmas than the popular superstitions of the old faith." The second *C* tags this passage: "A Presbyterian minister who visited the northern islands in the beginning of the eighteenth century relates with much horror that in one parish of Orkney the people attached such a reverence to the remains of a ruined and roofless chapel called Our Lady's Kirk, containing a stone which was said to bear the footprints of St. Magnus, that it was found necessary even in the wildest weather to conduct the Presbyterian service there, as the congregation refused to attend it in any other place."

31.7–8, 17–19: Two *C*s appear on this page. The first marks this sentence: "The faces of the sick were fanned with the leaves of a Bible." The second *C* tags Lecky's assertion that "it was noticed that if any change should give a renewed ascendency to Popery the people were thoroughly prepared to embrace it. Other superstitions partook largely of paganism."

32.11–13: Twain wrote "Same thing" next to these lines: "The great virtue of the Highlander was his fidelity to his chief and to his clan. It took the place of patriotism and of loyalty to the sovereign. It was unbroken by the worst excesses of tyranny, and it was all the more admirable on account of that extreme poverty which, after the Union, made the Scotch nobles a laughing-stock in England."

33: This page features a marginal line running its entire length. Lecky is discussing the "absolute devotion of the clansmen to their chief."

34.14–17: A marginal line spans a contrasting of the Lowlanders who "surrendered Charles I for money" and the "poverty-stricken Highlanders, among whom the Pretender wandered."

35.14–19: A marginal line spans this passage: "The Highlanders were distinguished for their hospitality to those who came properly recommended to them, and several examples are recorded of the signal generosity of the inhabitants of the Western Islands to shipwrecked sailors at the very time when the practice of plundering wrecks was most scandalously prevalent on both the English and the Irish coasts."

36: Twain asked "Is it a compliment?" next to Lecky's footnote 2, a quote from Macky's *Journey through Scotland:* "'The people speak as good English here [at Inverness] as at London, and with an English accent; and ever since Oliver Cromwell was here they are in their manners and dress entirely English.'"

37.13–16, 18–23: These marginal lines tag a discussion of Scotland's lack of material comforts.

39: A marginal line marks footnote 2: "Nearly 100 men, women, and children, were seized in the dead of the night on the islands of Skye and Herries, pinioned, horribly beaten, and stowed away in a ship bound for America, in order to be sold to the planters."

40: Marginal markings span the length of the page and its footnotes describing Scotland in the eighteenth century as reminding one of "very barbarous times."

42.13–26, 30–32: Four capital *C*s extend along lines discussing England's attempt to "force Episcopacy, by savage persecution, upon a Presbyterian people." The next sentences are marked with a marginal line, next to which Twain inscribed a capital *P*: "Besides this, the natural poverty and the unhappy position of Scotland could not save it from the commercial jealousy of its neighbor. Though part of the same empire, it was excluded from all trade with the English colonies; no goods could be landed in Scotland from the plantations unless they had been first landed in England and paid duty there, and even then they might not be brought in a Scotch vessel." Given the subject matter and Twain's inscription at the chapter's head, the *P* no doubt stands for "Protection."

43.17–23, 27–31: Twain inscribed "Say a tenth of the country's population?" along the first group of lines and wrote "See 40 civ." along the second group. The passage is quoted from Fletcher of Saltoun's *Second Discourse on the Affairs of Scotland* and discusses the "numbers of idle vagabonds" living in extreme poverty.

44: Twain wrote the word *tramps* alongside the top of the page, a further passage from Fletcher of Saltoun's *Second Discourse on the Affairs of Scotland:*

"Many murders have been discovered among them, and they are not only a most unspeakable oppression to poor tenants (who, if they give not bread or some kind of provision to perhaps forty such villains in one day, are sure to be insulted by them), but they rob many poor people who live in houses distant from any neighborhood. In years of plenty many thousands of them meet together in the mountains, where they feast and riot for many days; and at country weddings, markets, burials, and other the like public occasions, they are to be seen—both men and women—perpetually drunk, cursing, blaspheming, and fighting together."

Marginal lines mark the remainder of the page, and Twain has underlined the phrase "to a condition of slavery" amid a discussion of the desperate conditions in Scotland that prompted one commentator to advocate the enslavement of the Scottish people as a solution to poverty.

46.5–7, 19–22: This page features two *C*s. The first marks this sentence: "Nor was the contemptuous repudiation of the English doctrine of passive obedience confined to the Highlanders. The Lowlanders in this respect scarcely differed from their northern fellow-countrymen, except in the more orderly and methodised character of their opposition." Twain inscribed the second *C* to the left of a marginal line tagging this passage: "It was in this respect the very antipodes to the Anglican Church and to the Gallican branch of the Catholic Church, both of which did all that lay in their power to consecrate despotism and to strengthen authority."

49: Footnote 1 is marked. It claims that English esquires have "all the barbarism imaginable," whereas the Scottish gentry are more refined.

50.19–21: A marginal line with a *C* to the left of it marks this passage: "The great majority of the Episcopal clergy refused to comply with this latter condition, which, by asserting that the Pretender had no right to the throne, was tantamount to abandoning the doctrine of the Divine right of kings." Footnote 1 is also marked: "The lower and middle classes were usually Presbyterian, the nobility and gentry Episcopalian."

54.5–7: A marginal line marks a discussion of the "repudiation of the religious doctrine of the Divine right of kings."

57.9–13: A marginal line extends along a discussion of protection: "The Scotch were excluded by their neighbors from all trade with the Colonies."

58.9, 28–33: Twain struck "~~restrictions upon~~" and substituted "prohibitions & permit" in this passage: "The necessities of the Government were such that the ministers appear to have supported a strange measure, which was carried, to remove the restrictions upon the importation of French wine, at a time when war was raging between England and France." Twain wrote "against bribe, patriotism & principle" alongside these lines: "It was hoped that in the recess the angry feeling would subside; and, as a means of softening some of the leaders, Athol, who, though he was Lord Privy Seal, had been prominent in opposition, was made a Duke; Tarbet, who had been conspicuous on the same side, was raised to the Earldom of Cromarty; and several other dignities were conferred."

62.15–21: A marginal line marks this passage discussing the importing and exporting of goods in Scotland, in particular the Navigation Act that destroyed "the whole shipping trade of the smaller country."

63.6–11: Twain placed a marginal line alongside a passage discussing the "curious law which encouraged the English Woolen trade by providing that every corpse should be buried in wool."

64.18–22: A marginal line spans Lecky's discussion of the unequal relations between England and Scotland.

65.11–15: Twain placed a marginal line alongside a passage charting abuses of Scotland by England.

66.8–12, 21–26: Marginal lines mark a discussion of the government's efforts to encourage Catholics "to remain passive." Below, Twain marked a passage in which Lecky discusses Ireland: "Duped and Sacrificed by the English Government, they threw themselves into a violent agitation, brought the country to the verge of Civil War, and obtained emancipation from a Tory ministry by the menace of rebellion."

73.1–17: A marginal line tags a passage describing the destruction of many chiefs and clans: "In this manner the moral condition of the Highlands was profoundly modified, and the way was prepared for the abolition of hereditary jurisdictions by the Pelham ministry in 1746."

74: Twain printed a *C* at the top of the page and lined the entire page. The page concerns the Episcopal Church's support for the Pretender: "For many years after the accession of the Hanoverian dynasty, the Pretender seems to have habitually designated the clergyman who was to fill a vacancy in the Scotch episcopacy."

75: Likewise, this page features a capital *C* at its top, above the page number. The page begins with *jurors* as it appears in this sentence: "As the Scotch bishops were, without exception, Non-jurors, their letters of orders were insufficient, and as it was impossible for Orders to be repeated, the effect of this law was to unfrock all the existing Episcopal clergy in Scotland, except the few who had been ordained out of the country."

78.13–79.16: Lecky has been outlining the "Effects of Legislation on Character," using Scotland as a microcosm to illustrate what can be done in a very short time. Twain inscribed a marginal line beginning on page 78 and continuing to page 79:

It is a singularly curious fact that when Pennant visited Scotland, in 1769, one of the features with which that acute English traveller was especially struck was the remarkable absence of beggars in a population that was still extremely poor. "Very few beggars," he said, "are seen in North Britain; either the people are full masters of the lesson of being content with very little, or what is more probable, they are possessed of a spirit that will struggle hard with necessity, before it will bend to the asking of alms."

If I have been fortunate enough in the foregoing pages to exhibit clearly the nature and the coherence of the measures I have enumerated and the magnitude of the economical and moral revolution that was effected, the history can, I think, hardly fail to have some real interest for my readers. There are very few instances on record in which a nation passed in so short a time from a state of barbarism to a state of civilization, in which the tendencies and leading features of the national character were so profoundly modified, and in which the separate causes of the change are so clearly discernible. Invectives against nations and classes are usually very shallow. The original basis of national character differs much less than is supposed. The character of large bodies of men depends in the main upon the circumstances in which they have been placed, the laws by which they have been governed, the principles they have been taught. When these are changed the character will alter too, and the alteration, though it is very slow, may in the end be very deep.

81.21–27: Twain inscribed a marginal line next to this passage: "The last traces of serfdom disappeared in England about the time of James I., but in Scotland colliers and labourers in the salt works were in a condition of serfdom during the greater part of the eighteenth century. They were legally attached for life to the works on which they laboured. Their children were bound to the same employment in the same place, and on the sale of the works their services were transferred to the new owner."

Alongside, Twain wrote "Slavery during greater part of 18th century. Up to 1775. Ceased only 100 yr ago."

82.11–14: Twain indited a marginal line marking this passage: "It was, indeed, the custom in England to regard the Scotch as the most slavish and venal of politicians, and the reproach was not wiped away till the Reform Bill of 1832 gave Scotland a real representation and created constituencies surpassing those of any other part of the kingdom in the average of their intelligence, purity, and liberalism."

84.7–16: A marginal line marks this passage:

> In spite of their admirable education, in spite of their Protestantism, in spite of their growing industry, the aspect of the Scotch population in the latter years of the eighteenth century was still extremely repulsive to an English eye. All the squalor of dress, person, and dwelling that now shocks the traveler in some parts of Ireland was exhibited in the Lowlands, and it was accompanied by a striking absence of the natural grace, the vivacity, the warm and hospitable spirit of an Irish population.

Twain scored footnote 2 column 2 from lines 1–15 with a marginal line and underlined "Lowlanders" and "Highlanders," writing "100 yr ago." The marked text begins with *behind* and is quoted by Lecky from Skrine's *Travels in the North of England and Part of Scotland:*

> "The common people of Scotland are more than a century behind the English in improvement; and the manners of the Lowlanders in particular cannot fail to disgust a stranger. All the stories that are propagated of the filth and habitual dirtiness of this people are surpassed by the reality; and the squalid, unwholesome appearance of their garb and countenances is exceeded by the wretchedness that prevails within their houses . . . Whole groups of villagers fly from the approach of a traveler like the most untamed of savages." On the other hand, the Highlanders "are courteous in their manners, civil in their address, and hospitable to the utmost extent of their little power."

86.1–9: Twain tagged this discussion of tyrannical Presbyterian ministers with a marginal line and a capital *C:*

Those who take any wide or philosophical view of religious phenomena will find it peculiarly difficult to sympathise with men who, assuming the genuineness, authority, and absolute infallibility of the whole body of canonical writings without question and without discrimination, excluded on principle all the lights which history, tradition, patristic writings, or Oriental research could throw upon their meaning; banished rigidly from their worship every artistic element that could appeal to the imagination and soften the character; condemned in one sweeping censure almost all Churches, ages, and religious literatures, except their own, as hopelessly benighted and superstitious, and at the same time pronounced, with the most unfaltering assurance, upon the most obscure mysteries of God and of religion, and cursed, with a strange exuberance of anathema, all who diverged from the smallest article of their creed.

87.10–14, 23–30: Twain imprinted a marginal line with a capital *C* twice. The first *C* appears next to this passage: "The last and one of the very worst instances in British history of the infliction of death for the expression of religious opinions was the execution, in 1697, of Thomas Aikenhead, a young man of only eighteen, for the enunciation of some sceptical opinions which he was afterwards most anxious to recant, and this judicial murder was mainly due to the Scotch clergy." Twain's second *C* adjoins this discussion: "In no part of the British empire—I imagine in no part of Protestant Europe—were prosecutions for witchcraft so frequent, so persistent, and so ferocious as in Scotland, and it was to the ministers that the persecution was mainly due. They employed all their influence in hunting down the victims, and they sustained the superstition by their teaching long after it had almost vanished in England."

88: Three capital *C*s span lines 1–10 and a line scores the entire page. Twain underlined "laymen" and "of the clergy" and at the top of the page wrote "Within 15 yr of Salem—that they find so much fault with— where *nobody* was burnt." The text of the first ten lines follows:

Hundreds of wretched women have on this ground been burnt in Scotland since the Reformation, and the final sentence was preceded by tortures so horrible, various, and prolonged that several prisoners died through the torment. As late as 1678 no less than ten women were condemned to the flames on a single day on the charge of having had carnal intercourse with the devil.

Even when the superstition had to a great degree died away among educated <u>laymen,</u> the influence <u>of the clergy</u> over the populace was such that acquittal itself was sometimes insufficient to save the life of the victim.

The remainder of the page introduces a contemporary account that continues through page 90.

89: Twain inscribed marginal lines the length of page 89 and placed a capital *C* next to these lines, some of which he underlined: "On being visited, however, by the magistrates, she at once asserted her innocence, declared that her previous confessions were all lies, and were made '<u>to</u> <u>please the minister and the bailies,</u>' and succeeded in obtaining her release." Twain then wrote "<u>After</u> Salem above 10 years. 1704–5" at the top of page 89. He also underlines "three hours' sport" and "woman was killed" in the last lines of the page:

Her two daughters rushed in and fell upon their knees before the mob, imploring at least to be permitted to speak one word to their mother before she expired; but they were driven away with fierce threats. At last, after "<u>three hours' sport,</u> as they called it," the <u>woman was killed;</u> the populace compelled a man with a sledge and horses to drive several times over her head, and they placed her mangled corpse under a heap of stones at the door of the woman who had given her shelter on the previous night, whom they threatened with a similar fate.

90: Marginal lines span the length of the page, and two capital *C*s also appear, alongside this passage:

Under the teaching of the Scotch clergy, the dread and hatred of witches rose to a positive frenzy; and the last execution for witchcraft, as well as the last execution for heresy, in the British Empire, took place in Presbyterian Scotland. As late as 1727 a mother and daughter were convicted of witchcraft; the daughter succeeded in escaping, but the old woman was burnt in a pitch-barrel. <u>The associated Presbytery, in 1736, left a solemn protest against the repeal</u> <u>of the laws against witchcraft as an infraction of the express word</u> <u>of God.</u>

Next to the passage Twain wrote "34 yrs after Salem" and underlined as indicated, and he wrote "43 yrs after" at the end.

91.1–8, 15–end: The first line has a *C* to the right of it and tags this passage:

> A picture of Christ, attributed to Raphael, formed part of a small collection which was exhibited in 1734 at Edinburgh and Perth. In the latter city it was at once denounced from the pulpit; a furious mob, shouting "Idolatry!" "Popery!" and "Molten images!" surrounded the house where it was. It was saved with difficulty, and soon after the Seceders solemnly enrolled among the national sins of Scotland the fact that "an idolatrous picture of our Lord and Saviour Jesus Christ was well received in some remarkable places of the land."

Twain imprinted three parallel lines, one of which extends to the end of the page, marking this passage:

> The Scotch Sabbath became a proverb throughout Europe. Even after the Revolution, the magistrates in Edinburgh employed men called "seizers," whose function was to patrol the streets and arrest all who were found walking on Sunday during sermon time. On that dreary day it was esteemed sinful to walk in the fields, to stand in the streets, to look out of the window, to suffer little children to play, to travel even on the most urgent occasions, to pursue the most innocent secular recreation or employment, to whistle, to hum a tune, to bathe, or, in the opinion of some ministers, even to shave. Very few things affect so largely the happiness and the true civilisation of a people as the manner in which they are accustomed to spend the only day of the week in which, for the great majority of men, the burden of almost ceaseless labour is intermitted.

Twain wrote "Like A.E." to the right of the second marginal line. Boewe transcribes this as "Like at E." ("Twain on Lecky" 5), but a period is clearly visible after the second character. The abbreviation might stand for American Episcopalianism.

92.1–12: A marginal line marks a passage treating the "Scotch Sabbath," during which "every element of brightness and gaiety on that day was banished, every form of intellectual and aesthetic culture was rigidly proscribed."

93.21–end: A marginal line scores this passage:

Luxury increased, and the severity of domestic discipline which
had once prevailed rapidly disappeared. In the early years of the
century we are told, "Every master was revered by his family, hon-
oured by his tenants, and awful to his domestics. His hours of eat-
ing, sleeping, and amusement were carefully attended to by all his
family, and by all his guests. Even his hours of devotion were
marked that nothing might interrupt him. He kept his own seat by
the fire or at the table with his hat on his head, and often particular
dishes were served up for himself that nobody else shared of. His
children approached him with awe, and never spoke with any degree of freedom before him. The consequence of this was that except at meals they were never together." There was a reverence for
parent and elderly friends and generally an attention to the old
which in the latter part of the century was unknown. The position
of servants was still very humble.

94.1–5, 19–26, 31–34: Twain imprinted a marginal line adjoining this
passage: "They had 'a set form for the week of three days broth and salt
meat, the rest meagre, with plenty of bread and small beer.' Until vails
were abolished, the yearly wages of menservants were only from 3l. to 4l.,
those of maidservants from 30s. to 40s." A further marginal line marks
this passage:

The intercourse of men with women, however, though not less
pure, was much less reserved than in the latter part of the century.
"They would walk together for hours or travel on horseback or in
a chaise without any imputation of imprudence." The character of
"a learned lady" was greatly dreaded, and it was acquired by a very
slight knowledge of the current literature of the time. Our infor-
mant has preserved from the recollections of her uncle a curious
record of the ordinary way of spending Sunday in a gentleman's
house in the first years of the century.

Twain left a *C* adjoining this discussion of the Scotch Sabbath: "At
one the chaplain again read prayers, after which they had cold meat or
an egg, and returned to church at two. The second service terminated at
four, when they betook themselves to their private devotions, except the
children and servants, who were convened by the chaplain and exam-

ined." Twain expresses the sentiments of many when he writes "Not preferable to hell." at the bottom of the page.

95.16–19: A capital *C* marks a discussion of the Scotch Sabbath: "They complained among other things that the people were now accustomed to walk or stand in the streets before or after service time on Sunday, that they even wandered on that day to fields and gardens, or to the Castle Hill, or stood idly gazing from their windows, and that 'some have arrived at that height of impiety as not to be ashamed of washing in waters and swimming in rivers upon the holy Sabbath.'"

96.12–16, 24–27: Twain imprinted a line next to this passage: "This kind of preaching became especially popular after the rebellion of 1745, when ideas of liberty were widely diffused. The phrase 'slavery of the mind' came then into common use. Nurses were dismissed for talking to the young of witches or ghosts, and the old ministers were ridiculed who preached of hell and damnation." Another marginal line occurs alongside this discussion: "We read of a Hell-fire Club in Edinburgh, and of a Sweating Club, whose members perpetrated infamous street outrages like those of the Mohocks in London, and it is certain that during a great part of the eighteenth century hard drinking and other convivial excesses were carried among the upper classes in Scotland to an extent considerably greater than in England, and not less than in Ireland."

97.11–14, 17–19, 22–23: A marginal line marks this passage: "It has been observed with truth that every popular schism in Scotland was inspired, not by a desire to innovate, but by a desire to restore the sterner discipline of the past." Twain left also a capital *C* alongside this discussion: "The empire of the Kirk over the greater part of Scotland, and over the poorer and middle classes, was but little shaken during the eighteenth century; and although it is scarcely possible for a Christian Church to exercise a supreme influence over a people without producing some excellent moral effects, it also contributed largely to narrow, darken, and harden the national character." Twain marked also the next sentence, inditing a triple marginal line from line 22 to line 23: "The general standard of external decorum was, indeed, so far higher than in England that it was said that a blind man travelling southwards would know when he passed the frontier by the increasing number of blasphemies he heard." Twain ended the page by leaving a marginal marking alongside this passage: "The industrial virtues, however, for which Scotchmen are so eminently distinguished, can only be very partially attributed to the influence of the Kirk; for they spring naturally and almost spontaneously from good secular education and from an advanced industrial civilisation, while in some other branches of morals no great improvement has been effected."

98.1–5, 17–19, 29–31: Twain inscribed a double marginal line next to this passage: "It is well known that the statistics of drunkenness and the statistics of illegitimacy show that in point of sobriety the Scotch nation ranks below either of the other parts of the kingdom." Twain wrote "Sobriety & Chastity" next to this passage. Twain also left a marginal line along with the notation "A of N.E." next to this passage: "The effects were what might have been expected. The extreme publicity given to these matters had no tendency to diminish the offence; the spectacle of the public penances attracted to the Kirk those who would certainly have found no other charm within its walls; and the excessive severity of the penalties imposed on the fallen led to very serious increase of child-murder." Twain also inscribed a triple marginal line and writes the word *bastardy* next to this discussion: "In the Northern districts the influence of the Kirk in this, as in other respects, appears to have been less felt; and it is somewhat remarkable that, in spite of all the efforts of the clergy, a great Scotch writer was able to state, long after the middle of the eighteenth century, that 'in the Highlands of Scotland it is scarce a disgrace for a young woman to have a bastard.'"

Volume 3, Chapter 10

1.11–19: A marginal line marks this passage: "Among the many objections to elective monarchy, the most serious is that it condemns the country in which it exists to perpetual conspiracies, tumults, and intrigues, which are fatal to the formation of settled political habits, and derange every part of the national organization."

3.21–24: Twain imprinted a marginal line, marking this passage: "But the evils which have resulted from the predominance of such a way of thinking in a community are so great that they have led many who have no personal sympathy with the superstitious estimate of royalty, as a matter of expediency, rather to encourage than oppose it."

45.15–21: Twain marginally marked these lines and wrote the comment "Confused & obscure—an unusual fault in Mr. Lecky's English" next to this sentence: "But the most important of all the accessions to the party of Bute was Fox, the old rival of Pitt, in whose favour Grenville was displaced from the leadership of the Commons, who in consideration of the promise of a peerage, undertook to carry the peace, and who, having vainly attempted to draw the Duke of Cumberland and other great Whig peers into the same connection, threw himself, with all the impetuosity of his fearless and unscrupulous nature, into the service of the court."

Volume 3, Chapter 11

163.2 Twain revised Lecky's prose, changing "if it were rigidly applied" to "if it had been rigidly applied"† in the second line of the page by adding "had been"† above his markings.

192.24–31: Twain imprinted a marginal line alongside Lecky's discussion of Swift's tract "Essay on Public Absurdities": "It is imbued with the strongest prejudices of his party. He speaks of the folly of giving votes to any who did not belong to the established religion of the country. He condemns absolutely standing armies. He deplores that persons without landed property could by means of the boroughs obtain an entrance into Parliament."

Volume 3, Chapter 12: America, 1763–1776

296.23–25: Twain inscribed a double marginal line next to this passage: "Political power was incomparably more diffused, and the representative system was incomparably less corrupt than at home, and real constitutional liberty was flourishing in the English colonies when nearly all European countries and all other colonies were despotically governed."

325: This page discusses protection and is dog-eared.

327: This page discusses protection and is dog-eared.

Volume 3, Chapter 13

536.16–23: Twain left a marginal line next to this passage:

The sentence of excommunication might be imposed by them for many offences; but it was most commonly employed as a punishment for contempt of the Ecclesiastical Court in not appearing before it, or not obeying its decrees, or not paying its fees or costs. An excommunicated person in England was placed almost wholly beyond the protection of the law. He could not be a witness or a juryman. He could not bring an action to secure or recover his property. If he died without the removal of his sentence he had no right to Christian burial.

538.15–23: A marginal line tags a passage discussing the persecution of dissenters.

568.17–19: Twain left a marginal line alongside this discussion of the eighteenth century: "It is, that the immense changes which have taken place in the past century in the enlargement of personal and political liberty, and in the mitigation of the penal code, have been accompanied by an at least equal progress in the maintenance of public order and in the security of private property in England."

581.27–28: Marginal lines mark a passage detailing the abuse of impressment: "As we have already seen, the press-gang was often employed to drag Methodist teachers from a work which the magistrates disliked."

582.8–10: Twain marked this passage with marginal lines: "As merchant ships came in from America, and the sailors looked forward, after their long voyage, to see once more their wives and children, a danger more terrible than that of the sea awaited them, for it was a common thing for ships of war to lie in wait for the returning vessels, in order to board them and to press their sailors before they landed."

583.1–12: Twain impressed a long marginal line beside this passage:

The breadwinner being gone, his goods were seized for an old debt, and his wife was driven into the streets to beg. At last, in despair she stole a piece of coarse linen from a linen draper's shop. Her defence, which was fully corroborated, was that "she had lived in credit and wanted for nothing till a press-gang came and stole her husband from her, but since then she had no bed to lie on, nothing to give her children to eat, and they were almost naked. She might have done something wrong, for she hardly knew what she did." The lawyers declared that shop-lifting being a common offence, she must be executed, and she was driven to Tyburn with a child still suckling at her breast.

585.11–14, 19: Twain imprinted marginal lines next to this passage: "Two or three Acts in favour of insolvent debtors had been passed, granting them their liberty on condition of enlisting in the army or navy, and in 1702 a system had begun which continued up to the time of the Peninsular War, of permitting criminals, who were undergoing their sentence, to pass into the army." Below, this passage is marked: "The usual manner of disposing of criminals under sentence of transportation had hitherto been to send them to America, where they were sold as slaves to the planters; but the war that had just broken out rendered this course impossible."

586.1–10: Twain tagged this passage: "In estimating the light in which British soldiers were regarded in America, and in estimating the violence and misconduct of which British soldiers were sometimes guilty, this fact must not be forgotten. It is indeed a curious thing to notice how large a part of the reputation of England in the world rests upon the achievements of a force which was formed mainly out of the very dregs of her population, and to some considerable extent even out of her criminal classes."

587: This page bears a comment in Twain's hand that has been marked out. It is both written and excised with black pencil: "How [illegible word] about [illegible word]."

Volume 4

No marginalia noted in this volume.

Volume 5

110–111: No pages are marked in this volume, but a bookmark saves these pages. The bookmark is torn from a portion of a letter. On one side the words "S.L. Clemens, Dear Sir; Did you ever know" appear, and on the other "I am, yours respectfully, Elise Rathbone, Brooklyn, September 1st. Eighty seven."

Volume 6
[All marginalia in volume 6 occur in chapter 23.]

144.25–29: Twain imprinted a marginal line next to this passage: "In question of peerages the royal influence is always extremely great, and 'through his whole reign,' it has been said, 'George the Third adopted as a fixed principle that no individual engaged in trade, however ample might be his nominal fortune, should be created a British peer.'"

164.28–30: Twain imprinted a marginal line next to this passage: "Whatever controversy there might be about the comparative value of the additions made to human knowledge in the eighteenth and in preceding centuries, there could be no question of the fact that the eighteenth century was preeminently the century of the diffusion of knowledge."

166.1–5, 10–11: A marginal line appears alongside Lecky's discussion of the rise of lending libraries: "The exact date of their origin is disputed, but they certainly existed a few years before the middle of the century, and in its last thirty years they multiplied rapidly, not only in London, but in the provincial towns." A further mark tags this passage: "All important controversies became in their style and method more popular, and a vast literature of novels sprang into existence, at once producing and representing a greatly increased love of reading."

168: Marginal lines span most of the page. Lecky discusses the gradual changes in the country life as very slow indeed, perhaps providing a prototype for Camelot. The page begins with the word *life* in the following sentence: "In the middle of the eighteenth century there were still thousands of country gentlemen who had scarcely ever been farther from their homes than their country town, while among the poor the habits of life had been for generations almost unchanged." The last sentence of the page is a quote from the *Annual Register* of 1761: "'It is scarce half a century ago,' he says, 'since the inhabitants of the distant countries were regarded as a species almost as different from those of the metropolis as the natives of the Cape of Good Hope." In addition, Twain left a double marginal line from line 28–31: "Before the close of the eighteenth century there were already more than seventy provincial newspapers in England." Twain wrote the comment, "70 provincial papers. What kind?" next to this sentence.

169.1–5: Twain inscribed a marginal line next to this passage: "Their manners as well as dialect were entirely provincial, and their dress no more resembled the habit of the town than the Turkish or Chinese. . . . A journey into the country was then considered almost as great an undertaking as a voyage to the Indies."

170.1–3, 15–19: Twain placed a marginal line next to this sentence: "The spread of refined and intellectual tastes, and the great diminution among the country gentry of ignorance, coarseness, drunkenness, and prejudice might at first sight be regarded as an unmixed good, but it must not be forgotten that these things were purchased by the almost absolute disappearance of a class of men who, with some vices and with many weaknesses, have played a useful and memorable part in English life and history." Twain also marked lines next to this passage describing the life of the country gentleman: "He went to church regularly, read the weekly journal, settled the parochial disputes between the parish officers at the vestry, and afterwards adjourned to the neighboring alehouse, where he usually got drunk for the good of his country."

171.1–12: Twain imprinted marginal lines next to a description of the furnishings one might find in a gentleman's country house:

> Against the wall was posted King Charles's Golden Rules, Vincent Wing's Almanac, and a portrait of the Duke of Marlborough; in his window lay Baker's "Chronicle," Foxe's "Book of Martyrs," Glanvil on "Apparitions," Quincey's "Dispensatory," "The Complete Justice," and a book of Farriery. In a corner by the fireside stood a large wooden two-armed chair, with a cushion, and within the chimney-corner were a couple of seats. Here at Christmas he entertained his tenants, assembled round a glowing fire made of the roots of trees; and told and heard the traditionary tales of the village, respecting ghosts and witches, while a jorum of ale went round.

173.1–3, 28–35: Twain imprinted marginal lines as Lecky continues his discussion of the country gentleman in this passage: "The social consequence which the possession of a great estate produces; the 'land hunger' which becomes with some men a passion scarcely less strong than the passion for drink, and the excessive and wholly extravagant preservation of game which has grown up within the present century have all contributed to it; and the increased luxury of country life makes men desire to surround their country places with an increased area of productive land." Twain also lined this passage:

> This is, I believe, the experience of most wealthy landlords; and it is to this economical process much more than to any feudal laws that the concentration of land in a few hands has in modern times been due. The main governing influence of the transformation of manners which has been described in the preceding pages, is to be found in the improvement of roads and of means of locomotion, a

subject that meets us at every turn when examining the industrial and social, and even the moral, political, and intellectual history of the eighteenth century.

174.9–11, 29–33: A marginal line marks this passage: "With the increase of wealth, however, and consequently of locomotion, this system proved insufficient; and among the many great reforms that were adopted under Charles II. the introduction of turnpikes is not the least memorable." Triple marginal lines span this passage: "The improvement in travelling advanced very slowly. The new turnpike roads were extremely unpopular, and fierce mobs—sometimes taking for their rallying cry the words of the prophet, 'Stand ye in the ways, and see, and ask for the old paths'—frequently attacked and destroyed the turnpikes."

175.16–21: Twain placed marginal lines next to these sentences: "Defoe met a lady near Lewes driven to church in her coach by six oxen, along a road so stiff and deep that no horse could go in it, and he mentions that there were roads in this country of such a character that after heavy winter rains, a whole summer was insufficient to make them passable. Horace Walpole speaks of roads in a similar condition in the immediate neighbourhood of Tunbridge Wells."

176: A marginal line spans the entire page. Lecky proposes that "the last forty years of the eighteenth century produced a great and general revolution in English roads."

177: This page concerns the improvement of roads and bears a line along its entire length. It begins with *lay* in this sentence: "Beyond Newcastle to the north lay a country in which no wise men would travel except through absolute necessity."

178: This page likewise concerns the roads and features lines running the entire length. It begins with a discussion of the King's proclamation in 1635 that "no hackney-coach should be suffered in London or Westminster unless it was to travel at least three miles beyond it."

179: Marginal lines span the length of this page, which concerns the conditions of the roads.

180–81: A piece of paper marks these pages and has shadowed both. The pages concern the tremendous changes in travel that had occurred in England.

221.1–3: A triple marginal line marks this passage: "Handloom-weaving, once a flourishing trade—long maintained a desperate competition against the factories, and as late as 1830 a very competent observer described the multitude of weavers, who were living in the great cities, in houses utterly unfit for human habitation, working fourteen hours a day and upwards, and earning only from five to eight shillings a week."

225.1–19: A marginal line tags this passage:

In one case brought before Parliament, a gang of these children was put up for sale among a bankrupt's effects, and publicly advertised as part of the property. In another, an agreement was disclosed between a London parish and a Lancashire manufacturer in which it was stipulated that with every twenty sound children one idiot should be taken. Instances of direct and aggravated cruelty to particular children were probably rare, and there appears a general agreement of evidence that they were confined to small factories. But labour prolonged for periods that were utterly inconsistent with the health of children was general. In forty-two out of forty-three factories at Manchester, it was stated before the Parliamentary Committee in 1816 that the actual hours of daily work ranged from twelve to fourteen, and in one case they were fourteen and a half. Even as late as 1840, when the most important manufactures had been regulated by law, Lord Ashley was able to show that boys employed in the carpet manufacture at Kidderminster were called up at three and four in the morning, and kept working sixteen or eighteen hours; that children of five years old were engaged in the unhealthy trade of pin-making, and were kept at work from six in the morning to eight at night.

231.29–232.9, 33–35: Twain places marginal lines alongside Lecky's description of government control of religion and wages: "Religious belief and religious worship were rigidly prescribed by law and enforced by the severest penalties. Sumptuary laws regulated in minute detail private manners and expenses. Wages and prices were both determined, not by free competition, but by law."

232. In the margin on page 232 Twain commented, "The idea being drawn from Moses?" Twain left marginal lines next to this sentence: "Attempts to regulate manners by sumptuary laws came to an end, though Blackstone notices that when he wrote there was still in the Statutebook an obsolete law of Edward III. ordaining that no one should be

served at dinner and supper with more than two courses, except on some great holidays, when he might have three."

233.1–3, 12–27: Twain imprinted a marginal line next to this sentence: "A law of 1746 punishing profane swearing by fines proportioned to the rank of the culprit." Twain queried, "High rank low fine?" next to Lecky's comment. Twain writes "Universal suffrage would have broken that up promptly." next to a description of the many laws proscribing behavior:

> It provided that no one could lawfully exercise any art, mystery, or manual occupation without having served in it at least seven years as an apprentice; that no one should be bound as an apprentice who was not under twenty-one years, and whose parents did not possess a certain fortune; that every master who had three apprentices must keep one journeyman, and for every other apprentice above three, one other journeyman; that no one should be engaged as a servant or journeyman for less than a year; that the hours of work should be twelve in summer, and from dawn to night in winter, and finally that wages should be assessed for the year by the justices of the peace or town magistrates, who were also directed to settle all disputes between masters and apprentices. Another law which was passed under James I extended the power of the justices and town magistrates to fix the wages of all kinds of labourers and workmen.

234.32–34: Twain imprinted a line next to this passage: "In the last years of the century new and very stringent laws were made forbidding combinations of workmen to raise wages."

235.1–3, 26–35: Twain left a marginal line next to this discussion: "When, however, the law ceased to regulate wages, and the masters were at full liberty to concert to depress them, the combination laws against workmen became a glaring injustice." Twain scored this passage:

> I have already cited the law which made it penal for any woman to wear a dress made of Indian calico. In 1766 a lady was fined 200*l* at the Guild Hall because it was proved that her handkerchief was of French cambric. In the same year an attorney named Brecknock, who had been sent to prison by the House of Lords for publishing a book called the "Droit du Roi," avenged himself upon Lord Camden by laying an information before Judge Fielding, that the

Chief Justice and three other judges wore cambric bands in court, contrary to the Act of Parliament.

236.24–27: Twain imprinted a marginal line amid Lecky's discussion of the "poor law" that prevented laborers from traveling in order to gain high wages: "The poor law secured him an ultimate support in the parish in which he was settled, but it also gave the parochial authorities an almost unlimited power of preventing a new labourer from establishing himself in the parish and of forcibly removing poor men if they seemed likely to become chargeable on the rates."

237.1–2, 25–30: A marginal line tags this sentence: "The regulations of profits, by fixing the price of provisions and other goods, was now only retained in the case of bread, the assize of which continued to 1815, when it was abolished in London and appears to have become obsolete in other parts of the kingdom." A marginal line also marks this sentence:

The transition of industry from small establishments to vast factories, the wholly new conditions on which its success depended, and the magnitude and power which the different industrial classes assumed, made the regulations of Elizabeth and of the Stuarts altogether impracticable, and they at last led to the great measures of 1814 and 1824, which repealed the Apprentice Act and a number of other old laws, preventing workmen from combining or from emigrating, regulating the rate of wages, the hours of work, and the manner of conducting any business or manufacture.

240.21–30, 31–33, 36–38: A marginal line scores this passage:

As Dugald Stewart has truly said, it was its main object "to demonstrate that the most effectual plan for advancing a people to greatness is to maintain that order of things which Nature has pointed out; [by allowing every man, as long as he observes the rules of justice, to pursue his own interest in his own way], and to bring both his industry and his capital into the freest competition with those of his fellow-citizens." Restrictive duties, prohibitions and bounties, by which Legislatures have endeavoured to force industries into particular channels, are alike condemned, as well as all attempts to regulate private expenses by sumptuary laws.

The brackets in this passage indicate Twain's bracketing within the marginally lined section. Outside of the marginally lined passage, Twain bracketed lines 31–33, which contain this sentence: "The natural effort of each man to improve his own position, when exerted with freedom and security, is represented as the mainspring of national progress." Likewise, Twain also bracketed part of lines 36–38 and this passage: "whatever lowers the cost of the products which a nation requires is equivalent to an increase in the national wealth."

243.13–16, 37–39: This page bears a marginal line alongside these sentences: "But many other and very various influences have been tending in the same direction. The greatly increased sensitiveness of philanthropy which characterises our century, and the immense extension of the newspaper press, have together brought into clear and vivid relief vast numbers of miseries, wants, and possibilities of improvement, which in former years had been unknown or unrealised, and it becomes the natural impulse of multitudes to seek an immediate remedy in Government interference." Next to Lecky's statement "With the great transfer of power to uninstructed democracies the impulse towards Government interference has naturally increased," Twain wrote "NO" in the margin.

246.14–end: Marginal lines mark this passage:

Another class of laws had acquired a great additional severity by the lapse of time. Legislators had endeavoured to protect property by punishing with death those who stole a sum of money which in their time was considerable, and the penalty was retained when the change in the value of money had made that sum insignificant. In this way, as an old lawyer forcibly complained, "While everything else had risen in its nominal value and become dearer, the life of man had continually grown cheaper." It was also the constant practice of Parliament in the eighteenth century, when new offences arose or when old offences assumed a new prominence, to pass special Acts making them capital. Hence an enormous and undigested multiplication of capital offences, which soon made the criminal code a mere sanguinary chaos. Previous to the Revolution the number in the Statute-book is said not to have exceeded fifty. During the reign of George II. sixty-three new ones were added. In 1770 the number was estimated in Parliament at one hundred and fifty-four, but by Blackstone at one hundred and sixty; and Romilly, in a pamphlet which he wrote in 1786, observed that in the sixteen years since the appearance of Blackstone's Commentaries it had considerably increased.

247.1–23: Twain marginally lined passages outlining the absurdity of the English penal code.

248.12–13: A double marginal line marks this sentence: "Unwilling to convict culprits for small offences which were made punishable by death, they recently acquitted in the face of the clearest evidence; and, as witnesses in these cases were also very reluctant to appear, criminals— among whom the gambling spirit is strongly developed—generally preferred to be tried for a capital offence rather than for misdemeanour."

250.11–15: Marginal lines mark this passage: "Outside Parliament, Paley, in a well-known passage of his 'Moral Philosophy,' justified the English system on the ground that it swept into the net every crime which under any possible circumstances could deserve death, leaving it to the executive to single out for condign punishment such cases as presented particular features of danger or aggravation."

251.3–5, 7–10, 15–17, 27–30: Four short marginal lines mark several passages on this page. The first marks this passage: "One writer, near the close of the century, mentions that he was present when a girl of twenty-two was hanged for receiving a piece of check from an accomplice who had stolen it." The second line marks this passage: "Such crimes were at this time scarcely ever capitally punished, but the poor girl had unfortunately drunk too freely before the trial, and was insolent in the dock. The prosecutor, a simple, honest man, who had no idea that such a punishment would be inflicted, was driven almost distracted by remorse, and did not long survive the shock." The third marks this passage: "I have already mentioned the repeal of the laws condemning prisoners who refused to plead to be pressed to death, and all gipsies to be hanged, and the substitution in 1790 of the gallows for the stake, in the capital punishment of women." Finally, a squiggly line tags this passage: "It is a curious illustration of the caprice of national sentiment, that English opinion in the eighteenth century allowed the execution of criminals to be treated as a popular amusement, but at the same time revolted against the Continental custom of compelling chained prisoners to work in public, as utterly inconsistent with English liberty."

252.11–14, 19–22, 28–29, 32–34: This page bears four marginal lines.

The first marks a passage discussing "the senseless and savage rule which deprived prisoners accused of any capital offence, except treason, of the assistance of counsel," and the second notes Blackstone's criticism of that rule. A line also marks this text: "It appears still to have been the rule that criminal trials should be compressed into a single day." The last marginal line marks this passage: "In the more lucrative branches of the profession no such hurry was shown. Civil suits, and especially suits in Chancery, were often protracted for years, and sometimes even for generations, by merciless legal subtleties, and in this way countless fortunes were engulfed, and countless hearts were broken."

253.13–16, 22–27: Twain marginally lined this passage, underlining some words: "Drunkenness is too frequently apparent where it ought of all things to be avoided. I mean in jurymen and witnesses. The heat of the court, joined to the fumes of the liquor, has laid many an honest juryman into a calm and profound sleep, and sometimes it has been no small trouble for his fellows to jog him into the verdict, even where a wretch's life has depended on the event." Twain imprinted as well a marginal line alongside this passage: "The American War put an end to the old system of disposing of criminals by selling them for the term of their sentence to American planters. This system began in 1718, continued for fifty-six years, and appears to have been remarkably successful."

255.13–19, 23–29, 31–end: The first marginal line tags a passage describing the zeal of the advocate for prison reform, John Howard, whose "whole life was devoted to a single object, and the researches he made into the condition of prisons in every part of the United Kingdom as well as in all the principal countries on the Continent, revealed to the world a mass of maladministration and atrocious cruelty which made a deep and lasting impression." Broken marginal lines mark passages describing the cruelty Howard witnessed and chronicled in *On Prisons*. Later marginal lines detail the "dark, damp, subterranean dungeons reeking with pestilential effluvia."

256.3–15, 26–32: The first marginal line marks a passage asserting that "the gaol fever raged with such a deadly virulence that Howard computed that every year it carried away far more than perished by the gallows." The second marginal line marks this passage: "Many country prisons were in an almost ruinous condition. A gaol at Ely was so dilapidated that for some time it was the custom to secure the prisoners by chaining them on their backs on the floor, with an iron collar and spikes about their necks, and a heavy iron bar over their legs. This case was one of unusual atrocity; but in most country prisons, heavy chains and iron collars were in constant use, though the gaoler was often ready to remove or lighten them for money."

257.1–4, 15–19, 21–23, 31–34: The first marginal line marks this sentence: "At Salisbury, Howard found two debtors, daily chained by a staple fixed outside the prison door in order that they might sell nets, purses, and laces made in the prison; and at Christmas felons chained together were permitted to go begging through the City." The second line marks this passage: "In most prisons debtors and felons, men and women, young boys or girls fresh to the paths of crime, and confined for the most trifling offences, and the oldest and most hardened criminals habitually mixed together during the whole day, so that the prison became the most deadly and most certain school of vice, and innumerable crimes were planned within its walls." The third line marks this passage: "In some counties the gaol delivery was but once a year. At Hull it was but once in three years." The fourth marginal line adjoins this passage: "These few lines may be sufficient to give a general outline of the abuses of English prisons in the early years of George III., but the reader who would form an adequate conception of their magnitude must himself turn to that ghastly procession of detailed evidence, collected from every gaol in the kingdom, which is to be found in the treatises of Howard. A long and searching investigation into the condition of prisons on the Continent completed his task, and it had an importance which is not limited to its immediate subject."

258.8–14, 18–24, 32–end: Twain inscribed a marginal line next to this passage: "There were no doubt prisons in Germany and Italy, in the bishopric of Liege and in Russia, which were even more horrible than any in England. Though torture had been in general abolished or disused throughout Europe, Howard still found it regularly employed at Osnabruck, Hanover, Munich, Hamburg and Liege, and in Austrian Flanders, and he found recent traces of it in some other quarters." Twain imprinted four marginal lines next to this passage: "But on the whole, England, which stood so high among the nations of the world in political, industrial, and intellectual eminence, ranked in most matters relating to the treatment of criminals shamefully below the average of the Continent. Nowhere else were the executions so numerous. Nowhere else were they conducted with such revolting indecency, and in scarcely any other country were the abuses in prisons so gross, so general, and so demoralising." The page ends with a double marginal line next to this passage: "In the Dutch Republic, institutions, both for the correction and reformation of prisoners, had been brought to almost the highest perfection; nearly every important prison reform of the nineteenth century appears to have been anticipated, and Howard found in the Dutch prisons and Rasphouses not only a model of all he desired, but also a conclusive proof of the efficacy of such methods in diminishing crime." Next to the marked text, Twain wrote "Republic."

259.25–26: As Lecky continued his discussion of prison conditions in various countries, Twain wrote "Two republics beat them all." in the top left margin. A double marginal line marks a passage noting that the "beneficent Act was passed appointing for the first time regular chaplains for the county gaols of England." The underlining is Twain's.

260.7–end: A marginal line marks a great deal of text, including this sentence: "The treatment of debtors in England was indeed one of the most astonishing instances of the astonishing corruption of English law." The marginal lines extend the length of the page with "made up, and not defended at all," "68,728*l*," and "285,950*l*" underlined. The marking continues through the last sentence to the next page with deep underlining of "political liberty" in the underlined and marginally marked lines "Can it be deemed surprising that many foreigners who valued good administration, public order, and cheap justice more than representative institutions and political liberty, should have preferred their own system to that of England?"

261.12–14: A marginal line appears next to Lecky's observation that "the diet and treatment of prisoners should always be such as to make imprisonment a deterrent punishment to the most needy, and that hard labour is an essential element in every sound prison system."

262.18–21, 33–end: Along the length of the page Twain opines, "English liberty was for gentlemen only." He also leaves double marginal lines adjoining this sentence: "By the law of England, no one at this time, with a few strictly specified exceptions, was permitted to shoot or fish even on his own grounds, unless he possessed a freehold estate of at least 150*l*; the sale of game was absolutely prohibited, and although the penalties of poaching were not so severe as they became under George IV., it was still possible for young men to be publicly whipped for having killed a hare." I have indicated Twain's underlinings. At the bottom of the page Twain impressed three parallel marginal lines alongside a passage discussing the "almost absolute impossibility of finding any honest means of livelihood" in England.

263: Twain wrote "True to-day. 1888." alongside Lecky's quoting of Coquhoun: "'The period,' he says, 'is not too remote to be recollected, when it was thought a disgrace for a woman (excepting on holiday occasions) to be seen in the taproom of a public-house; but of late years the obloquy has lost its effect, and the public taprooms of many alehouses are filled with men, women, and children, on all occasions.'"

264: A marginal line spans the length of this page that begins with *malefactors* in this sentence: "Probably the most important measure for the suppression of crime during the period we are considering, was an Act which was passed in 1773 making it possible for felons and other malefactors who escaped from England to Scotland or from Scotland to England to be arrested in either country and sent back to the place where their offences were committed."

265.1–10, 27–31: These marginal lines mark passages describing the danger of the roads in and around London.

266.16–21, 25–27: These marginal lines mark passages discussing the suppression of duelling.

267.1–8, 14–19, 26–29: The first marginal line tags this passage: "On the Occasion of Pitt's duel with Tierney in 1798, Wilberforce desired to bring the subject before the House of Commons in the form of a resolution, but he found that he could not count upon more than five or six members to support him, and accordingly relinquished his intention. The immense number of conspicuous men, and especially of conspicuous statesmen, who fought duels during the eighteenth century is very striking." A broken marginal line marks this sentence: "These are but a few out of many examples that might be given. No revolution of public sentiment has been more remarkable than that which in the space of little more than a generation has banished from England, and in a great measure from Europe, this evil custom which had so long defied the condemnation both of the Church and of the Law." The underlining is Twain's. Twain left a marginal line next to these sentences: "It is impossible, I think, to trace the history of crime, of the treatment of criminals, of the treatment of debtors, and of the maintenance of order, without acknowledging the enormous improvement which has in these fields, at least, been effected in England, as in most other countries, since the eighteenth century. The tone of life and manners has become indisputably <u>gentler and more humane,</u> and men recoil with a new energy of <u>repulsion from brutality, violence, and wrong</u>." The underlining is Twain's; note that the phrase "gentler and more humane" is underlined twice. Twain continued to underline many words and phrases on the remainder of the page as a chronicle of practices that ceased since the eighteenth century: "<u>the lunatics in Bedlam</u> were constantly spoken of <u>as one of the sights of London</u>"; "<u>maintenance of the African slave trade was a foremost object of English commercial policy</u>"; "<u>men and even women were publicly whipped through the streets</u>"; "<u>when skulls lined the top of Temple Bar, and rotting corpses hung on gibbets along the Edgware Road.</u>"

268.1–8, 10–12, 16–25, 30–34: Compiled in this list are Twain's continued underlinings with *not* the first word of page 268: "prisoners <u>exposed in the pillory not unfrequently died through the ill usage of the mob, and when the procession every six weeks of condemned criminals to Tyburn was one of the great festivals of London</u>"; "<u>abolition of the old modes of recruiting for the army and navy</u>"; "<u>the character of public amusements</u>"; "the <u>treatment of boys at school</u>"; and "the <u>comfort and health of their servants</u>" all mark improvements from past practice. Twain scribbled the comment "<u>of ladies</u>" next to this sentence in lines 10–12: "The wholesale <u>cattle stealing</u> of the Highlands, highway robbery, piracy and <u>kidnapping</u> are now things of the past." The underlining is again Twain's. The sentences from line 16–25 also contain many underlined portions, given here again in a list: "<u>intolerance at least finds no longer any sanction in English law</u>"; "<u>duelling has disappeared; drunkenness has become very rare</u>"; "gambling, though it has probably greatly increased in the form of reckless and dishonest speculation, has <u>in other respects declined</u>"; "<u>and banished profane swearing from conversation.</u>" And yet, not all was improvement, and Twain underlined these passages from line 30–34: "<u>growing vice in high quarters</u>"; and "<u>scandals in the royal family; the public relations of the Duke of Grafton, when Prime Minister, with Nancy Parsons.</u>" The page ends with Twain's leaving a marginal line next to this sentence: "Bills for preventing the intermarriage of the offending parties were carried through the House of Lords in 1771 and in 1779, but on both occasions rejected by the Commons."

269.1–4, 8–10, 21–24, 33–35: Twain imprinted a bold exclamation point next to the first four lines of the page alongside Lecky's discussion of an

English belief that the French "had formed a deliberate and subtle design to corrupt her morals, and had for that purpose sent over a number of ballet dancers." The remaining marginal lines tag sentences treating English divorce law and morality.

270.4–6, 9–22, 31–35: The first two marginal lines adjoin passages discussing English divorce law. The last marginal line marks this passage: "It is possible also, that it may have been more largely affected than other departments of morals, by that decline of theological beliefs which was so manifest in the closing years of the eighteenth century, and which is certainly not less apparent in our own day."

271. 3–10: A double marginal line marks this passage: "In its closing years, it is true, the Methodist and Evangelical movements, and the strong conflicting passions aroused by the French Revolution, somewhat altered its character; but in general it was an unimpassioned and unheroic age, singularly devoid of both religious and political enthusiasm, and much more remarkable for intellectual than for high moral achievements. It was pre-eminently a century of good sense; of sobriety of thought and action: of growing toleration of humanity; of declining superstition; of rapidly extending knowledge; of great hopefulness about the future."

The endleaf bears this list: "240, 247, 250, 269."

Appendix 4

TWAIN'S MARGINALIA IN THOMAS CARLYLE'S *THE FRENCH REVOLUTION*. 2 VOLS. NEW YORK: HARPER AND BROTHERS, N.D. [ALL MARGINALIA WERE MADE IN BLACK PENCIL. BOTH VOLUMES ARE INSCRIBED "SUSAN L. CRANE QUARRY FARM 1888."]

Volume 1, Book 1, "The Bastille"; Chapter 2, "Realized Ideals"

6.30–35: This page bears a marginal line next to Carlyle's discussion of democracy: "Boston Harbor is black with unexpected Tea: behold a Pennsylvanian Congress gather; and ere long, on Bunker Hill, DEMOCRACY announcing, in rifle-volleys death-winged, under her Star Banner, to the tune of Yankee-doodle-doo, that she is born, and, whirlwind-like, will envelop the whole world!"

Volume 1, Book 1, "The Bastille"; Chapter 4, "Louis the Unforgotten"

21.21: Heavy black underlining of "in Joan of Arc's country" as it appears in the following sentence discussing Dame Dubarry: "What a course was thine: from that first truckle-bed (in Joan of Arc's country) where thy mother bore thee, with tears, to an unnamed father."

23.24–27: This page bears a marginal line where Carlyle describes the aristocracy's forgetting that their lives are in danger. The marginal line begins with "but a word mispronounced" and continues through the next sentence: "The new Louis with his Court is rolling towards Choisy, through the summer afternoon: the royal tears still flow; but a word mis-pronounced by Monseigneur d'Artois sets them all laughing, and they weep no more. Light mortals, how ye walk your light life-minuet, over bottomless abysses, divided from you by a film!"

Volume 1, Book 2, "The Paper Age"; Chapter 3, "Questionable"

35.22–24: Next to these lines there is a marginal line and the note "see page 56." following this sentence: "It will accumulate: moreover, it will reach a head; for the first of all Gospels is this, that a Lie cannot endure forever."

Volume 1, Book 2, "The Paper Age"; Chapter 8, "Printed Paper"

56.8–9: This page contains a marginal line with the comment "See—page 35" next to Carlyle's statement: "All this (for be sure no falsehood perishes, but is as a seed sown out to grow) has been storing itself for thousands of years; and now the account-day has come."

Volume 1, Book 6, "Consolidation"; Chapter 3, "The General Overturn"

216: Twain struck through the *u* and wrote an *n* in the margin to correct the misprint of *month* in the phrase, "Some twenty mouths of heroic travail."

225.1: Twain canceled through the *w* of *two* and wrote *o* off to the side but then seems to have realized that Carlyle was correct after all and scribbled out his own writing, leaving the line "National Guards are un-skillful and of doubtful purpose; Soldiers are inclined to mutiny: there is danger that they two may quarrel, danger that they may *agree*."

Volume 1, Book 7, "The Insurrection of Women"; Chapter 2, "O Richard, O My King!"

241: There are no marks on this page, but it has been bent over. The page begins as follows: "For indeed self-preservation being such a law of Nature, what can a rallied Court do, but attempt and endeavor, or call it *plot*,—with such wisdom and unwisdom as it has?" The page ends with *Noncommissioned*, as it appears in the sentence "Further, as such Dinner may be rather extensive, and even the Noncommissioned and the Common man be introduced, to see and to hear, could not his Majesty's Opera Apartment, which has lain quite silent ever since Kaiser Joseph was here, be obtained for the purpose?"

Volume 1, Book 7, "The Insurrection of Women"; Chapter 10, "The Grand Entries"

274–75: A piece of newspaper marks and has shadowed these pages amid Carlyle's discussion of mobs arriving at Versailles. Page 274 begins with the line "Now too Lafayette, suddenly roused, not from sleep (for his eyes had not yet closed), arrives; with passionate popular eloquence, with prompt military word of command." Page 275 ends with the end of the first paragraph of chapter 11, "From Versailles."

Volume 1, Book 8, "The Feast of Pikes"; Chapter 6, "Je Le Jure"

315.1–11: This page bears a marginal line along the first paragraph of the chapter:

> With these signs of the times, is it not surprising that the dominant feeling all over France was still continually Hope? O blessed Hope, sole boon of man: whereby, on his strait prison-walls, are painted beautiful far-stretching landscapes; and into the night of very Death is shed holiest dawn! Thou art to all an indefeasible possession in this God's-world; to the wise a sacred Constantine's-banner, written on the eternal skies; under which they *shall* conquer, for the battle itself is victory: to the foolish some secular *mirage,* or shadow of still waters, painted on the parched Earth; whereby at least their dusty pilgrimage, if devious, becomes cheerfuler, becomes possible.

Volume 1, Book 8, "The Feast of Pikes"; Chapter 12, "Sound and Smoke"

347: Discussing kingship, Carlyle uses the metaphor of marriage in the last paragraph of the chapter: "Shall we say, then, the French Nation has led Royalty, or wooed and teased poor Royalty to lead *her,* to the hymeneal Fatherland's Altar, in such over-sweet manner; and has, most thoughtlessly, to celebrate the nuptials with due shine and demonstration,—burnt her bed?" Twain counters tersely: "The simile is false. The king broke <u>his</u> oath <u>while he took it.</u>"

Volume 1, Book 9, "Nanci"; Chapter 6, "Bouille at Nanci"

375: At the bottom of the page Twain, or someone else, has marked out Twain's comment that "He didn't lose the diamond here, but at [indecipherable word] two years earlier." Both the writing and the excision are in black pencil and appear next to this line in Carlyle's book: "Could tumult awaken the old Dead, Burgundian Charles the Bold might stir from under that Rotunda of his: never since he, raging, sank in the ditches, and lost Life and Diamond, was such a noise heard here."

Volume 1, Book 10, "The Tuileries"; Chapter 4, "To Fly or Not to Fly"

400.1: To correct a printer's error, Twain struck *m* in *Perpignam,* substituting *n.*

402.16–20: A marginal line runs alongside Carlyle's discussion of the origin of the term *sansculotte:* "There they fan one another into high loyal glow; drink, in such wine as can be procured, confusion to Sansculottism; show purchased dirks, of an improved structure, made to order; and, greatly daring, dine."

Volume 1, Book 10, "The Tuileries"; Chapter 6, "Mirabeau"

417.14: At the end of the chapter a wishful Carlyle muses, "Had Mirabeau lived one other year!" Under this Twain wrote, "How glad the world should be that he didn't."

Volume 2, Book 1, "Parliament First"; Chapter 4, "No Sugar"

27: This page is folded over, and although it bears no marks, it features the question, "how shall literary men do without coffee?" How, indeed?

Volume 2, Book 4, "Regicide"; Chapter 8, "Place de la Revolution"

215: No markings are visible on this page, but the corner has been turned down. The page begins with the phrase "at one in the morning" in the following sentence: "The voter Lepelletier lies dead; he has expired in great pain, at one in the morning;—two hours before that Vote of *No Delay* was fully summed up." The page ends with the words "impressively to the" in the sentence "A King dying by such violence appeals impressively to the imagination; as the like must do, and ought to do." Twain may have bent the page because of Carlyle's comment, "curses and falsehoods do verily return 'always *home*,' wide as they may wander." Twain marked two similar statements on pages 35 and 56 in book 2 of volume 1.

Volume 2, Book 8, "Thermidor"; Chapter 5, "The Prisons"

378.31–32: A marginal line tags this section treating terror in the prisons: "Rigor grows, stiffens into horrid tyranny; Plot in the Prison getting ever rifer."

Volume 2, Book 9, "Vendemiaire"; Chapter 8, "Finis"

429–30: At the end of the book, immediately following the last line, Twain wrote an extended criticism of Carlyle's work that spilled over onto the following page:

Finish Sept. 10th .88

This is a picture of the French Revolution, but in only a limited way, [scratched-out word] a history of it. It is as if one gave you a picture [scratched out a word] of God manufacturing by tedious & long processes, Hair, Bones, Flesh, Nails, Nerves, Muscles, Tendons, & piling them in separate piles, & adding a bucket of Blood—& stopping there: with the [scratched out word] remark, "Such was the process of the Creation of Man." Now what use were that, except he set up man & let us look at him & see if he was better or worse than this chaos & rubbish he was made out of?

The Revolution had a result—a superb, a stupendous, a most noble & sublime result—to wit, French Liberty, & in a degree, Human Liberty—& was worth a million times what it cost, of blood, & terror, & various suffering, & titanic labor. And this fair & shapely creation was not worth Carlyle's pains to paint. Nothing but the Process interested him—the Result was matter of indifference. He should have given a chapter showing what the French laws were, before the Revolution, & what they were when the Revolution's work was finished.

Notes

1. FOLLOWING THE "COMPASS OF FACT": RETHINKING MARK TWAIN'S COMPOSING PROCESS

1. Twain's recollection of the incident is from *Mark Twain's Notebooks & Journals, Volume 3: 1883–1891*, 79. Cable is quoted in Arlin Turner, pp. 134–35. One specialized study of some interest is Robert Allen Alexander's analysis in his unpublished dissertation of Cable's "influence on the evolution" of *Connecticut Yankee* (51). A short time after the incident in the bookstore, Twain and Cable sent this telegram, dated February 3, 1885:

> To O.W. Pond
> Plankinton House
>
> Milwaukee:
>
> Now wit you well, Sir Sagramore, thou good knight and gentle, that there be two that right wonderly do love thee, grieving passing sore and making great dole at thy heavy travail. And we will well that thou prosper at the hand of the leech, and come lightly forth of thy hurts, and be as thou were tofore.
>
> Sir Mark Twain. Sir Geo. W. Cable. (quoted in Turner 96)

2. For Mark Twain's debt to Malory see R. H. Wilson, "Malory in the *Connecticut Yankee*," *Texas Studies* 27 (1948): 185–205. In his essay "'The Master Hand of Old Malory': Mark Twain's Acquaintance with *Le Morte D'Arthur*," Alan Gribben examines the question of Twain's first experience with Malory and shows that Twain was already familiar with *Morte D'Arthur* by the time he toured with Cable. See also Howard Baetzhold, *Mark Twain and John Bull: The British Connection* (Bloomington: Indiana University Press, 1970), 133.

Howard Baetzhold establishes the time frame for Twain's composition of the book in "The Course of Composition of *A Connecticut Yankee*: A Reinterpretation," *American*

Literature 33 (1961): 195–214. Except where I qualify this chronology, it is the time frame I use throughout this study. According to Baetzhold's chronology, chapters 1–3 were written between December 1885 and March 1886; chapters 4–9 and 11–19 were written between early July 1887 and August 15, 1887; chapter 20 and the first paragraph of chapter 21 were written before July 1888; chapters 10 and 21–36 were written between early July and October 1, 1888; chapters 37–42 were written from October 1–5, 1888, and the book was completed by May 1889.

3. See the essay "Howells' 'Most Unliterary' Friend" in *Mark Twain's Library: A Reconstruction* (1:xvii). Gribben's criticism of Paine appears in the article "'I Detest Novels, Poetry & Theology': Origin of a Fiction Concerning Mark Twain's Reading," *Tennessee Studies in Literature* 22 (1977): 154–61. There are a number of pioneers in the field of Twain's reading: Henry A. Pochmann, "The Mind of Mark Twain" (master's thesis, University of Texas, Austin, 1924); Harold Aspiz, "Mark Twain's Reading: A Critical Study" (Ph.D. diss., University of California, Los Angeles, 1950); and Franklin L. Jensen, "Mark Twain's Comments on Books and Authors," *Emporia State Research Studies* 12 (1964): 5–53. Walter Blair, too, asserts that "Nothing could be more inaccurate than the popular belief that the humorist was a simple homespun philosopher all of whose insights came down from natural-born wit and experience rather than from book learning. Actually he ranged avidly and widely through literature of many sorts, constantly garnering material. He read enough French, English, and American history to become a really impressive (though opinionated) specialist in certain periods" (*MT&HF* 13).

4. Readers interested in the contentious exchange between Robinson and Wonham might wish to read letters to the editor published after the appearance of Robinson's article. See "Commentary," *Nineteenth-Century Literature* 51 (1996): 137–41. Susan Gillman similarly subordinates conscious artistry to subconscious motivation in her book *Dark Twins*. Her examination of Twain's aesthetic commentary becomes a search for metaphors expressing subconscious motivations. Pamela Boker's reading of Twain is more positive, but she similarly identifies the "return of the repressed" in Twain's fiction as his creative source (164). Years ago, Toby Tanner pointed out, apparently to no avail, that even with characters like Aunt Rachel in "A True Story," it was Twain who "managed to simulate and re-create the speech" so that "just as he intended, we feel that the story is actually her work" (136). This illusion is of crucial concern for realistic fiction, but although "real incidents . . . may make a story" as Boris Tomashevsky observes, the work remains always "wholly an artistic creation" (68).

5. This comment was written to an unknown correspondent, perhaps in 1891, according to Paine (*MTLAP* 2:543).

6. See especially Alan Gribben, "'Stolen from Books, Tho' Credit Given': Mark Twain's Use of Literary Sources," and Minnie Brashear's chapter, "Sam Clemens's Reading," in *Mark Twain: Son of Missouri*, pp. 196–224. For Twain's sources for *Life on the Mississippi* and *Adventures of Huckleberry Finn* see Horst Kruse's reasoned discussion in "Gerstaecker's *The Pirates of the Mississippi* and Mark Twain's *Adventures of Huckleberry Finn*," *American Literary Realism* 31 (1999): 1–14.

7. According to the note in *MTN&J* (3:134), the passage was written in early November 1887. In fact, the *Princeton Review* draft has been ignored by nearly everyone. Cindy

Weinstein's claim that the "notebooks Mark Twain composed during the years 1884–90 read more like the memos of an entrepreneur and budding engineer than of a writer of literature" is typical (147).

8. Keats to John Taylor, February 27, 1818, in *English Romantic Writers*, ed. David Perkins (New York: Harcourt, Brace and World, 1967), 1212.

9. William Dean Howells, "Editor's Study," *Harper's New Monthly Magazine*, April 1887, 825–26.

10. The phrase "local particularism" is from Erich Auerbach, *Mimesis*, 425. René Wellek discusses the "objective representation of contemporary social reality" in *Concepts of Criticism*, 240–41. See chapter 4 of Lilian Furst's *All Is True*, pp. 73–94. Twain's phrase "standard work" is from a letter dated November 27, 1871 (*LLMT* 166). Compare Twain's practice to that of the English realists, who, according to Lennard Davis, sought to produce "a factual fiction" (212).

11. See Howard Baetzhold's discussion of "realisation" in *Mark Twain and John Bull*, 59–61, and also my discussion of this in *Mark Twain's Ethical Realism*, 16–18 and 88–117.

12. For a discussion of the particulars see Gretchen Sharlow's "'Love to All the Jolly Household': A Study of The Cranes of Quarry Farm, Their Lives, and Their Relationship with Mark Twain" (master's thesis, Elmira College, 1991).

13. See Lorraine Lanmon's "Quarry Farm: A Study of the 'Picturesque'" for a thorough discussion of "Ellerslie" and other architectural elements of the farm.

14. George Parsons Lathrop's interview with Twain appeared in the *Hartford Daily Current* and is included in Susy Clemens's biography of her father, *Papa*, pp. 161–64. Jeffrey Steinbrink, too, contrasts the environment of Buffalo to that of Elmira, noting the "invigorating explosion of work at Quarry Farm" (173).

15. Edwin J. Park, "A Day with Mark Twain," *Chicago Tribune*, September 19, 1886, p. 12. (Reprinted in *Interviews with Samuel L. Clemens 1874–1910*, ed. Louis J. Budd [Arlington, Tex.: American Literary Realism, 1977], 41–43.)

16. Quoted in Rufus Rockwell Wilson and Otilie Erikson Wilson, "Mark Twain's Days in Elmira," in *New York in Literature* (Elmira, N.Y.: Primavera Press, 1947), 336–50; reprinted in *Mark Twain in Elmira*, ed. Robert D. Jerome and Herbert A. Wisbey Jr. (Elmira, N.Y.: Mark Twain Society, 1977), 3–15.

17. See the entry under William Lecky in Gribben, *Mark Twain's Library*, 1:400–403.

18. Park, "A Day," p. 12.

19. The draft prefaces Twain wrote for the book are included in appendix C of the University of California Press edition of *Connecticut Yankee*, pp. 516–18.

20. Louis J. Budd observes mordantly, "Ignoring the dates of his facts from Twain's favorite historians, bitterly disappointed Hank accused the church of not only failing to oppose slavery but spreading a slave mentality" (*Social Philosopher* 128).

21. See also James D. Williams, "Revision and Intention in Mark Twain's *A Connecticut Yankee*." Ronald Johnson, for example, situates the novel in its "contemporary" context, although by no means its historical context as I have described it. He reads the novel as one of the "artifacts of a specific period in American culture, a time of growing discord in the United States, particularly seen in the intensifying battle between industrial owners and workers" (74). Similar views are expressed by Martha Banta, Forrest Robinson

(*In Bad Faith*), John Carlos Rowe, and Jane Gardiner. Gardiner discusses the "general confusion and disorientation" suffered by society and by Twain (455). Peter Messent believes that "the cultural analysis and criticism in Twain's work can easily be missed by the reader. It is quite possible, as I argue in my chapter on *A Connecticut Yankee in King Arthur's Court* (1889), that he missed it, too" (19).

22. Like Kim Moreland, Lawrence Howe derides "Hume, Macaulay, Lecky, and Taine, who postulated that history was a continuous march of progress" (119).

23. Many critics cite Twain's inner conflicts as the source of conflicts within the novel. See Baetzhold, *MT&JB*, p. 131, and Justin Kaplan's comment that "Hank Morgan is Mark Twain" (297). Judith Fetterley, too, sees the book as offering Twain "the opportunity for indulging in a fantasy of omnipotence" (667), and James Cox sees the violence of the ending as "symbolically a crippling of the inventive imagination, as if Mark Twain were driven to maim himself in an effort to survive" (210). Cindy Weinstein's explanation that the "seemingly random episodes of violence" in *Connecticut Yankee* are due to an ideology demanding that "texts should not only erase the signs of labor . . . but must also figure the erasure of themselves" (131) is deceptively complex.

24. See appendix C of the University of California Press edition of *Connecticut Yankee*, pp. 516–18. Twain voiced similar sentiments a short time later in his speech "On Foreign Critics," in which he asked the question, "How old is real civilization?" (942).

25. See Alan Gribben's essay, "The Dispersal of Samuel L. Clemens' Library Books" for the full, horrifying story.

2. TWAIN'S "CLOUD OF WITNESSES": THE 1885 AND 1887 MARGINALIA IN LECKY'S *SPIRIT OF RATIONALISM*

1. For a description of the marginalia see Mary Boewe's "Twain on Lecky: Some Marginalia at Quarry Farm," *Mark Twain Society Bulletin* 8 (1985): 1–6.

2. See Mark Twain, *Mark Twain's Notebooks & Journals, Volume 3:1883–1891*, ed. Robert Pack Browning, Michael Frank, and Lin Salamo (Berkeley: University of California Press, 1979), 125. Mary Boewe confirms the date of the purple marginalia in Lecky's *Spirit of Rationalism* in "Twain on Lecky: Some Marginalia at Quarry Farm."

3. For a fascinating account of Twain's idea for the book at a very early stage see Howard Baetzhold's "'The Autobiography of Sir Robert Smith of Camelot': Mark Twain's Original Plan for *A Connecticut Yankee*," *American Literature* 32 (1961): 456–61.

4. See also David L. Newquist's "Mark Twain among the Indians" and James McNutt's "Mark Twain and the American Indian: Earthly Realism and Heavenly Idealism." In chapter 20 of his book *Fatal Environment* Richard Slotkin analyzes the "multi-layered satire" (516) of *Connecticut Yankee*, discussing in particular Twain's relationship to frontier ideology. There are several fine studies of the use of Americanisms in *Connecticut Yankee*: Dennis Berthold, "The Conflict of Dialects in *A Connecticut Yankee*" and Allen Guttmann's "Mark Twain's Connecticut Yankee: Affirmation of the Vernacular Tradition?" are particularly valuable. Deborah Wyrick's "Hank Morgan: Linguistic Entrepreneur" and Thomas Zlatic's "Language Technologies in *A Connecticut Yankee*" are also worth reading. Americanisms are at the heart of many such interpretations, but just as

significant as how Hank's language reveals his character is the way the conflict of dialects keeps ever before the reader the fact of historical change.

5. The excised passage is recorded in "Emendations of the Copy-Text," *A Connecticut Yankee in King Arthur's Court*, ed. Bernard L. Stein (Berkeley: University of California Press, 1979), 669.

6. Readers may wish to consult Stanley Brodwin's excellent essay, "Mark Twain's Theology: The Gods of a Brevet Presbyterian," *The Cambridge Companion to Mark Twain*, ed. Forrest Robinson (New York: Cambridge University Press, 1995), 220–48. A popular but worthwhile article is Jeff Garrison's "Mark Twain, 'A Dusty Christian,'" *Presbyterians Today* 87 (July/August 1997): 17–19.

7. Rodney O. Rogers, "Twain, Taine, and Lecky: The Genesis of a Passage in *A Connecticut Yankee*," *Modern Language Quarterly* 34 (1973): 436–47. Stephen Biko is quoted in *Black Consciousness in South Africa*, ed. Millard Arnold (New York: Vintage, 1979), xx.

3. MACAULAY'S "STATELY SENTENCES": TWAIN'S 1885 AND 1887 MARGINALIA IN *THE HISTORY OF ENGLAND*

1. Alan Gribben identifies the editions of Macaulay's *History of England* owned by Twain's family: Livy's copy, the two sets donated by Twain, and a fourth set that Twain ordered from a bookseller. See *Mark Twain's Library*, 1:435–36. The passage excised from *Following the Equator* is quoted in Gribben, *Mark Twain's Library*, 1:436.

2. Marginalia in one of Twain's copies is reported in Chester L. Davis, "Mark Twain's Marginal Notes on Macaulay," *Twainian* 10 (July–August 1951): 1–2.

3. Although Macaulay remained one of Twain's favorite authors, he was not exempt from even more strident criticism: "So far as I know, only one author has ever made a memorable speech before a lawmaking body in the interest of his trade—that was Macaulay. I think his speech is called great to this day by both authors and publishers; whereas the speech is so exhaustingly ignorant of its subject and so trivial and jejune in its reasonings that to the person who has been both author and publisher it ranks as another and formidable evidence, and possibly even proof, that in discarding the monkey and substituting man, our Father in Heaven did the monkey an undeserved injustice." *The Autobiography of Mark Twain*, ed. Charles Neider (New York: Harper, 1959; reprint, New York: HarperPerennial, 1990), 280 (page citations are to the 1990 edition). Occasional passages in *Connecticut Yankee* present individual Catholics in a favorable light even as the Church itself is condemned vigorously. In contrast, Twain portrays Father John in *The Prince and the Pauper* as a good man in a noble profession. One feels some empathy even for the "mad hermit" of chapters 20 and 21.

4. Park, "A Day," 41–43.

5. Information regarding Twain's response to Arnold is from Baetzhold, *Mark Twain and John Bull*, 110–19. See also John Hoben's discussion in "Mark Twain's *A Connecticut Yankee*: A Genetic Study," *American Literature* 18 (1946): 197–218. Hoben discusses Arnold as a productive irritant for Twain, but his chronology has been superseded by Baetzhold's. See the "Alterations in the Manuscript" section of the University of California Press edition of *Connecticut Yankee*, p. 737.

6. See the entry for page 196, line 8 in the "Emendations of the Copy-Text" section of the University of California Press edition of *Connecticut Yankee*, p. 667.

7. James D. Williams, "The Uses of History in Mark Twain's *A Connecticut Yankee*," 104.

8. Quoted in Gribben, *Mark Twain's Library*, 1:436.

9. Gribben, *Mark Twain's Library*, 2:712. For Twain's comments on Macaulay see *MTN&J*, 3:142–44. See also Chester L. Davis, "Twain's Marginal Notes," 1–2.

10. Regrettably, the Langdon mansion no longer exists. Despite some attempts to preserve the building, it was razed in 1939. See George Winner's "The Decline and Fall of the Langdon Home," *Mark Twain in Elmira*, 28–35. The books in the Langdon library have been scattered, although Elmira College does have an extensive collection of them.

4. "THE MEN OF OLD IDEAS MUST DIE OFF": MARK TWAIN AND LECKY'S *ENGLAND IN THE EIGHTEENTH CENTURY*

1. A piece of a letter sent to Twain by Elise Rathbone and used by him as a bookmark in the fifth volume of Lecky's work is dated September 1, 1887. Twain doubtless paged through the volumes even before giving them to Theodore Crane, and he may even have read part of the fifth volume, leaving the bookmark as evidence; one hopes that even Twain would have had some compunction about inscribing extensive scholia in a gift book, at least prior to its presentation.

2. See the "Alterations in the Manuscript" section of the University of California Press edition of *Connecticut Yankee*, p. 734.

3. See Baetzhold, "Course of Composition," 204.

4. Lecky got much of his information about English law and the prison system from John Howard's *The State of the Prisons in England and Wales* and from Blackstone's *Commentary*. Twain may have consulted those sources directly at some point, as he left himself these notes: "Book 4, ch 27, Blackstone. Read it." and "Get Howard's 'State Prisons'" (*MTN&J* 3:423).

5. See especially Twain's marginalia in Lecky (2:9, 42; 6:231, 232, 233, 234, 236, 237, 240, 243).

6. The draft prefaces Twain wrote for the book are included in appendix C of the University of California Press edition of *Connecticut Yankee*, pp. 516–18.

5. THOMAS CARLYLE'S "BUCKET OF BLOOD": TWAIN'S REREADING OF *THE FRENCH REVOLUTION*

1. For a discussion of Twain's reading of Carlyle see Gribben, *Mark Twain's Library*, 1:128–29. The edition of Carlyle I discuss in this chapter is not the edition Shelley Fisher Fishkin describes finding at Quarry Farm with a "shiver of excitement" (*Lighting Out* 79). That edition contains markings but no written comments and belonged in all probability to Ida Langdon, niece of Mark Twain and an English professor at Elmira College.

2. For a description of the manuscript at this point see the "Alterations in the Manuscript" section of the University of California Press edition of *Connecticut Yankee*, p. 733.

3. See Baetzhold, "Course of Composition," 204. For the canceled passage about a "peaceful" revolution see the "Alterations in the Manuscript" section of the University of California Press edition of *Connecticut Yankee*, p. 734.

4. For details of the stroke and its effect on *Connecticut Yankee* see Gretchen Sharlow, "Theodore Crane: A New Perspective," *Mark Twain Society Bulletin* 13 (1990): 1–5. Sharlow details how Theodore Crane's suicidal thoughts as he languished for months after the stroke contributed to the deathbed scene of *Connecticut Yankee*.

5. See the "Alterations in the Manuscript" section of the University of California Press edition of *Connecticut Yankee*, p. 821.

CONCLUSION

1. See Henry Nash Smith's introduction to the University of California Press edition of *Connecticut Yankee*, pp. 14–15.

2. See also Howard Baetzhold, "Backgrounds of 'The Autobiography of Belshazzar,'" *Mark Twain Society Bulletin* 9 (1986): 1–4.

Bibliography

Alexander, Robert Allen. "Twain and Cable, Twins of Genius: The Origins and Evolution of *A Connecticut Yankee in King Arthur's Court* and *Bonaventure*. Ph.D. diss., Flor-
ida State University, 1997.

Althusser, Louis. "Ideology and Ideological State Apparatuses (Notes towards an Investigation)." In *"Lenin and Philosophy" and Other Essays,* trans. Ben Brewster, 127–86.
New York: Monthly Review, 1971.

Andrews, Kenneth R. *Nook Farm: Mark Twain's Hartford Circle.* Seattle: University of
Washington Press, 1969.

Aristotle. *Physics.* Trans. Robin Waterfield. New York: Oxford University Press, 1996.

———. *Poetics.* In *Introduction to Aristotle,* trans. Ingram Bywater, ed. Richard McKeon,
624–67. New York: Modern Library, 1947.

Arnold, Millard, ed. *Black Consciousness in South Africa.* New York: Vintage, 1979.

Aspiz, Harold. "Lecky's Influence on Mark Twain." *Science and Society* 26 (1962): 15–25.

———. "Mark Twain's Reading: A Critical Study," Ph.D. diss., University of California,
Los Angeles, 1950.

Auerbach, Erich. *Mimesis: The Representation of Reality in Western Literature.* Trans.
Willard Trask. Princeton, N.J.: Princeton University Press, 1953.

Baetzhold, Howard G. "'The Autobiography of Sir Robert Smith of Camelot': Mark
Twain's Original Plan for *A Connecticut Yankee.*" *American Literature* 33 (1961): 456–61.

———. "Backgrounds of 'The Autobiography of Belshazzar.'" *Mark Twain Society Bulletin* 9 (1986): 1–4.

———. "The Course of Composition of *A Connecticut Yankee:* A Reinterpretation."
American Literature 33 (1961): 195–214.

———. *Mark Twain and John Bull: The British Connection.* Bloomington: Indiana University Press, 1970.

———. "'Well, My Book Is Written—Let It Go. . . .': The Making of *A Connecticut
Yankee in King Arthur's Court.*" In *Biographies of Books: The Compositional Histories of*

Notable American Writings, ed. James Barbour and Tom Quirk, 41–77. Columbia: University of Missouri Press, 1996.

Bakhtin, Mikhail. "The *Bildungsroman* and Its Significance in the History of Realism (Toward a Historical Typology of the Novel)." In *Speech Genres and Other Late Essays,* trans. Vern W. McGee, ed. Caryl Emerson and Michael Holquist, 10–59. Austin: University of Texas Press, 1986.

Banta, Martha. "The Boys and the Bosses: Mark Twain's Double Take on Work, Play, and the Democratic Ideal." *American Literary History* 3 (1991): 487–520.

Bell, Michael Davitt. *The Problem of American Realism: Studies in the Cultural History of a Literary Idea.* Chicago: University of Chicago Press, 1993.

Berthoff, Warner. *The Ferment of Realism: American Literature, 1884–1919.* New York: Free Press, 1965.

Berthold, Dennis. "The Conflict of Dialects in *A Connecticut Yankee.*" *Forum* 18 (1977): 51–58.

Blair, Walter. *Mark Twain and Huck Finn.* Berkeley: University of California Press, 1960.

Blake, William. "London." In *English Romantic Writers,* ed. David Perkins, 63–64. New York: Harcourt, Brace and World, 1967.

Boewe, Mary. "Morgan vs. Merlin: The Case for Magic and Miracle in *A Connecticut Yankee in King Arthur's Court.*" *Quarry Farm Papers* 4 (1994): 29–39.

———. "Twain on Lecky: Some Marginalia at Quarry Farm." *Mark Twain Society Bulletin* 8 (1985): 1–6.

Boker, Pamela A. *The Grief Taboo in American Literature: Loss and Prolonged Adolescence in Twain, Melville, and Hemingway.* New York: New York University Press, 1996.

Branch, Edgar M. *Mark Twain and the Starchy Boys.* Elmira, N.Y.: Elmira College Center for Mark Twain Studies at Quarry Farm, 1992.

Brashear, Minnie. *Mark Twain: Son of Missouri.* Chapel Hill: University of North Carolina Press, 1934.

Briden, Earl F. "Through a Glass Eye, Darkly: *The Skeptic Design of Life on the Mississippi.*" *Mississippi Quarterly* 48 (1995): 225–37.

Bridgman, Richard. *Traveling in Mark Twain.* Berkeley: University of California Press, 1987.

Brodwin, Stanley. "Mark Twain's Theology: The Gods of a Brevet Presbyterian." In *The Cambridge Companion to Mark Twain,* ed. Forrest Robinson, 220–48. New York: Cambridge University Press, 1995.

Budd, Louis J., ed. *Interviews with Samuel L. Clemens 1874–1910.* Arlington, Tex.: American Literary Realism, 1977.

———. *Mark Twain: Social Philosopher.* Bloomington: Indiana University Press, 1962.

Burke, Kenneth. *A Grammar of Motives.* Berkeley: University of California Press, 1974.

Cady, Edwin H. *The Light of Common Day: Realism in American Fiction.* Bloomington: Indiana University Press, 1976.

Camfield, Gregg. *Sentimental Twain: Samuel Clemens in the Maze of Moral Philosophy.* Philadelphia: University of Pennsylvania Press, 1994.

Cardwell, Guy. *The Man Who Was Mark Twain: Images and Ideologies.* New Haven: Yale University Press, 1991.

Carlyle, Thomas. *The French Revolution.* 2 vols. New York: Harper and Brothers, n.d.

———. "On History." In *The Works of Thomas Carlyle.* Vol. 14. New York: Collier, 1897.

Carter, Everett. "The Meaning of *A Connecticut Yankee.*" *American Literature* 50 (1978): 418–40.

Chandler, Raymond. "Introduction." In *Trouble Is My Business.* New York: Vintage, 1988.

Chase, Richard. *The American Novel and Its Tradition.* New York: Doubleday, 1957.

Clark, Charles H. "Mark Twain at 'Nook Farm' (Hartford) and Elmira." *Critic* 6 (January 17, 1885): 25–26. Reprinted in *Critical Essays on Mark Twain, 1867–1910,* ed. Louis J. Budd, 76–80. Boston: G. K. Hall, 1982.

Clemens, Clara. *My Father Mark Twain.* New York: Harper, 1931.

Clemens, Susy. *Papa, an Intimate Biography of Mark Twain.* Ed. Charles Neider. New York: Doubleday, 1985.

Cook, Nancy. "Finding His Mark: Twain's *The Innocents Abroad* as a Subscription Book." In *Reading Books: Essays on the Material Text and Literature in America,* ed. Michelle Moylan and Lane Stiles, 151–78. Amherst: University of Massachusetts Press, 1996.

Cox, James M. *Mark Twain: The Fate of Humor.* Princeton, N.J.: Princeton University Press, 1966.

Cummings, Sherwood. *Mark Twain and Science: Adventures of a Mind.* Baton Rouge: Louisiana State University Press, 1988.

Daugherty, Sarah B. "William Dean Howells and Mark Twain: The Realism War as a Campaign That Failed." *American Literary Realism* 29 (1996): 12–28.

Davis, Chester L. "Mark Twain's Marginal Notes on Macaulay." *Twainian* 10 (July/August 1951): 1–2.

Davis, Lennard J. *Factual Fictions: The Origins of the English Novel.* Philadelphia: University of Pennsylvania Press, 1996.

Dewey, John. *Art as Experience.* New York: Perigee, 1980.

Dickinson, Leon T. "The Sources of *Prince and the Pauper.*" *Modern Language Notes* 64 (1949): 103–6.

Doody, Margaret Anne. *The True Story of the Novel.* New Brunswick, N.J.: Rutgers University Press, 1996.

Doyno, Victor A. *Writing Huck Finn: Mark Twain's Creative Process.* Philadelphia: University of Pennsylvania Press, 1991.

Emerson, Everett. *The Authentic Mark Twain: A Literary Biography of Samuel L. Clemens.* Philadelphia: University of Pennsylvania Press, 1984.

Ensor, Allison. "Mark Twain's 'Dream of a Knight-Errant': The Origin and Development of *A Connecticut Yankee in King Arthur's Court.*" *Tennessee Philological Bulletin* 15 (1978): 5–16.

Fetterley, Judith. "Yankee Showman and Reformer: The Character of Mark Twain's Hank Morgan." *Texas Studies* 14 (1973): 667–79.

Fishkin, Shelley Fisher. *Lighting Out for the Territory: Reflections on Mark Twain and American Culture.* New York: Oxford University Press, 1997.

———. *Was Huck Black? Mark Twain and African-American Voices.* New York: Oxford University Press, 1993.

Fleishman, Avrom. *The English Historical Novel: Walter Scott to Virginia Woolf.* Baltimore: Johns Hopkins University Press, 1971.

Foley, Barbara. *Telling the Truth: The Theory and Practice of Documentary Fiction.* Ithaca: Cornell University Press, 1986.

Foner, Philip S. *Mark Twain: Social Critic.* New York: International Publishers, 1958.

Forster, E. M. *Aspects of the Novel.* New York: Harcourt, Brace and World, 1927.

Foucault, Michel. "Nietzsche, Genealogy, History." In *The Foucault Reader,* ed. Paul Rabinow, 76–100. New York: Pantheon, 1984.

Fulton, Joe B. *Mark Twain's Ethical Realism: The Aesthetics of Race, Class, and Gender.* Columbia: University of Missouri Press, 1997.

——. "Thomas Carlyle's 'Bucket of Blood': New Mark Twain Marginalia in *The French Revolution.*" *American Literary Realism* 29 (1997): 49–63.

Furst, Lilian. *All Is True: The Claims and Strategies of Realist Fiction.* Durham: Duke University Press, 1995.

——. *Realism.* London: Longman, 1992.

Gardiner, Jane. "'A More Splendid Necromancy': Mark Twain's *Connecticut Yankee* and the Electrical Revolution." *Studies in the Novel* 19 (1987): 448–58.

Garrison, Jeff. "Mark Twain, 'A Dusty Christian,'" *Presbyterians Today* 87 (July/August 1997): 17–19.

Gillman, Susan. *Dark Twins: Imposture and Identity in Mark Twain's America.* Chicago: University of Chicago Press, 1989.

Girgus, Sam B. "Conscience in Connecticut: *Civilization and Its Discontents* in Twain's Camelot." *New England Quarterly* 51 (1978): 547–60.

Glazener, Nancy. *Reading for Realism: The History of a U.S. Literary Institution, 1850–1910.* Durham: Duke University Press, 1997.

Gribben, Alan. "The Dispersal of Samuel L. Clemens' Library Books." *Resources for American Literary Study* 5 (1975): 147–65.

——. "The Formation of Samuel L. Clemens' Library." *Studies in American Humor* 2 (1976): 171–82.

——. "Good Books and a Sleepy Conscience: Mark Twain's Reading Habits." *American Literary Realism* 9 (1976): 294–306.

——. "Howells' 'Most Unliterary' Friend." In *Mark Twain's Library: A Reconstruction.* Vol. 1. Boston: G. K. Hall, 1980.

——. "'I Detest Novels, Poetry & Theology': Origin of a Fiction Concerning Mark Twain's Reading." *Tennessee Studies in Literature* 22 (1977): 154–61.

——. *Mark Twain's Library: A Reconstruction.* 2 vols. Boston: G. K. Hall, 1980.

——. "'The Master Hand of Old Malory': Mark Twain's Acquaintance with *Le Morte D'Arthur.*" *English Language Notes* 16 (1978): 32–40.

——. "'Stolen from Books, Tho' Credit Given': Mark Twain's Use of Literary Sources." *Mosaic* 12 (1979): 149–55.

Griffith, Clark. *Achilles and the Tortoise: Mark Twain's Fictions.* Tuscaloosa: University of Alabama Press, 1998.

Guttmann, Allen. "Mark Twain's Connecticut Yankee: Affirmation of the Vernacular Tradition?" *New England Quarterly* 3 (1960): 232–37.

Hansen, Chadwick. "The Once and Future Boss: Mark Twain's Yankee." *Nineteenth-Century Fiction* 28 (1973): 62–73.

Harris, Susan K. *The Courtship of Olivia Langdon and Mark Twain.* Cambridge: Cambridge University Press, 1996.

———. *Mark Twain's Escape from Time: A Study of Patterns and Images.* Columbia: University of Missouri Press, 1982.

Hegel, G. W. F. *Reason in History: A General Introduction to the Philosophy of History.* Trans. Robert Hartman. New York: Bobbs-Merrill, 1953.

Herman, Luc. *Concepts of Realism.* Columbus, S.C.: Camden House, 1996.

Hill, Hamlin. "Mark Twain: Audience and Artistry." *American Quarterly* 16 (1963): 25–40.

Hoben, John. "Mark Twain's *A Connecticut Yankee:* A Genetic Study." *American Literature* 18 (1946): 197–218.

Holub, Robert C. *Reflections of Realism: Paradox, Norm, and Ideology in Nineteenth-Century German Prose.* Detroit: Wayne State University Press, 1991.

Horn, Jason. *Mark Twain and William James. Crafting a Free Self.* Columbia: University of Missouri Press, 1996.

Howe, Lawrence. *Mark Twain and the Novel: The Double-Cross of Authority.* New York: Cambridge University Press, 1998.

Howells, William Dean. "Editor's Study." *Harper's New Monthly Magazine,* Apr. 1887, 824–29.

———. "Editor's Study." *Harper's New Monthly Magazine,* Nov. 1889, 962–67.

———. "Editor's Study." *Harper's New Monthly Magazine,* Jan. 1890, 318–23.

———. "My Mark Twain." In *Literary Friends and Acquaintance,* ed. David F. Hiatt and Edwin Cady, 256–322. Bloomington: Indiana University Press, 1968.

Irving, John. *A Prayer for Owen Meany.* New York: Ballantine Books, 1989.

James, Henry. "The Art of Fiction." In *The Art of Criticism: Henry James on the Theory and Practice of Fiction,* ed. William Veeder and Susan M. Griffin. Chicago: University of Chicago Press, 1986.

———. *The Letters of Henry James.* Ed. Percy Lubbock. 2 vols. New York: Scribners, 1920.

———. "The Novel of Dialect: W. D. Howells." In *The American Essays of Henry James,* ed. Leon Edel, 250–57. New York: Vintage, 1956.

Jefferson, Ann. *Reading Realism in Stendhal.* Cambridge: Cambridge University Press, 1988.

Jensen, Franklin L. "Mark Twain's Comments on Books and Authors." *Emporia State Research Studies* 12 (1964): 5–53.

Jerome, Robert D., and Herbert A. Wisbey Jr., eds. *Mark Twain in Elmira.* Elmira, N.Y.: Mark Twain Society, 1977.

Johnson, James L. *Mark Twain and the Limits of Power: Emerson's God in Ruins.* Knoxville: University of Tennessee Press, 1982.

Johnson, Ronald M. "Future as Past, Past as Future: Edward Bellamy, Mark Twain, and the Crisis of the 1880s." *American Studies in Scandinavia* 22 (1990): 73–79.

Kaplan, Amy. *The Social Construction of American Realism.* Chicago: University of Chicago Press, 1988.

Kaplan, Justin. *Mr. Clemens and Mark Twain.* New York: Simon and Schuster, 1966.

Kearns, Katharine. *Nineteenth-Century Literary Realism: Through the Looking Glass.* New York: Cambridge University Press, 1996.

Keats, John. Letter to John Taylor, February 27, 1818. In *English Romantic Writers,* ed. David Perkins, 1211–1212. New York: Harcourt, Brace and World, 1967.

Ketterer, David. "Epoch-Eclipse and Apocalypse: Special 'Effects' in *A Connecticut Yankee." PMLA* 88 (1973): 1104–14.

Kiskis, Michael J. "Mark Twain and Collaborative Autobiography." *Studies in the Literary Imagination* 29 (1996): 27–40.

Kolb, Harold. *The Illusion of Life: American Realism as a Literary Form.* Charlottesville: University Press of Virginia, 1969.

Krause, Sydney J. *Mark Twain as Critic.* Baltimore: Johns Hopkins University Press, 1967.

Kruse, Horst. "Gerstaecker's *The Pirates of the Mississippi* and Mark Twain's *Adventures of Huckleberry Finn." American Literary Realism* 31 (1999): 1–14.

———. *Mark Twain and* Life on the Mississippi. Amherst: University of Massachusetts Press, 1981.

Ladd, Barbara. *Nationalism and the Color Line in George W. Cable, Mark Twain, and William Faulkner.* Baton Rouge: Louisiana State University Press, 1996.

Lanmon, Lorraine Welling. "Quarry Farm: A Study of the 'Picturesque.'" *Quarry Farm Papers* 3 (1991): 1–30.

Lathrop, George Parsons. Interview in the *Hartford Daily Current.* Reprinted in Susy Clemens, *Papa, an Intimate Biography of Mark Twain,* ed. Charles Neider, 160–64. New York: Doubleday, 1985.

Lauber, John. *The Inventions of Mark Twain.* New York: Hill and Wang, 1990.

Lawton, Mary. *A Lifetime with Mark Twain: The Memories of Katy Leary, for Thirty Years His Faithful and Devoted Servant.* New York: Haskell House, 1972.

Lecky, William Edward Hartpole. *A History of England in the Eighteenth Century.* 6 vols. New York: D. Appleton and Company, 1887.

———. *History of European Morals from Augustus to Charlemagne.* 2 vols. New York: D. Appleton and Company, 1900.

———. *History of the Rise and Influence of the Spirit of Rationalism in Europe.* 2 vols. New York: D. Appleton and Company, 1884.

Leon, Philip W. *Mark Twain and West Point.* Toronto: ECW Press, 1996.

Levine, George. *The Realistic Imagination: English Fiction from Frankenstein to Lady Chatterley.* Chicago: University of Chicago Press, 1981.

Lowry, Richard S. *"Littery Man": Mark Twain and Modern Authorship.* New York: Oxford University Press, 1996.

Lukács, George. *History and Class Consciousness.* London: 1971.

———. *Studies in European Realism: A Sociological Survey of the Writings of Balzac, Stendhal, Zola, Tolstoy, Gorki and Others.* London: Merlin Press, 1972.

Macaulay, Thomas Babington. "History." In *Critical and Historical Essays.* Boston: Houghton Mifflin, 1900.

———. *The History of England from the Accession of James II.* 5 vols. Philadelphia: J. B. Lippincott, 1869.

————. *The Life and Letters of Lord Macaulay.* Ed. G. Otto Trevelyan. 2 vols. New York: Harper and Brothers, 1876.

————. *Selections from the Writings of Lord Macaulay.* Ed. G. Otto Trevelyan. New York: Harper and Brothers, 1877.

Malory, Sir Thomas. *Morte Darthur.* Globe edition. Ed. Sir Edward Strachey, Bart. New York: Macmillan, 1871.

"Mark Twain and His Book." *New York Times,* Dec. 10, 1889, 5.

Martin, Jay. *Harvests of Change: American Literature, 1865–1914.* Englewood Cliffs, N.J.: Prentice-Hall, 1967.

Marx, Karl. *The Eighteenth Brumaire of Louis Bonaparte.* New York: International, 1963.

McKeon, Michael. *The Origins of the English Novel 1600–1740.* Baltimore: Johns Hopkins University Press, 1987.

McLean, Marianne. *The People of Glengarry: Highlanders in Transition, 1745–1820.* Buffalo: McGill-Queen's University Press, 1991.

McNutt, James C. "Mark Twain and the American Indian: Earthly Realism and Heavenly Idealism." *American Indian Quarterly* 4 (1978): 223–42.

McWilliams, Jim. *Mark Twain in the* St. Louis Post-Dispatch, *1874–1891.* Troy, N.Y.: Whitson, 1997.

Meindl, Dieter. *American Fiction and the Metaphysics of the Grotesque.* Columbia: University of Missouri Press, 1996.

Messent, Peter. *Mark Twain.* New York: St. Martin's, 1997.

Michaels, Walter Benn. "An American Tragedy; or, The Promise of American Life: Classes and Individuals." *Representations* 25 (1989): 71–98.

Michelson, Bruce. "Realism, Romance, and Dynamite: The Quarrel of *A Connecticut Yankee in King Arthur's Court.*" *New England Quarterly* 64 (1991): 609–32.

Mill, John Stuart. *On Liberty.* In *Utilitarianism, Liberty, and Representative Government,* 81–229. New York: E. P. Dutton, 1951.

Mizruchi, Susan L. *The Power of Historical Knowledge: Narrating the Past in Hawthorne, James, and Dreiser.* Princeton, N.J.: Princeton University Press, 1988.

Montaigne, Michel de. "Of Friendship." In *Montaigne: Selected Essays.* Trans. Charles Cotton and William Hazlitt. New York: Modern Library, 1949.

Moreland, Kim. *The Medievalist Impulse in American Literature: Twain, Adams, Fitzgerald, and Hemingway.* Charlottesville: University Press of Virginia, 1996.

Newquist, David L. "Mark Twain among the Indians." *MIDAMERICA* 21 (1994): 59–72.

Nietzsche, Friedrich. *The Genealogy of Morals: An Attack.* Trans. Francis Golffing. New York: Doubleday, 1956.

Paine, Albert Bigelow. *Mark Twain: A Biography.* 3 vols. New York: Chelsea House, 1980.

Park, Edwin A. "A Day with Mark Twain." *Chicago Tribune,* Sep. 19, 1886. Reprinted in *Interviews with Samuel L. Clemens 1874–1910,* ed. Louis J. Budd, 41–43. Arlington, Tex.: American Literary Realism, 1977.

Pizer, Donald. *Realism and Naturalism in Nineteenth-Century American Literature.* Carbondale: Southern Illinois University Press, 1966.

Pochmann, Henry A. "The Mind of Mark Twain." Master's thesis, University of Texas, Austin, 1924.

Pound, Ezra. "Hugh Selwyn Mauberly." In *The Norton Anthology of Modern Poetry*. 2d ed. Ed. Richard Ellmann and Robert O'Clair. New York: Norton, 1988.

Prendergast, Christopher. *The Order of Mimesis: Balzac, Stendhal, Nerval, Flaubert*. Cambridge: Cambridge University Press, 1986.

Regan, Robert. *Unpromising Heroes: Mark Twain and His Characters*. Berkeley: University of California Press, 1961.

Richards, David. *Masks of Difference: Cultural Representations in Literature, Anthropology, and Art*. New York: Cambridge University Press, 1994.

Ricouer, Paul. *Time and Narrative*. Vol. 1. Trans. Kathleen McLaughlin and David Pellauer. Chicago: University of Chicago Press, 1983.

Robinson, Forrest G. *In Bad Faith: The Dynamics of Deception in Mark Twain's America*. Cambridge, Mass.: Harvard University Press, 1986.

———. "The Innocent at Large: Mark Twain's Travel Writing." *The Cambridge Companion to Mark Twain*, ed. Forrest Robinson, 27–51. New York: Cambridge University Press, 1995.

———. Response to Henry B. Wonham. "Commentary." *Nineteenth-Century Literature* 51 (1996): 140–41.

———. "An 'Unconscious and Profitable Cerebration': Mark Twain and Literary Intentionality." *Nineteenth-Century Literature* 50 (1995): 357–80.

Rogers, Franklin R. *Mark Twain's Burlesque Patterns*. Dallas: Southern Methodist University Press, 1960.

Rogers, Rodney O. "Twain, Taine, and Lecky: The Genesis of a Passage in *A Connecticut Yankee*." *Modern Language Quarterly* 34 (1973): 436–47.

Rowe, John Carlos. "How the Boss Played the Game: Twain's Critique of Imperialism in *A Connecticut Yankee in King Arthur's Court*." *The Cambridge Companion to Mark Twain*, ed. Forrest G. Robinson, 175–92. New York: Cambridge University Press, 1995.

Rust, Richard Dilworth. "Americanisms in *A Connecticut Yankee*." *South Atlantic Bulletin* 33 (1968): 11–13.

Salomon, Roger. *Twain and the Image of History*. New Haven: Yale University Press, 1961.

Sewell, David R. "Hank Morgan and the Colonization of Utopia." *American Transcendental Quarterly*, n.s., 3 (1989): 27–44.

Shanley, Mary Lyndon, and Peter Stillman. "Mark Twain: Technology, Social Change, and Political Power." *The Artist and Political Vision*, ed. Benjamin Barber and Michael McGarth, 267–89. New Brunswick: Transaction, 1982.

Sharlow, Gretchen E. "'Love to All the Jolly Household': A Study of the Cranes of Quarry Farm, Their Lives, and Their Relationship with Mark Twain." Master's thesis, Elmira College, 1991.

———. "Theodore Crane: A New Perspective." *Mark Twain Society Bulletin* 13 (1990): 1–6.

Shi, David E. *Facing Facts: Realism in American Thought and Culture, 1850–1920*. New York: Oxford University Press, 1995.

Skandera-Trombley, Laura E. *Mark Twain in the Company of Women.* Philadelphia: University of Pennsylvania Press, 1994.

Slotkin, Richard. *The Fatal Environment.* Middletown, Conn.: Wesleyan University Press, 1985.

Smith, Henry Nash. "Introduction." In *A Connecticut Yankee in King Arthur's Court,* ed. Bernard L. Stein, 1–30. Berkeley: University of California Press, 1979.

———. *Mark Twain's Fable of Progress: Political and Economic Ideas in* A Connecticut Yankee. New Brunswick, N.J.: Rutgers University Press, 1964.

Steinbrink, Jeffrey. *Getting to Be Mark Twain.* Berkeley: University of California Press, 1991.

Stern, J. P. *On Realism.* London: Routledge, 1972.

Stitt, Megan Perigoe. *Metaphors of Change in the Language of Nineteenth-Century Fiction: Scott, Gaskell, and Kingsley.* Oxford: Clarendon Press, 1998.

Tanner, Toby. *The Reign of Wonder: Naivety and Reality in American Literature.* New York: Harper and Row, 1965.

Thacker, Andrew. "Foucault and the Writing of History." In *The Impact of Michel Foucault on the Social Sciences and Humanities,* ed. Moya Lloyd and Andrew Thacker, 29–53. New York: St. Martin's, 1997.

Thomas, Brook. *American Literary Realism and the Failed Promise of Contract.* Berkeley: University of California Press, 1997.

Tomashevsky, Boris. "Thematics." In *Russian Formalist Criticism: Four Essays,* ed. Lee T. Lemon and Marion J. Reis. Norman: University of Oklahoma Press, 1964.

Tuckey, John S. "Introduction." In *Mark Twain's Which Was the Dream?* ed. John S. Tuckey, 1–29. Berkeley: University of California Press, 1967.

Turner, Arlin. *Mark Twain and George W. Cable.* East Lansing: Michigan State University Press, 1960.

Twain, Mark [Samuel Clemens]. *The Autobiography of Mark Twain.* Ed. Charles Neider. New York: Harper 1959. Reprint, New York: HarperPerennial, 1990.

———. *A Connecticut Yankee in King Arthur's Court.* Ed. Bernard L. Stein. Berkeley: University of California Press, 1979.

———. "English As She Is Taught." In *"What Is Man?" and Other Philosophical Writings,* ed. Paul Baender, 240–55. New York: Gabriel Wells, 1923.

———. "Fenimore Cooper's Literary Offenses." In *Literary Essays,* 60–77. New York: Gabriel Wells, 1923.

———. "General Grant's Grammar." In *Mark Twain's Speeches,* 135–37. New York: Gabriel Wells, 1923.

———. *The Innocents Abroad or The New Pilgrim's Progress.* 2 vols. New York: Gabriel Wells, 1923.

———. *Life on the Mississippi.* New York: Gabriel Wells, 1923.

———. *The Love Letters of Mark Twain.* Ed. Dixon Wecter. New York: Harper, 1949.

———. *Mark Twain, Business Man.* Ed. Samuel C. Webster. Boston: Little, Brown, 1946.

———. *Mark Twain–Howells Letters: The Correspondence of Samuel L. Clemens and William Dean Howells, 1872–1910.* Ed. Henry Nash Smith and William M. Gibson. 2 vols. Cambridge, Mass.: Harvard University Press, 1960.

——. *Mark Twain to Mrs. Fairbanks.* Ed. Dixon Wecter. San Marino, Calif.: Huntington Library Publications, 1949.

——. *Mark Twain's Autobiography.* Ed. Albert Bigelow Paine. 2 vols. New York: Harper, 1924.

——. *Mark Twain's Correspondence with Henry Huttleston Rogers.* Ed. Lewis Leary. Berkeley: University of California Press, 1969.

——. *Mark Twain's Fables of Man.* Ed. John S. Tuckey. Berkeley: University of California Press, 1972.

——. *Mark Twain's Letters.* Ed. Albert Bigelow Paine. 2 vols. New York: Harper, 1917.

——. *Mark Twain's Letters Volume 1: 1853–1866.* Ed. Edgar Marquess Branch, Michael B. Frank, and Kenneth M. Sanderson. Berkeley: University of California Press, 1988.

——. *Mark Twain's Letters Volume 2: 1867–1868.* Ed. Harriet Elinor Smith and Richard Bucci. Berkeley: University of California Press, 1990.

——. *Mark Twain's Letters Volume 3: 1869.* Ed. Victor Fischer and Michael B. Frank. Berkeley: University of California Press, 1992.

——. *Mark Twain's Letters to His Publishers, 1867–1894.* Ed. Hamlin Hill. Berkeley: University of California Press, 1967.

——. *Mark Twain's Notebooks and Journals, Volume 3: 1883–1891.* Ed. Robert Pack Browning, Michael Frank, and Lin Salamo. Berkeley: University of California Press, 1979.

——. "My First Lie and How I Got Out of It." In *"The Man That Corrupted Hadleyburg" and Other Essays and Stories,* 167–69. New York: Gabriel Wells, 1923.

——. "On Foreign Critics." In *Collected Tales, Sketches, Speeches, and Essays 1852–1890,* ed. Louis J. Budd, 942–44. New York: Library of America, 1992.

——. *The Prince and the Pauper.* Ed. Victor Fischer and Lin Salamo. Berkeley: University of California Press, 1979.

——. "Reply to the Editor of 'The Art of Authorship.'" In *Collected Tales, Sketches, Speeches, and Essays 1852–1890,* ed. Louis J. Budd, 945–46. New York: Library of America, 1992.

——. "Study and Stimulants." In *Study and Stimulants; or, The Use of Intoxicants and Narcotics in Relation to Intellectual Life,* ed. A. Arthur Reade, 120–22. London: Simkin, Marshall, 1883.

——. "The 'Tournament' in A.D. 1870." In *Collected Tales, Sketches, Speeches and Essays, 1852–1890,* ed. Louis J. Budd, 418–20. New York: Library of America.

——. *A Tramp Abroad.* 2 vols. New York: Gabriel Wells, 1923.

——. "What Is Man?" In *"What is Man?" and Other Philosophical Writings,* ed. Paul Baender, 124–214. Berkeley: University of California Press, 1973.

——. *"What Is Man?" and Other Philosophical Writings.* Ed. Paul Baender. Berkeley: University of California Press, 1973.

——. "What Paul Bourget Thinks of Us." In *Literary Essays,* 148–70. New York: Gabriel Wells, 1923.

——. "William Dean Howells." In *"What is Man?" and Other Essays,* 228–39. New York: Gabriel Wells, 1923.

————. *The Writings of Mark Twain: "Definitive Edition."* 37 vols. New York: Gabriel Wells, 1923.

Wang, Ban. *The Sublime Figure of History: Aesthetics and Politics in Twentieth-Century China.* Stanford: Stanford University Press, 1997.

Weinstein, Cindy. *The Literature of Labor and the Labors of Literature: Allegory in Nineteenth-Century American Fiction.* New York: Cambridge University Press, 1995.

Wellek, René. *Concepts of Criticism.* Ed. Stephen G. Nichols. New Haven: Yale University Press, 1963.

White, Hayden. *Metahistory: The Historical Imagination in Nineteenth-Century Europe.* Baltimore: Johns Hopkins University Press, 1973.

Wiggins, Robert. *Mark Twain: Jackleg Novelist.* Seattle: University of Washington Press, 1964.

Williams, James D. "Revision and Intention in Mark Twain's *A Connecticut Yankee.*" *American Literature* 36 (1964): 288–97.

————. "The Uses of History in Mark Twain's *A Connecticut Yankee.*" *PMLA* 80 (1965): 102–10.

Wilson, R. H. "Malory in the *Connecticut Yankee.*" *Texas Studies* 27 (1948): 185–206.

Wilson, Rufus Rockwell, and Otilie Erikson Wilson. "Mark Twain's Days in Elmira." In *New York in Literature,* ed. Rufus Rockwell Wilson and Otilie Erickson Wilson, 336–50. Elmira, N.Y.: Primavera Press, 1947. Reprinted in *Mark Twain in Elmira,* ed. Robert D. Jerome and Herbert A. Wisbey Jr., 3–15. Elmira, N.Y.: Mark Twain Society, 1977.

Winner, George. "The Decline and Fall of the Langdon Home," *Mark Twain in Elmira,* ed. Robert D. Jerome and Herbert Wisbey Jr., 28–35. Elmira, N.Y.: Mark Twain Society, 1977.

Wonham, Henry B. *Mark Twain and the Art of the Tall Tale.* New York: Oxford University Press, 1993.

————. Response to Forrest Robinson. "Commentary." *Nineteenth-Century Literature* 51 (1996): 137–40.

Wyrick, Deborah Baker. "Hank Morgan: Linguistic Entrepreneur." *Postscript* 2 (1985): 97–105.

Zlatic, Thomas D. "Language Technologies in *A Connecticut Yankee.*" *Nineteenth-Century Fiction* 45 (1991): 453–77.

Index

About the Author

Joe B. Fulton is Assistant Professor of English at Dalton State College in Georgia. He received a B.A. in Russian from Purdue University and a Ph.D. in English from Southern Illinois University at Carbondale and is the author of *Mark Twain's Ethical Realism*.